I0814915

THE GREEN FUSE

THE GREEN FUSE

ESSAYS IN MAKING SENSE OF GARDENS

PETER DALE

REAKTION BOOKS

To BCY – who else? who
Was always 'there . . . to spell
The new words – finger
Writing in the air' –

And who would say 'too' –
Beautifully, simply, those
Very long o's – so that it
Rhymed with 'true'. And who

Would remember, as he always did,
'To feed the wild, the hungry wild birds'.

Published by
REAKTION BOOKS LTD
2–4 Sebastian Street
London EC1V 0HE, UK

www.reaktionbooks.co.uk

First published 2025

EU GPSR Authorised Representative
LOGOS EUROPE, 9 rue Nicolas Poussin, 17000, La Rochelle, France
email: contact@logoseurope.eu

Printed and bound in Great Britain by Bell & Bain, Glasgow

A catalogue record for this book is available from the British Library

ISBN 978 1 83639 028 2

CONTENTS

Introduction

In the famous closing lines of his satirical novel *Candide*, Voltaire (1694–1778) has his eponymous character give an answer to life, the universe and everything: 'mais il faut cultiver nôtre jardin.'[1] There's nothing for it but to go and work in the garden. Of course, there's nothing whatsoever in the book to encourage its original readers of 1759 to take the advice seriously. Nor, on the face of it, is there anything very compelling about life now to make us take *our* gardens very seriously. And yet we do. The evidence from publishing, broadcasting and commerce is compelling, and so is that of our own eyes in the places in which we live: as things stand now, we take gardens and gardening really rather seriously. Or we allow gardens to take up a serious, significant part of our time, our money, our scarce space and our lives. 'Gardening is the most popular pastime in Britain and America.' 'Gardens are to life-style what image is to life.' 'Gardening is the new sex.' The list of claims could go on and on, and perhaps like life itself, the more absurd they become, the more they ring with a kind of truth.

By asking the question 'What do gardens mean?', this book examines why we take these set-apart places seriously. Some answers come readily to hand. Gardens and gardening, it seems, can be 'explained' in terms of fashion statements, or boastful exhibitionism, or plantsmanship, or hobby-horsing, or expressions of terrestrial mastery, or even as outdoor larders (those sixteenth-century deer parks, those twenty-first-century allotments and so on) – and, as explanations go, all of these are more or less plausible.

You could go on from there to say that some gardens are explicable as rich people's toys, some are expressions of municipal pride, some were conceived as safe havens for children and as quiet spots for adults, and those explanations can ring true too . . . sometimes. Or you could take the imaginative, intellectual plunge and see them sometimes as recoveries of lost Edens, as attempts to create (or recreate – memory, mythic or otherwise, seems so important here) glimpses of an Earthly Paradise. These places can be – *can* they? – the virtual spaces of our disappointed but forgiving, hopeful imaginations.

But there are also other, and more neglected, ways of looking for answers to the question 'What do gardens mean?' What are we doing when we talk about nature (and the natural) in the context of a garden, which, in reality, is anything but a 'natural' place? We don't really mean 'natural' at all, do we? But even if they aren't natural, gardens are full of living things, and their lives are, in some important sense, independent of ours. Seen in that way, are gardens analogous to zoos? After all, one of the byways of the history of gardens – and one of the more intriguing ones too – involves a lot of overlap with the history of zoos ('zoological gardens'). Systematic botanical gardens bear more than a passing resemblance to those very same places. But instinctively we want to reject the analogy. It offends against our ideas of nature and liberty. And yet the very word *paradise* seems originally to have meant a walled, set-apart place, and the word *garden* – whatever it may mean now – is still historically cognate with *yard*, *gird* and even *garth*.

Are we still treating our gardens, however subliminally, as things to be protected from the outside world, as zones set apart from wilderness? And what do we mean now by that word *wilderness*, which immemorially we have used in the sense of being the antithesis to *garden*? Where is wilderness now? Is it what remains of nature and the natural? Or is it the new man-made wilderness of the urban jungle? Or a bit of both? In any case, the issue begs the question of *walls*. What are we fencing in, and what (or who) are we trying to keep out?

We're familiar now with certain kinds of gardens being decoded for us. The English landscape gardens – those places which, above all, force upon us the serious claim that gardens are, or can be, art – have now got their own exegetical literature, with whose help they can be 'understood' in much the same way as *Ulysses* becomes accessible through a study guide. Which is all very well and, I'm sure, all very true, but it doesn't actually explain much about how or why we really do respond to these places.

An understanding of the finer points of the Whig agenda at Stowe actually does very little indeed to frame the view for us, and it is the view, if anything, which brings us back time after time. It's interesting to have the Virgilian references explained at Stourhead – interesting but not formative. To have views pointed out which are so clearly (and beautifully) modelled on Poussin is fine too. But the Poussins – Nicolas (1594–1665) and his brother-in-law Gaspard (1615–1675) – were not English, nor are their views, nor is the light in their paintings. And their classically inflected visions of Arcadia are not even remotely associable with the home-grown versions of Wordsworth (1770–1850) or Blake (1757–1827), Wainwright (1907–1991) or the Brontës. Perceived in this way, Stourhead, Rousham and Stowe are, quite unfairly, reduced to expensive (albeit more tasteful) versions of the patio garden built to remind you of your holiday in Ibiza. Bring on the cast-concrete donkeys (with panniers of marigolds) and the barbecued Chusan palm tree.

Rather more interesting – and certainly more appropriate to the majority of us – is the possibility that we might have had the perception of our own gardens (and their Englishness) mediated to us through an unconscious but pervasive memory of the garden of England seen through the eyes of people such as John Constable (1776–1837) or Francis Towne (1739–1816) or Helen Allingham (1848–1926): painters, illustrators, people whose ways of seeing may have shaped ours. Certainly, perceiving – comparing, criticizing, applauding – our own gardens in terms of other people's is a practice so common as to provoke no surprise or interest, but how much conceptual to-ing and fro-ing goes on even now between gardens and paintings, gardens and photography, gardens and reading, or even gardens and music? I believe the answer is much more than we'd usually credit. It's no accident, for example, that by far and away the most historically influential garden devised in England (a) has never actually been built on the ground, (b) was conceived by a blind man, one who perceived and imagined everything but actually saw nothing, and (c) is in a book that few in the last century or so have read in its entirety, but whose influence deeply (though invisibly) stains the memory of all of us through the medium of our cultural consciousness.

I mean the vision of Eden in Book IV of Milton's *Paradise Lost* (1667) (illus. 7). And, while we're on the subject of memories so deep that their sources are almost invisible, why is it that – when you scratch more and more deeply beneath the surface – so many people seem to have wanted to be able to associate their gardens, when they were making them, with (the myth of?) their own childhoods? What is actually going on there in terms of our own agendas, our own pursuits of meaning in life?

At Stourhead – which is more or less contemporaneous with *Candide*, as it happens – we can respectfully nod in the direction of a specialized knowledge of Ovid, Virgil, Claude and Poussin, but what really grips us is something that, though it may have originated in language, cannot be comprehensively or accurately translated back into words: beauty. Given the option of choosing between the received explanation of the meaning of Stourhead (classically referential, pictorially extrapolated, et cetera) and the suggestion that the garden represents the solace of a very rich man from whom death nevertheless systematically stripped away the things of real value (his entire family), the answer seems clear enough.

It would appear that the (superficially) intended meaning of the garden is not the real one – or not the whole of it by any means.

The same might be said, but this time ironically, of Nelson's Walk at Stowe. From that august name we absorb a resonance of a great man, of a nation revering its patriots and so on, but how do we stand when (and if) we stumble on the truth of the dedication? This was *not* Horatio Nelson of Trafalgar, but (surname only) Nelson of the Potting Shed, a jobbing labourer there. As it happens – but only in passing – there was also a Gurnet's Walk and a Roger's Walk. Naming parts of the garden after his gardeners was a homely idea Lord Cobham borrowed from Pliny, the classical precedent impeccable. Once again we have to contemplate a fairly volcanic shift in the meaning of a garden depending on what we know about it from sources that aren't intrinsically horticultural at all, and certainly not what they appear to be on the surface.

The way we perceive (in these cases, gardens, but the same is true for all sensory encounters) is mediated through all sorts of other experiences: *intertextuality* in the jargon of academic literary criticism, the way our reading of one book is coloured by the previous experience of having read others. But this theoretical principle, understood in its narrow, discipline-specific sense, falls short of what really happens, at least in gardens, because it is not only other gardens that colour our perception, but paintings, photographs, books, poems, childhoods, holidays, family lore and escapism, and – as if that weren't enough – it is often the case that it is not so much the objective impression of those things themselves that makes its mark, but very personal, subjective, selective and highly edited memories of them.

More often than not, the fusing of present experience with knowledge mediated through memory is something we welcome, enjoy and even cultivate. And as the brew thickens, so it becomes richer. But it's possible to contaminate an otherwise innocent perception to the point where we might prefer to avoid it altogether, rather than negotiate a sustainable balancing act between the pleasure we used to enjoy and the tainted knowledge of it acquired later. It's a problem familiar to a lot of music lovers: can you really turn a blind eye to the poison of his vile politics when you watch or listen to the music dramas of Richard Wagner (1813–1883)? The same might be true to a degree of our perceptions of some of the eighteenth-century landscapes we revere. Jane Austen (1775–1817) hints at but leaves us to make explicit the connection between Mr Bertram's rolling acres at Mansfield Park and the income from his slave plantation in Antigua. And although this example is drawn from fiction, the same thing is an incontrovertible fact of, for example, what were said to have been the incomparable gardens of William Beckford (1760–1844) at Fonthill Abbey. The same connection lurks directly or indirectly behind a great many other gardens (and houses too, of course), and not least among those whose creators' incomes were derived from banking: in the eighteenth century, that would have meant – with the exception of one or two local banks, one or two Quaker banks – directly or indirectly embracing investments in slavery. Among these banking gardeners it is hardly possible to overlook Henry Hoare (1705–1785) of Stourhead.

Does it matter? Does any of the information we can muster about the circumstances and purposes of the makers of historical gardens matter now? In principle the answer is certainly yes, but it will matter far more to the student of garden history than it will to the ordinary visitor. The latter's approach is broadly aesthetic and cultural, while the former is all too often likely to overlook the aesthetic altogether, and more's the pity because if you abstract the sensuous and the perception of beauty from the meaning of gardens you are left only with items on that list with which we began: gardens as statements of power, wealth and fashionable taste; gardens as romper rooms for men with noisy, macho machines; gardens where that mild but familiar mania for control can be expressed – those of the 'lawn and order' tendency – or as gentle exercise plots for ladies and the elderly; gardens as lavatories – and eventually graveyards – for pets; or gardens as cabinets of curiosities assembled by plantsmen. Pretty dull stuff as far as most of us are concerned.

Voltaire meant us to construe Candide's advice as ridiculous – simple-minded, blinkered, laughable nonsense – but here we are now, more than 260 years later, all too visibly compelled by that very same 'il faut'. To some extent, what has happened between 1759 and where we are now accounts for the difference. We are separated by the philosophical, political and aesthetic tendencies we call Romanticism, by the growth of towns and cities on unimaginable scales, by wars whose violence and scope superseded any previous classifications of collective madness, by heavy industry being replaced by industries so light you wonder where the dignity once conferred by work has now gone. We now look for meaning in our lives in places where it was either inconceivable or else taken for granted in days gone by. There are probably other factors too though, and some of them – as cultural indices of the sort of people we are now and the lives we lead – are neither negligible nor uninteresting. One of those is that insidious shift, mentioned earlier, in where we now perceive wilderness to lie. Another is perhaps quite closely allied to it and consists of the developing, if reluctant, sense we have of ourselves as partners in – but not, after all, the masters of – nature. That piece of sense can only press harder and harder upon us as such time as we have left goes by. As that revisionist pressure increases, it seems to me that gardens are going to loom larger and larger in our consciousness as transitional, mediating zones between ourselves and nature.

If the rainforests are now perceived as the lungs of our world, it may be that gardens will come to function as that same bruised world's conscience – in which case the meaning of gardens is going to become more and more discussed, more and more considered.

And if that takes us back through at least some of a completed circle to our own aboriginal perception of gardens as somehow numinous and sacred places, I shouldn't be surprised. I'm neither a new-ageist nor a card-carrying Christian/Muslim/Buddhist, but I'm not ashamed to report an interest in (the vacuum of?) my own spirituality, and I hope that parts of this book are evidence of objective interests being compatible after all with what gardens occasionally and subjectively brush my soul with: mystery, something magical, profound melancholy (sometimes), beauty I neither deserve nor entirely understand.

Horace Walpole (1717–1797) included his 'History of the Modern Taste in Gardening' in the fourth volume (1771) of *Anecdotes of Painting in England*, though it was probably written much earlier. It too is the contemporary of Voltaire's famous swipe at his coevals, and indeed at us. Central to Walpole's essay is the celebrated idea that 'all nature [is] a garden.'[2] For better or for worse, that idea has coloured and driven almost everything to do with gardens and gardening ever since, and whether we are paid-up members of the local eco-warrior battalion or just confused about whether or not we should complain about the thistle seeds coming over the fence from the neighbour's 'wild garden', we all pay some measure of lip service to it. But the trouble is: is it true? And, if it is true, why then should we bother with gardens at all? That, in essence, is the question which this book sets out to explore. Why do we bother?

The chapters of this book examine gardens and gardening in the light of other cultural activities, some very specific, others more general: the reading of books, the practice of religion(s), looking at paintings, listening closely to music, and then remembering, perhaps memorializing, dreaming, idealizing, trying to reconcile the urban with the rural. The ways these activities make sense, from time to time, of our experience of gardens are specifically located in the 'Interludes' – chapters on particular gardens where those moods (of bookish study, painterly evocation and emulation, et cetera) are strongly embodied and reflected.

The title – *The Green Fuse* – is borrowed from Dylan Thomas (1914–1953):

> The force that through the green fuse drives the flower
> Drives my green age; that blasts the roots of trees
> Is my destroyer.[3]

The word 'fuse' here is both archaic (for a flower stem) and contemporary (in its connotations of detonation and electricity). The idea in the poem – and seminal in all religions – that creation and destruction may share both an energy and a *telos*, a purpose, dissolves at a stroke so much of the sentimentality that bedevils popular perceptions of gardens. The way the monosyllabic and alliterative plod of the words in that first line eventually blossoms into the word 'flower' seems like a metaphor for what I have tried to do in looking again at aspects of what is often overlooked, or taken for granted, in gardens, and in finding meaning in these places where conventionally it is commerce, fashion or leisure pursuits that generally hold sway.

1

Mazes and Labyrinths

To MAZE, v. a. to perplex, bewilder, or confuse.[1]

Anatomically, the labyrinth is the maze-like zone of the inner ear. Less scientifically but just as vividly, the exposed surface of the human brain suggests something similar: the maze-like geography of a fantastic planet. So does the coiled gut of an animal. The analogy between the microcosm of a single human being and the macrocosmic world at large has its compelling reasons when the appearance of the brain is compared with the surface of the full moon on a cloudless night. The sight is no less mysterious, beautiful and charged with awe for the fact that it is also very familiar. Traditionally, to gaze at it for too long is to court danger. That lunar light, cast by the celestial body on to and into the lesser orb of the mind of man, makes for lunacy. To be bathed in its soft, magical light is one thing; to be *touched* is another.

The classic maze has seven coils, or spirals, or circles. But is there a difference between a maze and a labyrinth? Perhaps. A labyrinth is said to be unicursal. There is only one path, and no misleading deviations. But why then did Theseus need Ariadne's thread? In his *Thésée* (1946), André Gide (1869–1951) suggests at least one solution, which may or may not be correct. The thread is his link to the past, his own past. It is really himself that he is seeking. And that may not correspond with what most people have in mind when they venture into a labyrinth. In practice, there are multicursal labyrinths, as well as mazes with only one track and no blind alleys. I think the two terms must, by now, be more or less interchangeable, but they still resonate slightly differently. To my ear, the word *labyrinth* suggests the dark, the subterranean and perhaps the subconscious. *Maze*, on the other hand, suggests something open-aired and more playful. It probably doesn't matter.

There's a long and esoteric tradition of so-called sacred architectures involving the ratios of naturally occurring phenomena, or celestial patterns, or cyclic events. These, it seems, have been plotted on to sacred landscapes and reified in sacred buildings ranging from Neolithic sites to Gothic cathedrals. To their builders it must have seemed that in such geometric/geomantic forms as these, it might be possible to achieve the impossible: things such as the finite straight line and the curve reconciled in the endless circle, things such as the enigma of where we come from and where we go to. The sense of the maze somehow seems to involve reconciliation too, but in a spirit of play, deadly serious though that might be.

Sometimes the confederacy of geometry and cosmography is emphatic. The labyrinth on the floor of the nave at Chartres Cathedral – its size – exactly replicates the rose window above it. If the west wall holding the window were let down through ninety degrees, the rose would fit perfectly over the labyrinth. The length of the journey through the labyrinth is also exactly equal to the length of the cathedral itself. Similarly, the journey through the maze under the west tower of Ely Cathedral is equivalent to the tower's height. Perhaps, inside the great Romanesque and Gothic churches, there was also an intention that the receding view down the vaulting of the roof or along the arcades should be numerologically significant: the gradually diminishing succession of half-spheres in groups of seven (Southwell, Durham, Gloucester, Chartres itself and countless others), eleven (Canterbury and others) and occasionally fifteen (Toulouse). The turf maze on the common in the East Anglian town of Saffron Walden is said to involve a journey of one mile. The place is locally associated with stories of competitive races run by men to win the attention of girls. The undertones of this maze being, among other things, a metaphor for the womb – its entrance a vulva – are hard to ignore. Originally, there was a tree in its centre.[2] I suppose we should expect that – the tree as *axis mundi* – but it's gone now. Francis Dashwood (1708–1781), who certainly used similar sexual metaphors in his garden at West Wycombe in Buckinghamshire, may have had this anatomical metaphysic in mind when he had his workmen hack out a labyrinth in the cliff above his garden. It's still there. The Belgian artist Jan Vercruysse (1948–2018) made designs for a series of labyrinths and pleasure gardens that look innocent and geometrically abstract when seen close up, but viewed from a certain distance, clear representations of human sexual congress appear.

The maze gives lessons in achieving goals in simple but important ways. Typically, the maze demonstrates that the shortest route is unlikely to be the best, that to get nearer to the centre you must first go farther off, that mechanical method in following a route is fallible, that the goal may not justify the journey, and finally (that precept of so much mystical wisdom) that every journey, every unwinding of an ambition, involves not just the going but the coming back. Every maze could be inscribed with that legend from T. S. Eliot: 'In my beginning is my end.'[3] And in almost the same way, every maze-goer might be haunted by Robert Frost's difficulty with 'The Road Not Taken', the opportunity lost and the resulting difference to the rest of one's life, something imposing inescapably life-lasting consequences.

One of the ways in which mazes have been explained is that sometimes they suggest traps – or at least moral coils – for ourselves: the convolutions of Dante's *Inferno*, and Rosamund's Bower (where Henry II kept – or trapped: after all, it was built as a maze – his mistress, his love and his conscience). They are bewildering places, no matter how safe and reassuring the centre, once achieved,

1 Gustave Doré's illustration to *The Divine Comedy* (1861). The traveller's furtive backward look, foot-stumbling brambles and tentacle-like tree roots hint at sinister tensions.

may feel. Disorientation, dislocation, disturbance are their itinerary if not exactly their métier.

There's at least one other idea, also originating in our Judaeo-Christian centuries, which may bear even more closely upon mazes in the first instance, and then upon our attitudes to nature in the second. Made of hedges – miniaturized trees – a maze resembles a forest, though one highly structured to suggest chaos, disorientation. The forest, in Christian history, is often (and archetypically) seen as a labyrinth, a place of confusion and temptation, a zone of evil – a Black Forest indeed – the dark places harbouring the ravenous wolves that threaten the safety of Christian souls. Conventionally, Christians – or Little Red Riding Hood, or a Knight of the Round Table, or a traveller through Dante's *selva oscura* – would shun the forest (illus. 1). Or, if that weren't possible, they'd try to get through it and out to the other side as quickly as possible. How much that idea was responsible for medieval forest clearances then, and damage to our eco-consciences even now, is only just beginning to be recognized, but when the final reckoning is taken, it is likely to have been colossal.

Of course, there seems always to have been a subversive counterculture, originating, I should think, in the royal monopoly of forests as places to hunt in, and thus that divisive distinction between, on the one hand, chasing and killing animals for fun and, on the other, killing them but only to sustain and preserve your own life. Sherwood Forest was a menacing labyrinth only to the wicked (the Sheriff of Nottingham and his henchmen). To the virtuous – albeit the economically and socially excluded, the outlawed – the forest was a beneficent haven. The Green Man surely belongs to this counterculture too. But the mainstream perception of forests – at least from the Yahwist hatred of the groves of Baal, if not even earlier – saw them as evils to be uprooted, burnt and extirpated, places to be plundered if there were economic advantages in doing so, or as dark, labyrinthine places to be avoided. In

England, it was not until the publication of John Evelyn's *Sylva* in 1664 that forests began to be seen as places to respect or even to enjoy. And even then, Evelyn had to present his argument not in terms of aesthetics or conscience but by way of the hard-headed economics and patriotic symbolism of shipbuilding, though some of the illustrations in later editions of *Sylva* (or *Silva*) are indeed beguilingly beautiful (illus. 2).

The western paradigm of the maze is Greek. The sea god Poseidon demanded that Minos, King of Crete, sacrifice a beautiful white bull to him. Minos refused, and in revenge Poseidon

2 Engraving from Alexander Hunter's edition of John Evelyn's *Silva; or, A Discourse of Forest-Trees* (1786), drawn by John Miller. Note the gall wasp (on the left), which by irritation causes the tree to make its so-called 'apples'.

caused Pasiphae, the king's wife, to become sexually infatuated with the bull. The eventual issue of the unnatural union of woman and bull was the Minotaur. Minos lacked the courage to slay the hybrid creature (the original bull, the male parent, was carried off by Heracles). But something had to be done. So Daedalus, the celebrated master of all crafts, was commissioned to build a labyrinth to contain and hide the shameful, powerful beast. Thus trapped, the Minotaur spent his days in darkness and half-brute, half-human puzzlement. Sometimes his furious movements caused the earth to tremble, but still he couldn't get out. Nevertheless, he required the sacrifice of seven youths and seven maidens (that number again) every one, three or seven years. Over the span of the first cycle of years, three sets of sacrificial victims were successively supplied. But on the fourth occasion, a young Athenian hero named Theseus conspired with the king's daughter Ariadne to enter the labyrinth and kill the Minotaur. Ariadne's part in the plot was to supply Theseus with the famous red thread which, unravelled throughout the journey to the centre of the labyrinth, would lead him safely back again. That done, she and the victor would flee the furious Minos.

The story – the subduing of the inchoate and wild (the beast, perhaps, within ourselves) which otherwise consumes the best of our nature – furnishes one of the most persistent and culturally penetrating patterns known to humanity. It is enormously paradigmatic of so much of our subconscious. Our own local versions would have to include the stories of Beowulf and the monster Grendel, St George challenging and then mastering the Dragon, and then Gawain and his combat with his conscience and the Green Knight. But in this Cretan ur-version, Theseus takes the limelight, though if it weren't for Ariadne and her skills at the spinning wheel, all his valour would have been vainglorious. He would still have vanquished the man-bull, but he would never have got out again. He would have won only to lose.

Ariadne, for her part, had won Theseus' love thus far, but only to be abandoned by him on the island of Naxos. (She was taken up by Dionysus, he of sexual and musical, religious and vinous, terpsichorean and bardic, ecstasy.) Yet her part in the story is critical for the understanding of mazes and labyrinths. Schematically, these places pit space against time. Through them you race, twisting and turning, competing with the time it takes to accomplish the journey and to reach the centre. But time itself travels inexorably onward and in a straight line. Once again, the geometries – the infinite circle and the finite line – are seemingly contradictory. Even though most mazes predate timepieces, we have inherited plenty of stories about their having been used to measure time, how long a journey takes. Virgil's description of the *lusus Troiae* (in Book v of *The Aeneid*) is only the most literary of dozens of local traditions. The rub (and the lesson Ariadne teaches us) is therefore that there must be not only a going but a coming back and that only by reversing the trajectory can you cancel its consequences. It is almost like instruction in a sort of linear, temporal gravity: what goes up must come down; what goes forward must also return. And, what is more, your return brings you back precisely to where you began. The primal blood bond of Ariadne to her half-brother, the Minotaur, exerts a pull in the opposite direction to that of her attraction to his would-be slayer, Theseus. The two opposing dynamics cannot easily be reconciled. Something of this irony seems to leer out of Randoll Coate's Sun Maze (1996) at Longleat. If you stare at the pattern long enough, you begin to see the head of what looks like a man-bull laughing out of it. Or perhaps it is Dionysus, and the joke is on us twice over?

Robert Runcie (1921–2000), in the address at his enthronement as Archbishop of Canterbury in 1980, spoke at some length of a dream in which he was finding his way through a maze. This prompted the designing and building of the Archbishop's Maze (Randoll Coate and Adrian Fisher) at Greys Court near Henley-on-Thames and, as a result, probably significantly accelerated the modern renaissance of maze making generally. The wit of Coate's other mazes is all his own, I think. For example, in his Imprint of Man (1975), a foot-shaped maze in Gloucestershire, there are allusions to our genders and the triune Trinity, our five senses and the four elements, the planets and the zodiac signs. Best of all is the toe dangling itself in the water of the adjacent river. This is fun on a multi-dimensional, many-layered scale – in the mind and on the ground.

I have a minor notion that labyrinths might have been suggested to the ancient mind not only by all those things discussed so far – the brain, the womb, the web (Ariadne and threads again), the journey, the moral and the philosophical maze, time distracted from its linear course and so on – but by the idea of the fingerprint. 'Look! The Gods have been here. They have left evidence of their mighty touch on the landscape.' Celtic knots, however geometricized, suggest this playful allusion quite strongly. The spirals on the kerbstone at Newgrange in County Meath are said to be astronomical, and so they probably are, but I like to think also that the ancients would have looked for signs of the grasp of the god who had flung down mighty stones such as this, and that they weren't disappointed when they examined the forensic evidence: the encoiled prints of the fingers on the stone itself (illus. 3). Something of the same could be said of the patterns left on a muddy shore when the tide goes out – suggestive indeed of fingerprints. And who but a god could be heaving about such colossal volumes of water? A very recurrent Greek motif (albeit even more highly stylized and geometricized) suggests possibly the same thing, especially if a pair of them are locked together: the ubiquitous Greek key pattern. Indeed, the same motif recurs in centuries of early Chinese art. And then in the iconography of western painting, the clouds, the great waves of light, in van Gogh's *Starry Night* do the same. Perhaps it is another archetype. It is certainly the case that the maze has become a staple of umpteen computer games.

3 W. F. Wakeman's illustration of the kerbstone at Newgrange, County Meath, published in David MacRitchie's *Fians, Fairies and Picts* (1893). Dating from around 3200 BCE – older than Stonehenge and the pyramids – this piece of ancient sculpture has been endlessly reproduced and never quite understood.

It may also turn out to be the case that the quite extraordinary (but coincidental) similarity between mazes and printed electronic circuits may generate a new, specifically postmodern phase in the maze as an expressive metaphor for our own times. Likewise, the very difficult undertones of the idea of carbon footprints.

If the current vogue for garden mazes began in earnest in the early 1980s, the serious recovery of the metaphors themselves, so suggestively implicit in the very idea of a maze, belongs to the 1960s and to Michael Ayrton (1921–1975). Ayrton – painter, illustrator, sculptor and savant of the *Brains Trust* – had written a novel about Daedalus called *The Maze Maker* (1967). Its theme, in the abstract, was how knowledge of forms (the labyrinth, the honeycomb and so on) informs, in its turn, the forms of knowledge available to us, be they historical, mythological, physical or imaginative. Its subject,

Daedalus, was father of Icarus and maker of those ill-omened wings, designer of the labyrinth at Knossos, inventor of the lost-wax method of casting metals and enabler of the prodigious coupling of Pasiphae and the bull. Poseidon, behind Minos' back, had twisted Daedalus' arm to design and build the simulacrum of an alluring cow. Carefully, Daedalus calculated what would be the stresses upon the structure so that it would withstand the furious impact of the bull. And the all-too-willing Pasiphae was installed inside to receive the bull's ardour and semen.

Ayrton's fascination with Daedalus, the father of all arts and crafts, had been long-standing and, over the years, productive of many of his works in all sorts of media. That novel was only the most recent, but it was the one that had the greatest consequences. In the autumn of 1967, the year *The Maze Maker* was published, Ayrton was approached at a New York party by Armand Erpf, an extremely successful financier who lived on a private estate called Arkville in the Catskill Mountains, north of New York City. Erpf had read *The Maze Maker*. The story goes that he said to Ayrton little more than 'I want one [a maze],' and that was that.[4] Without much conviction, Ayrton made some preliminary plans and sent them. Erpf telephoned and then wrote to confirm the commission. Ayrton visited the site and – unlikely as it might seem – was extraordinarily reminded of the Greek landscape. Erpf possessed wealth worthy of Croesus himself, Ayrton learnt – wealth enough to float even his wildest dreams. And so he set to work in earnest.

The commission from Erpf included two sculptures – bronzes, the largest Ayrton had ever made – one for each of the paired chambers (*labrys*-like) at the centre of the maze. The first is of the Minotaur himself, tense and agonized with the duality of his nature, and the second is of Daedalus with Icarus on his shoulders (and straining away from him – both a burden and an achievement). They are powerful things. The maze itself is constructed of brick and stone. There are nearly 518 metres (1,700 ft) of narrow passages inside it. The whole is over 61 metres (200 ft) across – the largest labyrinth since the now lost Etruscan maze-defences for the tomb of Lars Porsena at Chiusi

With this place, an achievement whose scale exceeds that of any of his successors, Ayrton opened the new era of maze making. The now quite common use of mirrors in mazes began with him too (though we remember Gide's earlier idea of Theseus seeking himself). But much more importantly still, he established a recovery and new growth in the philosophical underpinning of the whole idea.

What has any of the foregoing got to do with gardens? In truth, the answer is probably only a little, but nevertheless very meaningfully so. A lot of mazes are not outdoors at all. Even those that are do not often touch more than tangentially – or only by accident – upon the fundamental elements from which gardens themselves are made, both in terms of ideas and as practice: growth, cyclic vegetation, landscape, enclosures and distances. (The Arkville maze is made of bricks, not yew hedges.) But a big maze is too big to be housed. It needs must be outdoors. And hedges are cheaper than walls. Slightly raised turf coils and paths of exposed earth or gravel between them are cheaper still. Mazes made of maize – the plant – are fun for the pun and agriculturally productive too, as well as costing little to make and being a lure to visitors who will pay to tread their paths. The lavish temporariness of a maze brushed into a dewy lawn on an early morning in late August – there fleetingly and gone a few hours later – is perhaps the last word in the garden-as-metaphor, even though the very brevity of its life militates against there being anything compellingly associative about such a maze and the garden in which it briefly occurs.

But perhaps there is still more to them than that. Perhaps – though mazes are rarely placed at the heart of a garden – the metaphors and ambivalences that they pose are nonetheless close to the centre of the issues which gardens deeply engage with, whether we consciously know and intend it to be so or not. They are, after all, patterns, artifices (like gardens themselves) designed to lead us on to a sense of integration, perhaps even of integrity, with time and space, earth and air. But they do so with the menace – albeit playfully perhaps – of confusion, disorientation and perplexity. They borrow from nature and the wild only to tame it possibly, to govern it perhaps, but at any rate to reinterpret it. Mazes subsist in the transitional world between order, meaning and safety (the garden at its most regulated) and the wild, the wilderness and bewilderment (nature at its most resisting rawness). They depend upon an eclipse, an occlusion, of reason – upon not being able to observe the whole and thus to plan and control our behaviour inside them – upon being incapable of seeing the Sacred Wood for the Disenchanted Trees.

The *Hypnerotomachia Poliphili* (the first word of whose title is itself a maze of almost definitive difficulty, but together its two words mean 'Poliphilo's strife of love in a dream') is the first important book about the spirit of gardens. Attributed to Francesco Colonna, it was published by Aldus Manutius in Venice in 1499, in a strange labyrinthine language of hybridized Latin and Italian. The story relates Poliphilo's dreamlike quest for his beloved Polia, and again and again the journey takes him to mazes and labyrinths. From the very outset, he finds himself having to traverse a maze-like forest compounded of distinctly disenchanting trees; he utters a prayer to 'the blessed Ariadne of Crete', beseeching her to deliver him from this 'tangled Labyrinth'.[5] And then, in a deep visionary sleep 'beneath an ancient, furrowed oak'– a dream within a dream – he sees a vast pyramid at the end of a fertile valley, surmounted by an obelisk, and the inside of the pyramid turns out to be another maze.[6] Later there will be a water maze – an allegory of life's difficult choices and their consequences – and, once it is reached,

Cytherea (the goal of the entire quest) turns out to be shaped, like the water maze, by concentric circles lined with hedges. This mazing narrative became, at least in some measure, the model and paradigm of many a subsequent garden (and quite a few books too). Further attention is given to it in Chapter Four, the 'Interlude' on Ilnacullin.

Mazes are never more essentially human (and thus emblematic of our human nature) than when we consider them as exercises in play. It cannot be an accident, or merely a coincidence, that the great maze at Versailles was designed by Charles Perrault (1628–1703), a Master of Play if ever there were one (and the obvious progenitor in our times of Angela Carter (1940–1992), whose creepy tales are often essentially labyrinthine). Perrault, the maze maker, is better known now as the reteller and popularizer of some of the most psychologically penetrating of all children's stories, 'Little Red Riding Hood' and 'Sleeping Beauty' among them. Mazes play games with us, but they are also didactic. They share that with the spirit of the great eighteenth-century English landscape gardens at the same time as they deviate strongly from them in that they are contra-rational and that mazes and labyrinths are necessarily (if inscrutably) formal and geometrical. They touch upon the essence of the meaning of other gardens too – other styles, other traditions in that long but not unbroken catena from the ancient Persian to the contemporary back garden – in that they are enclosures, artifices of walled-off, hedged-off space. The critical difference, however, is in the way that the walls face, as it were. The garden enclosure shuts out (the world, our cares and the neighbours) while the maze shuts in, not the world without, but you within it.

2

Gardens and Time

When lilacs last in the door-yard bloom'd,
And the great star early droop'd in the western sky in the night,
I mourn'd . . . and yet shall mourn with ever-returning spring.
WALT WHITMAN (1819–1892)[1]

It is the word 'door-yard' that fixes the first line in the memory. It is that which pre-empts any cloying in the sweet sentiment of the lilacs. It is the ordinariness of place – dust on the stone perhaps, and a step, a hole in the fence, even a privy-shed over which the lilacs grow – which indelibly lodges the flowers, their temporariness as well as their quiet beauty, into the same memory as Abraham Lincoln's death.

Should we lose faith with the poem when we learn that the chronology may not be quite right? Lincoln's death took place on 15 April 1865. The lilacs would have been quite unusually, almost implausibly early that year (though Lilac Time is quite a moveable feast, the buds being famously wary of late frosts). Some paschal flower – primroses, anemones – would have seemed more likely. The man who died was shot on Good Friday. His life lingered on for a few more hours, yet he died before Easter dawned.

But the association of lilac with Lincoln's death is stronger than scruples about fact and history. Here, as elsewhere, memory's claim to be taken seriously depends partly upon its refusal to be impartial and partly upon the fact that memory alone can arrest time, wind time backwards and, characteristically, recover and reconstruct it, thus resisting objectivity at the same time as making events and the sensation of events live again through imagination and partiality. These things are nearly central to the argument of this chapter, just as they are to the success of Whitman's poem. He places the mourning in terms of three indices of time: the passage of a day and a night (the 'great star . . . in the western sky'), the season of lilac blossom and the cycle of the 'ever-returning spring'. But he artfully disturbs the proper hierarchy of these temporal framings: the lilac, not the day span, comes first. And last. We register the hint of *never again* when 'lilacs *last* in the door-yard bloom'd'.

It would be a simple and easy matter to construct a rough and ready calendar according to times of blossom. To begin the year there would be Christmas roses, the Glastonbury thorn and snowdrops, followed by forsythia in March and then daffodils, primroses, pussy willows, tulips, magnolias and the May (the blossom of the hawthorn), bluebells and Queen Anne's lace, lilac and wisteria, through the rosy, dog-daisy days of June, July and August – lime blossom, ivy blossom, nectar-drunk bees – colchicums in September, and then into autumn Michaelmas daisies and cyclamen, heather on the hills and pine cones in the woods, closing perhaps with poinsettias inside the house at Christmas. We could all do this, with individual variations according to the character of our own gardens.

Britain and Ireland along with most of Europe (but only parts of the USA) are lucky enough to know four broad seasons, but even within them there are smaller tides and phases too – shorter-spanned but vivid seasons-in-miniature identified with and named after the plants which reach their apogee in them: the Blackthorn Winter, Cherry Blossom Time, Bluebell Time, Lilac Time, Blackberry Picking, the Mushroom Season. So engrained are the habits of associating phases of the year with plants that, when they are expressed well, they can sometimes achieve the weight of proverb. Cleopatra speaks of her 'salad days', and so do we of ours, without thinking twice about the curious image.[2] The children's rhyme 'Here we come gathering nuts in May, nuts in May, nuts in May;/ Here we come gathering nuts in May, on a cold and frosty morning' assumes a humorous complicity in its calendrical nonsense.[3] You do *not* gather nuts in May, but in the autumn, and though you have frosts in winter, it is the sun that you enjoy in May. But the very word *anthology* actually means, in its original Greek, a 'collection of flowers'. You could easily mark the phases of the year with exactly appropriate botanical quotations from poetry.

> Loveliest of trees, the cherry now . . .[4]

Or

> The holly and the ivy,
> When they are both full grown . . .[5]

Or, indeed,

> When lilacs last in the door-yard bloom'd . . .

Gardens provide us with chances to become involved in alternative patterns of time which are independent of, and perhaps essentially at variance with, ordinary chronometrical time. That is one of the deepest and perhaps most subversive ways in which they impinge upon us; one of the ways in which they seem to us to mean something, to make sense. This is important – all the more so perhaps when we consider, historically and in the here and now, how much we are measured and driven, slave-like, by time even when (since we are its inventor) we should be its masters. The Roman day lasted twelve hours – from dawn till dusk, irrespective of the season – so an hour in summer was something like twice as long as an hour in winter. Correspondingly, a working day for a medieval labourer would have been about twice as long in July as it was in November.

The relative brevity of life (the most personally significant span of our time) once pressed a quality upon time which we, enjoying so much more of it in quantitative terms, are less able to understand now – until, that is, we remind ourselves of the psychological reality behind expressions such as 'time dragged' or 'time rushed by'. On the other hand, perhaps the sheer monotony of so much of the labour that would have engrossed the lives of so many people (and actually still does, but in different forms now) might have meant that time was a burdensome thing anyway unless you ignored it.

The ways in which we have calibrated and regulated time reflect a tension between the abstract (the mathematically objective and astronomically correct) and the subjectively, waywardly human. In most other matters of mensuration – length and volume, weight and shape – we have tended to impose ourselves, or parts of ourselves (our bodies), into the measurements. But time, in reality so abstract, has shouldered us away, and the abstract has triumphed over the organic. We have forced ourselves to measure it not by reference to or analogy with ourselves, but from the motions and patterns of the non-human, physical cosmos. The sovereignty of time – waiting for no man – is expressed irresistibly through its abstraction. Even something as obvious as the difference between looking at a (circular, recurring, ever-renewing) clock face and a set of figures (linear, never to happen again) on a digital clock may make a very telling impact upon how we understand time: does it indeed belong to us at all? What might really be meant by 'having the time of our lives' or 'having time to ourselves'?

And we chafe against it – the passage of time – not just because it is abstract, and cold, and essentially artificial for all its mathematical rigour, but because there are times when we don't *naturally* conform to it. Though we may blush at their unscientific imprecision, we tend intuitively to associate ourselves with other, less linear schemes of time, more 'natural' rhythms. The practice of music – making it, listening to it – is one of these. Another is the semi-regulated mode, the semi-natural rhythms, of our gardens, where we split some of the differences between nature and human nature. These things offer us meta-times, as it were. There is here, perhaps, a sense in which we remain intuitively alchemists even as we strut our stuff as grown-up, self-respecting chemists. At any rate, in some primitive but significant ways, our human nature remains deeply at odds with the abstract nature of the world in which we find ourselves, and this is perhaps never more so than in the way we perceive the medium of time and ourselves as its vectors. Emily Dickinson (1830–1886) wrote:

> The vastest earthly Day
> Is shrunken small
> By one Defaulting Face
> Behind a Pall –[6]

The only truly human unit of measurement, the only element in the whole artifice of measured time which corresponds organically with the rhythms of humans (but then only approximately), is the coinciding of the phases of the moon (just over 29 and a half days – or, to be precise, 29 days, 12 hours, 44 minutes and 2.98 seconds) with the cycle of menstruation in women (the Latin word *mensis* means 'month'). All the rest is mathematical construct and, beautiful though the maths may be, it remains an artifice, an abstraction when applied to how we see ourselves, how we live and what for.

Historically, where you began the cycle (of time or of space) was just as likely to depend upon temperament, geography, politics or climate as upon the sort of geophysical data that we would use if we were starting now from scratch. Those first measurers were not, as we are now, heliocentric but geocentric. (But let us not be too superior: after all, we still speak of sunrise and sunset when, strictly speaking, we should be saying earthrise and earthfall.) To the ancients, the heart of it all – the centre of their cosmos – was their great local mountain, or the great lake, which suggested to them the apex or very bowel of their earth. Another favourite fixed axial point was the great world tree (the *axis mundi* again). Trees implied gardens, and the Garden itself became the *fons et origo* of the world, written first into Near Eastern myth and then into Christianity. It was the Garden of Eden that saw our Genesis. Thus, and in deeply subversive ways, all of us – and gardeners in particular – have historically felt the compulsion to look not to something new, futuristic, but to something lost, something we would dearly wish to recover.

Then came the objective, geophysical fixture of magnetic north, slightly refined before long into true north. Other fixed points came and went. 'Nought degrees' was eventually established through Greenwich rather than its rival Paris, and that was a reflection of politics and power rather than of any supra-temporal application of science or reason. One day, perhaps, it will move again as evidence of some other imperial boast. Rome reckoned distances from Trajan's Column, imperial Britain from Nelson's. The French Revolutionaries started time all over again, with Year One commencing on 22 September 1792 (though Gregorian time was reinstated there in 1806). Parts of Asia still adhere to the Islamic Calendar, whereby the new era began with the flight of Muhammad from Mecca in 622. The Chinese New Year begins on the first day of the first month in the traditional Lunar Calendar – and that usually means a date in February.

It is in the tension between *measuring* time quantitatively and *treasuring* time qualitatively – and that imponderable question of whom it is that time actually belongs to anyway – that we encounter the rub. Probably it is felt most sharply when we strive to reconcile 'making a living' with 'having a life'. That the two so rarely coincide is a fundamental difficulty of the human condition, a residue (as it seems sometimes) of a sort of primal, post-Edenic curse upon us all. And that is another sense in which gardens can mean something, because they can suspend time, translate it, alter it; because 'working in the garden' is a pleasure and not the drudgery so many of us perceive and feel in being 'employed', because this represents a radical (edenically recovered) inversion of how and why we might live.

> 'Twas later when the summer went
> Than when the Cricket came –
> And yet we knew that gentle Clock
> Meant nought but Going Home –
> 'Twas sooner when the Cricket went
> Than when the Winter came
> Yet that pathetic Pendulum
> Keeps Esoteric Time.
>
> EMILY DICKINSON[7]

In practice, we all live in several time zones, sometimes simultaneously but more often sequentially. There is the mechanical time that governs most of our work, the periodicity of our salaries, the six o'clock news and the rest, but, like (and sometimes because of) music, we are also – and usually more willingly – subject to other patterns of time. These are flexible and variable, not mechanical and precisely 'accurate'. They both reflect and, to some extent, determine how we feel.

In practice – and not just in our dreams, and not just because we are led there by Salvador Dalí (1904–1989) – in moments of absent-mindedness, in moments of vision, all our clocks are apt to melt . . . sometimes. An hour spent with a novel or in the theatre may encapsulate the entire lives of the people depicted within. An hour only, and yet we don't feel cheated by a distortion of ellipsis or contraction. We sense and are satisfied by what seems entire, complete, an integrity. The paradox is compounded when we notice that the hour passed 'in no time at all', such was our involvement. The fictions had worked some sort of magic in effecting, first, a synchronicity between the time we spent reading the book or watching the play or film with the time span of the people depicted inside it; and then a virtual suspension of time anyway. It was a shock to emerge from the matinée cinema to find it was dark outside. Some sort of adjustment into, and then out of, different time zones had to take place.

Language betrays the fact that though time itself may be a more or less objective construct, the way we think about it is not. What matters to us is not so much what time is, as what we feel about it. The word *temporary* (Latin *tempus*: 'time') should mean simply 'occurring in time' (as in 'temporal'), but there is a moral, emotional edge to it too. We can grin and bear with something if it is only temporary, or, alternatively, we make the very most of it if it is precious but ephemeral. Whatever the case may be, it is a word that we keep at arm's length. To consider ourselves as 'only temporary' requires some sangfroid, and so, generally, we don't. The way we behave and the things we do are governed not only by obligations to regimes of the clock and contractual obligations to employers but by how we feel: not only by circumstance but by temperament. Being *temperamental* – moody, inconsistent – often takes the form of refusing to conform to the obligations of time.

Temperament in music governs tuning first, but then mood, meaning and sense. Music, like us, moves in time, though time measured not in the mathematically abstract but in, and by, something far less mechanical, implied in the organically human (as well as musically technical) word *pulse* – an almost infinitely flexible medium which, not accidentally, also brings about a coincidence sometimes between music and the motions, the pulses, of our own hearts, the tempo of the music corresponding exactly with the pulse, beat, heart-motions at the core of our being. At other times – and actually much more frequently – music acts to change the rate of our cardiac pulses. In music, by the manipulation of pulse through changes of *tempi*, changes of metre and rhythmic inflexion, time (that is, crude metronomic time) is subverted and reformed. At its most remarkable is *hemiola*: bars measured literally, mechanically, in terms of one metre (say, a compound 6/8, as in a gigue) but being inflected as if they were a square two-in-a-bar, as in a march. Who actually minds (or even notices), for example, that the waltz in the second movement of Tchaikovsky's Sixth Symphony has not three but five beats to the bar? No one but the incorrigible number-cruncher. Because we do not after all dance to the music of time, but to the time of our lives. That, I suppose, is the heart of music's power both to stimulate and to calm, to disturb one matrix of order by superimposing another. It is a curious and telling thing that to play music perfectly (absolutely accurately in terms of conformity to metronomic pulse as, for example, a computer would or a drum machine) is also to ruin it. The life of music consists in its infinitely small and nuanced nonconformities.

That logic of local and personal time – the 'time of our lives', we say – reminds us of the retrospective sense of certain periods of time having had particular moods and modes quite independently of their temporal span. We speak with some consensus about the Age of Reason, the Long Eighteenth Century, the Age of Anxiety, the Fin de Siècle and so on. Some other, alternative calendars are with us still – all of them only for residual historical reasons. We still have an Academic Year; the Fiscal Year goes its own way; the Jewish New Year has its own date; Christmas and

Easter in the Orthodox churches generally differ from the dates upon which they are celebrated in the western churches. Particular modes of life – particular professions even – as well as particular moods impose different senses of the passage of time. Astrophysicists subsist in that most metaphysically delineated world of all, a region which ought really to belong to poetry, in which Time is indeed Space. Societies of hunters and nomadic herdsmen will always have been obliged to follow seasonal rather than calendrically precise annual rhythms: to shielings and summer pastures and then to winter shelters, following migratory flocks – the seasonal vagaries – of birds, schools of fish and herds of game.

> Nor will the sweetest delight of gardens afford much comfort in sleep, wherein the dullness of that sense shakes hands with delectable odours; and, though in the bed of Cleopatra, can hardly with any delight raise up the ghost of a rose.[8]

Sir Thomas Browne (1605–1682), who must stand as an *éminence grise* over any writer of gardens as well as of time, engages here with two distinct temporal modes: the first, the chronometrical, lurks behind the rhythms of sleeping and waking; the second, the more flexible and human, lies more deeply behind the intimations of mortality (the ghost of that rose and the Lethean dullness of 'sleep') and the sex and regenerative potency invoked in the presence of Cleopatra.

The solemn, resonant dignity of Browne's prose – sombre and mannered and very impressive – strides across the pages like the component yews of a Jacobean topiary garden, its shapes and postures almost (but not quite) absurd, its groupings constituting a veritable presence in the garden (as at Levens Hall in Cumbria or at Athelhampton in Dorset). The syntax curls and uncurls as if it were a knot garden. Browne's manner is, as I suppose he intended, his own greatest monument, his own abiding residue long after his death, his own answer to the problem of mortality and temporariness. Insofar as he was temperamentally capable of any sort of comedy at all, the beautiful half-cadence of 'and, though in the bed of Cleopatra' must be reckoned as one of the finest paraphrases ever of the tedious platitude 'life is not a bed of roses.' Only that weariness of the tone, in the context of Egyptian voluptuousness here, could hint at Browne's characteristically detached, anatomically mechanical (he was, after all, a doctor) and slightly disgusted view of sex, expressed occasionally elsewhere too. He could see the ridiculous side of it, if not quite the funny aspect: 'it is the foolishest act a wise man commits in all his life.'[9] Also characteristically, he was apt to frame intellectual observations in the context of gardens. He wished, for example, that our coitions might be accomplished like that of trees – silently, with purpose and efficiency undisturbed by passion.

Sensual he may not have been, but sensuous he certainly was, and extremely sensitive to the rhythms of time which gardens offer as alternatives to the clock. Here he is, bruised and starkly objective: 'Gravestones tell truth scarce forty years; generations pass while some trees stand, and old families last not three oaks.'[10]

To plant a tree is often to mark an event, or the closing of what we see as one epoch, or the anticipation of what may be another. Trees – most of them – last so long that the act of planting them constitutes a gesture at least towards extending our own influence well, well beyond the span of our own lives. To plant is to bequeath something to the future – the thought of which, but not the realization, we can enjoy – but in it there is also some gestural grit of defiance against our own mortality, our own temporariness. Trees last longer than we do but, like us, they don't last forever. They belong, like us, in the onward march of linear time, but their time is slower, longer and less personal than ours. They age better than we do. They finally close their lives blamelessly and unselfconsciously. Their timber, dead though it is, continues after them in ways that seem to mean, in a material sense at least, that trees are just as useful, or even more useful, dead than alive.

These characteristics of trees in time are not interchangeably ours too, but they blend with and develop some of the best of our own ambitions. When we set about to construct a map, if not of our permanence then at least of our continuity, it seems natural to call it our 'family tree'.

On a much, much smaller scale of time are the lives of annual plants; they're all over in four or five months, but no less complete and entire for their brevity. That we should have originated and enabled in the first place some of these things – by sowing their seeds and planting them out – connects us to their lives. That our lives are sustained, in some cases and in some measure, by their fruits, their seeds, their roots and their leaves makes the connection both literally and figuratively vital.

Between the plant whose whole life begins and ends in the same year and the long-lived tree, there is every degree and variety of length of life: peonies for fifty years, sorbus for thirty, hybrid tea roses for about ten, angelica for two. But, however long or short that may be, these living, vegetable things exemplify an integrity of being and purpose which we would probably be hard put to identify in our own lives. Every year there is generation – blossom, pollination and seed – and each time this happens there is beauty. That this beauty is often far, far in excess of what is necessary to achieve pollination may be a creature of our own imagination, but it means mightily to us, fiction or not. It is important to us to seem to have evidence that beauty – whatever its constituents and whatever its biological context – is, in the last analysis, gratuitous.

Somewhere in all this we are bound, sooner or later, to see our own lifespans relative to those of trees, herbaceous plants, insects and animals. We must see ourselves – in terms of the time that we last – as dwarfed by the life of a great tree; yet relative to the lifespans of most plants and all insects, we have all the time in the world. Or so it seems, until we remember that almost none of these things sees itself at all. Unlike us, they aren't self-conscious. It is not individual survival but the survival of their species which absorbs all their energies. Even when their lives are temporally short, relative to each one of us their existence is timeless. Edward Thomas (1878–1917) captures all of this – the temporariness of people, things, birds and the myth of forever-ness – in eight lines that construct and deconstruct time itself:

> There they stand, on their ends, the fifty faggots
> That once were underwood of hazel and ash
> In Jenny Pinks's Copse. Now, by the hedge
> Close packed, they make a thicket fancy alone
> Can creep through with the mouse and wren. Next Spring
> A blackbird or a robin will nest there,
> Accustomed to them, thinking they will remain
> Whatever is for ever to a bird.[11]

Gardens are fragile. Like us, gardens exist in space and time, and while individual plants may outlast us, gardens themselves most certainly do not unless they are cared for – by our descendants.

There is no more poignant occasion for realizing this than when witnessing the distress brought about by visiting a once planted, now neglected grave. In garden making we borrow from plants some tokens and talismans of abiding life but, uncared for, a garden becomes instead a lesson in spectacularly accomplished ruin. The whole idea of leaving our remains in certain cultivated places, and the intention that those places should be, even in these secular times, almost sacred to the memory of the people who lie there, is a hazardous one. A year's neglect and they are more like grisly memento mori, but kept well and for at least as long as someone still remembers the last person to have been laid there, such places, through the sense of generation and regeneration which trees and plants impart – even the lugubrious yew and the funereal conifers of the boundary hedges – convey some intimations of eternity perhaps, or at least of something abiding.

We can date the origins of this new landscaped style of interment and mourning – no longer in a necropolis but in a garden of remembrance – to early nineteenth-century France. In 1804 the widely imitated landscape cemetery of Père-Lachaise was opened on the outskirts of Paris. But even when a garden is not consciously intended in any sense as a theatre of memory for anyone dead (and that means the vast majority of gardens), there is still an unavoidable sense in which, striving to make them idyllic, we are recovering some myth of our own.

All the various sorts of time at work in a garden mesh like cogs, all of different sizes and all moving at different speeds. Linnaeus devised, on paper at least, a *horologium florae* whose hours were signalled by the opening and closing of particular flowers: the morning glory, Jack-go-to-bed-at-noon, the sowthistle, the daylily. But time measured naturally invites us to compare the span of our own lives with that of other living things. The last cog of all – but significantly not the largest – is the wheel of our own lives. And insofar as there can be no garden without also a gardener – not just in the sense that, uncared for, the garden will decay, but because it takes the one to make sense of the other – garden and gardener are indivisible.

Sundials were placed out of doors for the obvious reason that it was there that they would catch the sun. Now – their long, long reputation having gone before them for being unreliable, for being disabled by cloud, for being accurate only in high summer – they are to be found in gardens as much as ever, but as decoration, not as functional timepieces. Ironically, the first place you'd expect to find a sundial now is probably the last place in which you are, or want to be, conscious of time. It is not time that sundials encourage us to notice now but place, a place apart, where time, if it impinges at all, is occasional, is moveable, is almost an object of aesthetic rather than philosophical contemplation – a place where time itself has made time for us. A place, sometimes, where time is suspended.

The image embodies the idea. That fusion is meaningful.

Gerard Manley Hopkins (1844–1889) was not the first to have noticed that even children – who so generally behave as if they were immortal – are not quite entirely immune to intimations of mortality after all, but no one else has so precisely placed this wound and this vulnerability in their most telling context of all: a grove of trees. (But he was probably the first – by his idiosyncratic use of accents – to insist that the mensuration of time in poetry is not a matter of mathematical, number-crunched syllables, but the 'instresses' of sense.) This is his 'Spring and Fall: to a young child':

MÁRGARÉT, are you gríeving
Over Goldengrove unleaving?
Leáves, líke the things of man, you
With your fresh thoughts care for, can you?
Áh! ás the heart grows older
It will come to such sights colder
By and by, nor spare a sigh
Though worlds of wanwood leafmeal lie;
And yet you wíll weep and know why.
Now no matter, child, the name:
Sórrow's spríngs áre the same.

Nor mouth had, no nor mind, expressed
What heart heard of, ghost guessed:
It ís the blight man was born for,
It is Margaret you mourn for.[12]

3

The Garden as Theatre

It is arguable that almost all of the places in which we conduct our lives and our business are theatres of a sort, at least in the elemental sense that things happen there, words are spoken, deeds are done, and if we permit (or even when we don't), other people can watch if they wish to. After all, we 'perform' our duties, our ablutions, even miracles (if we can), play our parts in the dramas that life thrusts upon us and so on. At one extreme, you might think of Louis XIV's *lever*: his public rising from his bed. At another, your Finals' Examination Room. Think of those classrooms for surgeons, the anatomy theatres. Think of lecture theatres. But some places are more private than others, if only in the sense that though there may still be an audience, we can choose who they are. Humans, being social animals, have set aside only a few places which are truly and absolutely private. In that respect a garden is as much (or as little) a theatre as anywhere else.

The largest of the 'rooms' in Lawrence Johnston's garden at Hidcote in Gloucestershire is the Theatre Lawn. It is also the emptiest. At one end there is a large raised oval of turf – the stage – and that stage is magisterially held by an ancient beech. The whole space – stage and lawn – is walled by yew and is otherwise empty – except for you and your imagination. It is masterly.

At the other end of the scale (of how much is left to your own imagination) is that much-reviled thing: the garden of gnomes. Picture the scene: little chaps – they're always blokes, never women – with pointy hats. Some of them have homely beards, some are clean-shaven. Some carry shovels or fishing rods, or they push wheelbarrows. Some are very cheerful indeed; one is Grumpy. There may be a wishing well. If the denizens of this place were capable of movement, this would be a hive of wholesome industry. You would hear cheerful whistling and artless song: bright-coloured sounds to match their jocund, comfortable clothes. Waistcoats are the order of the day. On top of a low wall a (cast-concrete) cat is forever playing, not with a mouse or a fear-struck fledgling, but with a ball of wool. A hedgehog – clearly a close relative of Mrs Tiggy-Winkle – crosses the lawn. A ladybird is sunning itself on a reassuringly un-narcotic toadstool. Squirrels sport along the fence. A frog is caught forever in the moment of leaping from a lily pad, and so it goes on.

If you don't like gnomes, you could replace them with a child's fairy garden, or with Moth, Cobweb and Peasblossom, characters with more august thespian pedigrees, even though they are really still just sprites, pixies, boggarts and hobs. This particular lot are probably made from black-painted sheet steel. They will seem to have trodden printlessly, lissom-toed, across your lawn (but only when your back is turned and not on Thursdays, the gardener's day off, because he won't be there to move them while you're not looking). Install them, and they will turn the whole of your garden into 'the bottom of your garden' in the manner of Richard Dadd (1817–1886), or the Water Babies, or anything nostalgically but tastefully Victorian (illus. 9).

Or, if you hold that both gnomes and fairies are irredeemably naff, then you could people your garden with sculpture, originals or concrete casts: Flora and Strephon for the woodland glade, Hercules with his club for the end of the pleached lime avenue, and a sexy Aphrodite to set off the lilies on the broad water.

Chatsworth and Disneyland, Versailles and Tivoli (and all the countless lesser versions of them), in essence they all have at least this in common: the same impulse to see the garden as a theatre

– theatre of regressive fantasy (perhaps), or of Arcadian innocence, or of classical high-mindedness. We are the audience, and though we aren't written into the scripts and the actors themselves don't move, we are invited to become imaginatively involved in the plots. And we *do* move, and so our mingling with the actors, though more in the nature of tableaux than drama, nonetheless gives the scenes an air of movement. Our psychological involvement supplies still another level of dynamic. Snapshots of ourselves taken there *en scène* are the stills, as it were, of the visit, the drama.

In Le Nôtre's garden for Louis XIV (1638–1715) at Versailles, where the scale of things is at its greatest (park, acres, world), it is we who are shrunk, we who are dwarfed, we whose steps are unequal to the distances to be covered (the tour of Versailles was always intended to be made by carriage), and we who must look up if we are to catch the eyes of the heroes whose home this is. The statues, for their part, never deign to look down at us, but we, ant-like and tiny though we are, can still feel safe. These are gods who may sling thunderbolts, but we are so insignificant and diminutive that their artillery will pass harmlessly over our heads.

Classical gardens like this did not strike the people who made them as comic, still less as ironic, any more than contemporary gnomeries (where *we* are the giants) are a joke to those who devise them. Both are seriously meaningful in their separate ways even while both may be harbouring the absurd, the ridiculous, the laughable, at least to the coolly impartial eye.

The source of the word *gnome* is obscure. A fusion of the Greek *ge* and *nomi* (earth and dweller) seems possible. And it would make sense. In any case, gnomes are said to have made their first appearance in a British garden at Lamport Hall in Northamptonshire. There they were appropriately sited to look like gardeners-cum-quarryworkers on the large rockery of Sir Charles Isham (1819–1903).

In the 1840s he had imported these terracotta figures from Nuremberg, where they had long been talismans for miners, because gnomes and their kin had always been associated with life and work underground. There had been (and still is) a tradition there of spirits associated with mining. Sometimes rather sinister, sometimes just cheerfully mischievous, they went by the name of *Kobolde* (illus. 10). Isham had begun, in 1847, to plant up his rockery with small alpine plants and dwarf conifers. He was a spiritualist as well as a gardener. In his garden, there were reported sightings of 'several authentic cases of fairies'.[1] This particular theatre evidently had a life of its own.

The Irish variant of subterranean people has it that successive waves of invasion caused the autochthonous inhabitants to take flight, first to the wild places – the forest, the mountains and the caves – and then, with nowhere else to go, underground, condemned to work: bringing up sacks of good soil to make stony places fertile. Once giants, now they shrank. They became the Sidhe, the Little People, a magical race living out of sight but certainly not out of mind. On (or rather under) the land, the Sidhe became the genii of the places which the people above ground incautiously took for their own. The Sidhe, the Fairies, the Little People (pixies, imps, gnomes, leprechauns and the *púca*) continued their lives parallel to ours but almost invisibly. If we stole their treasures (the mineral fruits of their underground world – their crocks of gold – and thus their kinship with the German *Kobolde*), they might take their revenge on us by bringing the human house down when the tunnels beneath us collapse, or the air in the shaft explodes, or the fracking causes earthquakes. It's easy to see how miners in particular would want to keep on the right side of such folk. Otherwise, the Sidhe might cause the milk to turn in the butter-making or, far worse, lure away their children (who might follow, not always reluctantly – such are the magnetic lures of music, of storytelling, of other worlds).

> Come away, O human child!
> To the waters and the wild
> With a faery, hand in hand,
> For the world's more full of weeping than you can
> understand.[2]

Or it might be that they were not so much lured as snatched. Goethe's 'Erlkönig' (1782) suggests both. The German folkloric figure the Pied Piper reverted to luring. In the countryside of Ireland you can still hear them – the Sidhe, that is, not the gnomes – referred to as the Good People. The folk above ground still hedge their bets.

The great Irish garden at Mount Stewart in County Down remembers something of this (as well as the makers and keepers of this garden itself) by incorporating within its acres of woodland a family mausoleum. This, being infused with a distinctive Celtic, mythic spirit, is not some austere place, magnificent but deathly, like the Hawksmoor mausoleum visible from (but still – prudently? – outside) the garden at Castle Howard in Yorkshire, but a much more playful building, with a turret suggestive of both a fairytale castle and an ancient *dun*, peeping between the trees on the other side of the lake, almost but not quite within reach: the Land of Heart's Desire, Tír na nÓg, the Land of the Ever Young. This pre-Christian Irish Otherworld has none of the shuddering chilliness and gloom of the Greek Hades. On the contrary, such is its reputation for bliss that it was adopted as the trade name of a chain of stores selling children's clothes. The charming, fairytale, family mausoleum in the garden at Mount Stewart is in the best manner of the English architect William Burges (1827–1881), he of Castell Coch and of the Victorian interiors and new fortifications at Cardiff Castle.

Because there is so much to say about gardens in the English classical tradition – so much to explain, so much to decode – a great deal has been written about them. And rightly so. But what has been less discussed is that they are also – and, in some respects, much more simply – ravishingly beautiful places and, as a result of that, whatever may be the meanings they have (articulated through literary, painterly and political reference), these don't necessarily have to be understood before the beauty (if not the entire sense) of the place strikes the visitor. Moreover, in each case – Stourhead, Rousham, Stowe and the rest – the whole is greater than the sum of its parts.

That said, at Stowe there are more than ten temples (or 'fanes', or 'altars'). The chains of associations begin with their very titles. And it was this place that prompted the writing and publication of the first serious guide to an English garden: Benton Seeley's *A Description of the Gardens of Lord Viscount Cobham, at Stow in Buckinghamshire* of 1744. First, there are temples of Bacchus, Janus, Venus and Sleep, each one intended to be associated with and to stimulate quite particular moods, reflections and references. Each is the physical theatre of what we more usually take to be something abstract. Each is quite deliberately a frame of mind. Then there are temples which are just as intentional in their framing of our minds but whose dedication is straightway to the abstract: Concord (and Victory), Friendship, Honour, Vanity, Liberty and Virtue. Some of these are glossed even further. The Temple of Vanity is also named the Temple of Modern Virtue. The Temple of Virtue itself is glossed as the Temple of Ancient Virtue, and the Temple of Honour is also titled the Temple of British Worthies. In addition, there are the Fane of Pastoral Poetry and a Gothic Temple dedicated to Liberty and invoking Cobham's Saxon lineages.

The theme of these gardens (for they are in a very real, if anachronistic, sense theme parks) is more or less classical in origin and reference, but contemporary (that is to say, eighteenth century) in inference. And eclectic too: we know there were at various times (especially but not exclusively at Painshill) ephemeral constructions in the manner of 'Turkish Tents', 'Chinese Pagodas', 'Mogul Pavilions' and so on. Nevertheless, essentially the mood was a classical one, and its essence runs something like this: once upon a time there had been an Age of Gold, but the metal and temper of our time is iron at best, or baser still if studied closely and candidly. Virtue, however, did not die with the ancients. Their example is our legacy. It is accessible to us through ancient books, ancient archaeology and ancient languages, but you – the contemporary visitor – stand now in a living landscape and, because it lives, its informing spirits transcend place and time, history and language. This place actively informs us, our minds, our spirits and our senses. Here you will find classical virtues – a harmony of reason and nature (and the truth expressed through both of them), the liberty of the individual, the virtues of justice and the commonwealth, the wisdom of poetry and so on – rekindled and alive not only in the landscape itself but in you, your history and your nation. In the philosophical abstract, this is the distilled wisdom of Greek *sophia* and Roman *virtus*. Translated into mid-eighteenth-century political rhetoric, the garden as a whole and in its parts is a statement of allegiance to the Hanoverian Succession, a demonstration of pride in British imperial might or a declaration of commitment to the contemporary Whig agenda.

The garden at Stowe is a political argument. The more or less contemporary garden at Stourhead is more abstract. Other eighteenth-century landscape gardens – some of them made by Tories, but most by Whigs – share more or less the same intentions. It is true that Charles Hamilton's Painshill probably had no philosophical programme at all beyond the creation of an Arcadia, but that theme in itself would furnish an entire classical library. All of them incorporate the abstract spirit of a past age to quicken and breathe meaning into their own. All of them, to a greater or lesser degree, incorporate personifications of these abstractions in the form of statues, dedications, literary references and memorials.

In almost all of them there was an intentional correspondence between the paintings on the walls inside the house and the views to be gained in the gardens, between the scenes in the classical texts inside the library and the scenes outside. Inside and out, these things were to supply the frames of the minds of the people who lived or visited here.

In this sense, these entire places – houses and gardens – are theatres of ideas, of values and of evocations of the vibrant ghosts of the people who originally espoused those ideas and values. In both a technical and a general sense, they are fictions – something which itself is false but which enables something else to be recognized as true. The gardens are false in all sorts of ways, but because we're so used to fictions as powerful (and entertaining) vehicles of truth, we don't give it a second thought. Nevertheless, for a moment – but without any wish to deconstruct or damage the fictions – we should pause to consider these enabling tropes, because otherwise we will fail to understand these places. (And, in any case, their greatest glory – the sum of their meanings – is absolutely real. I mean again their consummate beauty.) Here are some of them. The statues aren't real people; they are simulacra in lead or dead stone of once living but now entirely absent people. The Valley (at Stowe) is not Grecian, despite its name. (The men at work scything the turf do not speak Greek. The intensity of the sun does not bake a Greek landscape, and there are no olives.) The Palladian Bridge does not cross an Italian stream or, indeed, any stream to speak of, and certainly not one whose (natural) volume would have justified such a large bridge. The texts – implicit or explicit and engraved or sign-written for your edification – are actually the silent voices of the voiceless: *eidolopoeia*, the voices of the dead. You are not listening to but lip-reading the past. Above all, you are not expected to worship at any of the altars or in any of the temples. This, perhaps the most invisible of all the fictions, is possibly the most penetrating. However you look at it, this is theatre.

In the case of Louis XIV and Versailles, Le Nôtre was instructed to design the garden there according to an iconographic programme. The Sun King took his pattern from the sun itself and from its personification in Apollo. The garden's main axes follow the points of the compass and thus geometrically resemble – if only from a bird's-eye view – a schematic sun. The prospect from the Grande Galerie was of a seemingly endless vista into the setting sun. Likewise, from the other side of the palace, the rising sun was framed by the garden, just as – an hour or two later, at least – the king himself would conduct his *lever*, his rising, within the golden chambers of the palace itself. The association of Sun King and Apollo has political, ideological and mythological implications, but the fiction doesn't require specific religious inferences to be drawn.

So it is too with the temples in the English landscape gardens. The philosophical tone of these places was intended to transcend particular cultural refractions, religion among them. That would have been in sympathy with the (progressive) deist thought of the time. Nevertheless, insofar as the presence of temples implied worship, that act would take place only inside the solipsistic theatre of your own thoughts, and not in any recognizably liturgical sense, albeit with your mind framed by the very present prompts of classical and ancient pastoral associations.

But then there is the case of Sir Francis Dashwood (1708–1781) and his classical garden at West Wycombe in Buckinghamshire. Not just classical but pretty flagrantly erotic. In Dashwood's mausoleum – his last words, as it were – Christian texts or even inferences were forbidden, and it was built explicitly on his instructions to lie partly within and partly without the consecrated ground of the parish churchyard. Syncretism – hedging your confessional bets – was not necessarily affectation. Dr William Stukeley (1687–1765), antiquarian (the first important writer to consider the significance of Stonehenge), physician and – eventually – divine, might strike us now as idiosyncratic and eccentric, but to his contemporaries he was held in high esteem. He promulgated the opinion – virtually the creed – that Druids had been proto-Christians. There was no conflict of culture or catechism for him here, but only continuity. His contemporaries did not actively demur.

I have dwelt at some length upon this quasi-religious appearance of gardens partly because the recurrent idea of gardens as the recoveries of Edens, which informs so much of the meaning of so many European gardens of whatever age or style, has inevitably brought biblical (and then Christian) undertones with it. However, these undertones shouldn't be allowed to monopolize the ways in which the gardens themselves make their meanings evident to us. The myth and the mythic cast of mind go deeper than particular sectarian complexions. The classical – and thus the pagan and Arcadian rather than the Christian and Edenic – complexion of these particular gardens we have been considering is just one of those historically local (European and indeed several eighteenth-century American) guises which the myth has assumed. A second factor is that the whole matter is evidence of one of the themes of this book – the garden as fiction, as a species of theatre – and of this particular fiction being almost as invisible as it is very close indeed to the heart of what gardens sometimes mean.

Nikolaus Pevsner (1902–1983) argued that the English landscape garden was brought about by thinkers – Pope, Burlington, Addison and so on – rather than by gardeners, but it's difficult to subscribe to that entirely if we bear in mind not only the (abstract) classical precedents and contemporary philosophical debates, but the material consequences as well: singularly beautiful places rather than just loci of embodied aesthetic ideals.[3]

And if required to supply an answer to the allied question – what then is the nature of the truth that these generative fictions reveal? – I don't think we have any choice but the Keatsian dictum, so hard to grasp with intellectual irons though it is: 'Beauty is truth, truth beauty.'[4] The obvious sense in which these places are far from simple is gainsaid by the extraordinary simplicity of the impression they make on the eye, intense and rich though that is. As a visitor – and the circuit of the garden completed, the moods absorbed – it is hard to leave places such as these without feeling that you have been improved somehow, that whatever is civilized (cultivated, educated, high-minded) about you has been refreshed and confirmed. But much stronger still are sensations of sheer, uncomplicated pleasure. You do feel that you have been drawn in artfully and by design, but you willingly consented and finally were glad to feel that you belonged there – naturally and without having to assume intellectual and educational airs and graces. The philosophical curriculum of these places is that by making (or recovering) a home for the ancients and for their gods we can also find ourselves at home, our minds framed by the experience, but what the places are really made of are beautiful prospects, harmonious proportions, the elements of space, colour, stone, water, trees and meadow making an absolutely convincing appearance of nature. That we know this can only have been achieved through the involvement of human beings sets the seal upon the experience. Nature and human nature are seen to be the indissoluble partners in the making of a real place – the sort of place which hitherto we had thought could exist only in the mind as an ideal. The Elysian Fields, the figments of our wishful, classicizing, theologizing imaginations, are open to real flesh-and-blood people after all.

One can imagine an impulse in the proprietors of both sorts of gardens (the high-minded classical and the demotic gnomes) to wish that their people, little or big, would come to life – essentially the same compulsion as drives the playwright. But equally, one can imagine the impulse being quickly reined in. It was all very well for Horace Walpole (1717–1797) in his 'History of the Modern Taste in Gardening' to applaud William Kent's famous 'leap' over the fence so that he 'saw that all nature was a garden', but, ironically, it was only because of the invention of another kind of fence – the invisible ha-ha, another of these gardens' fictions – that he could do so.[5] Without the ha-ha, the gardens would have been alive alright, but could the philosophic mind have been entirely philosophical about the liveliness of rutting deer, defecating fly-blown cows and the ineffably vacant minds of sheep? It would be all very well for the little windmill in the gnome garden to turn its sails, wind or no wind, or even for the sculpture in the landscape to move (sometimes it did: figures at the Villa d'Este moved by hydraulic action, and birds made of stone or lead 'sang'), but if the figures were not only to move but to go further and have a life of their own . . . the results might well be riveting to watch, but the theatre, the preordained frame of mind, would be wrecked, the play in ruins. The script is not the actors' own voices; they are ventriloquizing. That's part of the paradox of theatre itself: to be credibly realistic, to be alive, but not to have a life (or a mind) of its own. Something of the same problem faces all parents: at what point is the role of overseeing manager, director (scriptwriter?) in the lives of their children to be surrendered to the independent lives of the people they as parents originated?

To both of these points of view – the fully formed adult and the still enchanted child – Disneyland has found a solution: though the automata – of Mickey Mouse, the Incredible Hulk or whatever monster is currently spooking our imaginations – are fictions, it is we, the infantilized visitors, who are the children, irrespective of age.

By way of coda I want to consider one more, slightly more oblique, aspect of the idea of gardens as theatres. Theatres now are reckoned to be labouring under the embarrassment of two obstacles to open access: the prices they have to charge and the impression of being elitist palaces of culture that (they have been told) they give out. But they play on this too. Theatres are not only places to see but places to be seen in. They are loci of certain kinds of social interaction. If, historically and even now, access has sometimes been confined to high society, it makes no difference. The principle holds good no matter how wide or narrow is the social spectrum involved. Thus, *to have been seen* at Vauxhall Gardens or at Ranelagh in the 1740s, as well as having been there to make observations of your own, was part of the purpose of your visit. These places were the stage-sets of that timeless choreography of play and display, of impersonations and personifications – of playing and displaying. The sets (the component parts of the garden) we know were quite deliberately theatrical, and you yourself were part of the dramas being played out. The same thing goes on still in Copenhagen's Tivoli Gardens. The garden scenes are very contrived indeed (but very, very skilfully, discreetly and convincingly). The lake, seen from a variety of vantages, looks like a reproduction from the Willow Pattern merging into a scene from *Madama Butterfly*, or a fairy glade out of Hans Christian Andersen, or a classical landscape out of Hesiod, or a grove in the Everglades. At night, in summer, it is beautifully and cunningly lit (what theatre isn't?) to suggest a magical world. There are fantastically beautiful nocturnal insects (on invisible wires and made of perspex), misty gauzes of willow fronds half revealing, half concealing glades where shadows are warm and inviting (rather than threatening and sinister), and the whole place is full of scents and sounds, music and myrtles. The Tivoli Guard, children dressed as toy soldiers, complete the trope. What enemies could there be to spoil this idyll if toy soldiers and wooden rifles are sufficient to keep them at bay?

And you meet your friends here, or you make new ones. The cafés, the lakeside restaurants, the garden walks, the kiosks (have your silhouette drawn, try your strength with a mighty mallet, win the hoopla) and the superb children's playground – itself a sculpture park – are social venues. So it must have been in London's eighteenth- and nineteenth-century pleasure gardens. So it still is at Glyndebourne, though certainly not so demotically: to see and be seen, to be yourselves the incarnate drama, to play out a part in the garden theatre. And if this is merely a play on words, it is nevertheless a very old one which certainly predates the gardens under discussion and, indeed, the translation – by Richard Boyle (1694–1753), 3rd Earl of Burlington, patron of William Kent, one of the people credited by Pevsner with the invention of the English landscape garden – of Palladio's Olympic Theatre at Vicenza to the garden of his own country house at Chiswick in the 1720s.

The odd thing is that for most of us, most of the time, it is other people – the other actors? – who are anathema in a garden. They obstruct the views, they clutter and confuse the spaces, they disturb the air with their speech. We want to say that they are intruding upon the place, and so it may be, but the intrusion is most of all upon ourselves. Yet this is not necessarily a paradox, still less a flaw, in the metaphor of the garden as theatre and, therefore, as a *peopled* place. It is the ancient tension between seeing ourselves as social creatures and belonging to something larger, and yet as inviolably unique.

In sum, for all that gardens have often been configured in terms of performance and sometimes still are, part of their meaning may be that they are theatres not only of sculptures, of political and cultural ideologies, for ourselves and for other real people to perform and conform to, but (and more privately) of things less immediately real – private and particular memories and the ghosts of ideas – which matter on occasions to us even more than things that are solid, tangible and objective. These things – subjective impressions of particular places – are scattered among succeeding chapters.

4

INTERLUDE
Ilnacullin, County Cork, Ireland

You cannot reach Ilnacullin except by water. There's no bridge from the mainland, no road, no tidal causeway or stepping stones. You have to take the little boat from Glengarriff, and the island garden is a mile or so out into Bantry Bay. You thread a course between other small islands, other piles of rock. In summer at low tide, seaweed steams in the sun. There's time to dawdle by the colonies of seals. You look keenly at them, but they barely give you a second look. They lie on the rocks like slabs of primeval grey butter, or they perch on their stomachs, their backs stiff and their tail fins stuck out like rude tongues.

The man who guides your boat wears a shabby old yachting cap. He looks like a sailor of the old persuasion who can't swim on principle. Despite its somewhat dubious appearance, you trust the boat which he trusts himself to. (The boat is called the *Blue Pool*, and her livery is white but with blue braiding; it's better in Irish: *Poulgorm*.)

Away from the land a little, and you begin to assemble the elements of your sense of place. Behind you now, and out of sight, is Glengarriff, a pretty, old, spa town. The name means 'rough valley', but Glengarriff's appointments (a word they probably used in the original brochures for its Victorian hotels) are both genteel and accommodating. To the northwest and close by are the Caha Mountains. On a good day they glow soft purple, and you imagine miles and miles of unspoilt heather, but actually their surface is bare rock mostly. Knockboy rises to 705 metres (2,312 ft). It's blotched here and there with the darker shadows of clouds and speckled with the white of an occasional sheep. You know already that, for a few miles, the road over these mountains – the vast views, the surprises you get when you come out of tunnels – is one of the best drives in the world (illus. 4).

The small islands you passed in the bay clearly just rolled off these mountains, made a splash, and then settled in the sea. You begin to wonder which of them could be the garden. They all look the same, and they all look featureless: just rock and pine trees. But then the boat draws into a stony pool with a slipway running down into the water and a boathouse at the top. You can see the bottom through several feet of water. The boatman, who has stepped ashore, has only to lay on the gunwale hands big as shovels for the boat to rest safely against the stone ramp.

You wonder if you are in the right place. There's nothing to suggest that you have arrived at a garden. You notice all this and

4 W. H. Bartlett's illustration of Glengarriff, from *The Scenery and Antiquities of Ireland* (1842), vol. I. An imaginative view indeed of the Caha Mountains, but very beautiful too.

look behind you. There's nothing there either. Nothing but more anonymous rocky islands.

The journey to the garden, the sense of its separateness and of your own initiation into separation, is at the heart of the sense of this place. Likewise, the journey back, the reimmersion into the (relatively) giddy world of the busy pubs, the handful of shops and the hotels which constitute the town of Glengarriff. And then that mountain road north to Killarney.

You spot a sign that says 'To the Garden', and you climb (but quite carefully) up a path of polished, worn stones through what turns out only to be the shelter-belt of evergreen trees. In no time at all you are indeed in the garden. You step out on to a broad pavement, and before you stands an airy loggia. Down the shallow steps are a sunken garden and a pool. Closing this space and framing another, much larger prospect (the mountains beyond) is a small Italianate temple of Bath stone and red marble columns. You are in the great set piece of the island, which accounts for the proudly displayed subtitle: Ilnacullin, the Italian Gardens.

Some history is in order. In 1910 a Belfast-born man named Annan Bryce (1841–1923, MP for a Scottish constituency) bought the island from the British War Office. Apart from a Martello tower defending Bantry Bay from the French, there was only bald rock, a poor cottage, three or four very poor fields and a good deal of rough grazing. What little commercial value the place had must have consisted almost entirely in the turf dug out for fuel from between the rocks. But the strategic importance had been real enough once upon a time. In December 1796, 43 French ships carrying some 15,000 troops and the Irish patriot Wolfe Tone (1763–1798) set sail for Bantry Bay; they were battered by storms off the Irish Atlantic coast, and then the entire rebellion failed.

Having bought the island, Bryce set about having some spaces levelled, sometimes by pick and shovel and sometimes, when the rock wouldn't yield at all, by explosives. Tons and tons of topsoil were brought in by boat. After that, shelter-belts of pine and spruce were planted. On the whole, the climate here is kind, but the winds can be savage. Without this tall, tough girdle to the garden, salt spray would blight all but the most tolerant of plants. I imagine that *Griselinia littoralis* (a famously salt-tolerant small tree) was originally planted deliberately as a protecting understorey. Its success is evident not only in the calm air of the interior of the garden (though the ambient treetops sing a grand music sometimes) but in the thousands of self-sown seedlings everywhere. For years now, they've been weeding them out by the barrowful. Another plant to have become naturalized in this soft climate is *Gunnera manicata*, a very large rhubarb-like plant, its leaves easily big enough to shelter under in a rainstorm, its (inedible) stems brown-hairy and rough-pimpled. It flourishes in the garden itself, and then grows wild along the roadsides of the mainland too.

Bryce had a vision of a garden that would be home to all sorts of plants from the southern hemisphere (as indeed griselinia is). A rough and ready equivalence of latitude (with New Zealand and Australia) suggested the possibility, but he certainly knew a good deal of botany and horticulture too. And he had money. But above all, he had the imagination to project a visionary sense of place on to a desperately empty, fundamentally unyielding terrain. It is coincidence only that this beautiful mountainous landscape was also the scene of some of the worst privations of the Irish Famine, but it isn't an accident at all that its present fertility stems from vision as well as soil.

The vision was one we would all recognize, one stored in the treasuries of our own childhoods, and one that shuffles around in our adult heads still with proverbial expressions such as 'island of calm', 'island of treasure', 'oasis of peace' and 'island in the traffic of life'. There is a particular local resonance from Irish mythology. The Isles of the Blest, Hy-Brasil, were said to lie somewhere out of sight in this same western ocean which Bantry Bay spills into.

Bryce wanted not only to make a garden on Ilnacullin but to live there. The idea was for a big house on the site of the Martello tower. He called in the architect and garden designer Harold Peto (1854–1933), whose speciality was the translation of Italy and Arcadia into twentieth-century minds and places. Ilnacullin is his masterpiece. Peto knew what he was doing. He recreated in this Irish context an Isola Bella, or even a new Cytherea, the mythical island garden in Francesco Colonna's *Hypnerotomachia Poliphili* (Poliphilo's Strife of Love in a Dream) – that strange, beautiful book first published in 1499 which, above all others, informed the spirit of so many Renaissance gardens, and then cropped up again in Jean-Antoine Watteau's *Pèlerinage à l'île de Cythère* (1717) and

5 Illustration from Francesco Colonna's *Hypnerotomachia Poliphili* (1499). Familiar tensions are evident in this woodcut, one of the 174 that decorate a legendarily beautiful book: among them, nature versus the built environment, harmony versus discord (the broken *viola da braccio* that Logistica has dropped in disgust at Poliphilo's lust).

in Henri Duparc's beautifully evocative song 'L'Invitation au voyage' (1870; illus. 5).

Further on into the gardens, standing on a cliff and facing the mountains, is another temple. It is a little roofless theatre of classical columns, modest enough in its scale but massive in the gift of the mountains you can see from its parapet, a terrific *coup de théâtre*. And then there is a walled garden, which is mostly taken up now with nursery beds, but through the long slope from north to south is a masterly double border, backed by shrubs and rope-slung climbers, but lavishly planted with herbaceous things in front, taller things behind: abutilons, glad-ragging dahlias and exotic crinums. Then there's a tower in the wall, which separates this garden from your return to the casita lawn. They call it the Clock Tower, but it's really in the spirit of a sober Italian campanile. Ruskinian but without the caprice.

George Bernard Shaw (1856–1950) visited in 1923, and it seems likely that he wrote at least some of *Saint Joan* here, but at night he returned to Glengarriff, to the Eccles Hotel, a marvellous late Victorian pile that's still there.

My evocation of place probably overlooks the space here. Too much space in a garden imposes its own emptiness on you. Too little cramps. The whole island covers 15 hectares (37 ac). At least half of this is wilderness still. The garden is large enough, though, and there is indeed plenty of a sense of space. But it is almost always space enclosed. There are huge prospects, but only two of them: one from the temple mentioned earlier (which gives on to the mountains to the north) and one of the sea and rough shores to the south and west (which you gain from the Martello tower). All the rest is spacious but framed. There is a long, wide walk the length of the whole garden called the Happy Valley. It begins with a steep flight of stairs down from the mountain view and then drops gradually through the happiest of woodlands to a natural pool, after which it climbs again, eventually to the Martello tower.

The trees and shrubs are the botanical glories of the place. There are a great many seriously rare ones, most of them beautiful in leaf and flower, and all of them flourishing with a careless ease, which is another way in which this place makes its sense. There are several magnificent, full-grown *Rhododendron macabeanum*, leaves corrugated like skin pickled after seawater swimming, flowers in vast trusses of the loveliest primrose yellow, blotched sometimes with purple – they're here and a great many more besides. And tender cestrums, the very rare *Schima wallichii* (flowers like buttercups writ large, petals seemingly made of icing sugar) and specimens of Australasian plants growing better here than they do even in the southern hemisphere. There's the weeping Huon pine, and the most beautifully doleful, sorry-for-itself tree you'll ever see, *Dacrydium cupressinum*.

The last of the elements which go to make the sense of this place seems to have been an accident (or at least a piece of very good luck, though it probably didn't seem so at the time). The projected big house was never built. Annan Bryce died in 1923. His widow, Violet, carried on with the garden, and then so did his son Rowland. Best of all, a Scotsman called Murdo MacKenzie (1896–1983) became head gardener in 1928 and remained so until his retirement in 1971, long after the garden had become the property of the state in 1953. But after the First World War and then Annan's death, there was a lot less money available. MacKenzie's salary fluctuated. Or evaporated. Between 1938 and 1953, so impoverished had the enterprise become that he sometimes had to live only on his share of the fees paid by visitors.[1] But doggedly he stayed on. He knew his plants. His favourite was the rhododendron 'Lady Alice Fitzwilliam', but the plant I remember best is a rose. It sprawls in summer over a great domed rock, like the hairnet on an old lady's head: it may be *Rosa mulliganii*. It's a great character. MacKenzie – no-messing, Presbyterian, penny-pinched – made this place, ruled this place. At a sort of festschrift in his honour some years ago I heard a story about him spotting a party of visiting nuns, one of whom had plucked and then secreted the flower of a peony she liked underneath the skirt of her habit. Only just could he contain his vociferous contempt. He was hugely well regarded. He still is.

This place – its islandness especially – touches me deeply and has done so ever since I first visited it. I imagine it must do the same to others. For my part, it alerts me not only to its own magic and beauty but to better (but probably neglected) parts of myself: my own humanity, my own sensibility, even my sense of humour.

I close with three short passages from diaries compiled over the years. First something gentle:

> A Down's Syndrome child has a bright-faced dog on a leather lead. Together they tumble into the boat and now, back on to dry land, she stumbles along, head hung low. Because of the tilt of her head she is always looking at the ground, except when she catches the adoring grin of the dog. Then she smiles too, and the dog is rewarded. He is infinitely careful of the one he loves, even down to letting her believe that he needs her to lead him, rather than the other way around.

Something comic:

> A conspiracy of young gardeners is gathered to grouse about instructions from the Head Gardener. Today they must weed. '*Juniperus coxii*! There's fuck'en hundreds of those – fuck'en seedlings everywhere!' The confluence of Latin specific and the vulgar dog has its mischievous charms.

And something reflective:

Many seals basking on the rocks, and a few in the water. Climbing in and out, they're careful of the rough stubble of mussels under the beard of seaweed. It's hard to think of these engaging creatures as carnivores (but they are), just as, I suppose, it ought to be hard to think of some (gentle) people as meat-eaters.

5
The Green Chapel

Chapel – conventionally, the word is glossed as smaller places of worship situated, satellite-like, around the central nave and chancel of a great church, or a local branch of a larger trade union (particularly printers), and with a sense of privileged membership. Places of worship for dissenters were and still are often dubbed *chapels*. The god Mammon is generally worshipped in *temples*, banks and treasuries; there are *cathedrals* of power-generating engines (turbine halls and so on); *shrines* house sacred objects; *oratories*, *mosques* and *synagogues* are essentially prayer houses but are not private. There was no chapel or church, kirk or bethel, in Eden – no use or need for it probably.

The Garden of Forked Paths

My great-aunt had a garden: lawns and hedges, beds of roses, a diamond-shaped fish pond and gravel paths. For us children, it was somewhere full of places to hide and places hidden from us. And because of what was inscribed on to its only piece of furniture – a bench – the location was my first education in sacred places. There were mysterious old buildings, more than merely sheds most of them but less than barns, weather-boarded and protected with coats of thick bitumen, which gave off a drowsy fume in summer. But these were forbidden buildings. No verbal prohibition was needed; they were always locked. The largest, I learnt after her death, had been the school she had run for the Hertfordshire village of Bovingdon before the war. Had we known this as children, it would have seemed doubly forbidding.

There was a knoll on the largest lawn, and on it a garden seat of weathered, black teak. Along the back rail, carved into the wood, you could read:

> The kiss of the sun for pardon,
> The song of the birds for mirth,
> One is nearer God's heart in a garden
> Than anywhere else on earth.

I didn't know then the author of these words; years later I learnt that it was Dorothy Frances Gurney (1858–1932). That's quite interesting now, but not formative. What mattered, back then when I was a child, was my primitive inkling of what that word 'God' meant. Most of what I intuited was the idea that if He were in the vicinity, I had to behave myself. And that tended to put a damper on that part of the garden – my great-aunt's garden – in the first place, and then on every other garden, given the likelihood that God might be nearer than I thought.

Nevertheless, it was hard to behave well inside my head when my great-uncle, a man of august presence and military bearing – but also of small stature – mowed the lawn. There was a grand old motor mower, a pioneer of its kind, I suspect. It had no throttle and very little clutch. It either went forward or stood still, both of them impressively, for it was a formidable iron-clad thing. When Honk (that was Great-Uncle's name, but never to his face) steered the thing through 180 degrees around the top of a narrow rose bed, his feet left the ground and his little legs too. Also suspended was his dignity.

Between the mysteries of God, good behaviour and centrifugal force, the goblin of mischief would prod us in the ribs. I didn't know then that Gurney's word 'mirth' meant 'merriment', but I knew when *not* to laugh. And anyway, Honk would always have changed his clothes and resumed his customarily much more terrifying presence by the time we sat down for lunch.

I think I began, even then, to wonder if some words were all that they seemed, whether they could not actually mean more (or, indeed, less) than superficially seemed to be the case. Was God really close to you in a garden? Why did the legend on the bench remind me so vividly of those notices I found sometimes in galleries, marking a large, vacant patch of wall curiously unbleached by the light – notices signalling not a presence, but an absence: 'Leonardo da Vinci, *The Virgin of the Rocks*, removed for cleaning . . . conservation . . . its own safety'. Growing sensitivity to the possibilities of language – and to the impossibilities of some of the things it tries to convey – is part of growing up. If you're lucky, imagination and poetry span the gaps.

Sir Gawain – flower of Arthur's court, paragon of knightly virtue and champion of his own and the Round Table's honour – accepts the challenge of the Green Knight. He is to deliver the first blow there and then, but only on condition that, in a year and a day's time, he should travel alone, to arrive at a lonely place called the Green Chapel. There he must submit to a reciprocal blow.

It is the season of Christmas. The court is celebrating. The challenge and the challenger are discourteous intrusions. And foolish. How could there be a reciprocal blow, a debt of honour to repay, if the challenger were dead, as he certainly must be once the first blow – Gawain's – has been dealt?

The blow is struck. The head is severed but, dead or not dead, the Green Knight nevertheless raises himself, picks up his head and climbs on to his horse. The lips of the head speak:

Pay attention, Gawain. Make ready to honour your pledge
And keep your word to search till you find me again . . .
To the Green Chapel you must make your way –
I charge you so.[1]

The Green Knight rides off, and the court sees the hooves of his horse strike fire from the iron-hard, frost-rigid earth. Gawain has a year and a day to prepare either for meeting the challenge or for funking it: spring to hope, summer to fortify, autumn to bid his farewells and winter to dread. The journey of self-discovery corresponds exactly to the cycle of nature.

The journey, once begun, takes him into a desolate country – the mirror of his soul – with no shelter from either the deadliness of winter or the death he has contracted himself to suffer. But eventually he comes upon a castle, a fortress against his fear – perhaps – or else a trap for his turpitude. Once inside, he is warmly welcomed by the company of Christmas revellers, led by the lord of the castle, and by his beautiful wife. In the great hall, Gawain, flower of knighthood and teller of knightly tales, is a great success. Gawain, the very model of courtly virtues, becomes the darling of the assembly, of its lord and of his wife. And it is to her that he – the paragon of courtly love – pledges his soul in service.

The lord will go hunting. Gawain should stay behind and take his ease in readiness for the trials to come. He has told them of his great quest and obligation. Four days hence, early in the morning, he will be shown the path to the Green Chapel. It stands close by. But for now he should relax, his journey almost accomplished. In the meantime, by way of amusement, his host, Bertilak, persuades Gawain to commit himself to (another) reciprocal pledge: each should give up to the other, day by day, whatever it is they have won. And off Bertilak goes to the chase, leaving Gawain behind – with his wife.

Gawain, less the hunter than the prey, tries to resist both his own lust and the advances of Lady Bertilak. A kiss is all he will take. Faithfully, he gives that up on the return of Bertilak, who reciprocates with the gift of the finest cuts of venison from the quarry of the day, deer.

A second day, and a second assault on his virtue is again successfully resisted. Once more he takes only kisses, and once more he fulfils the terms of the contract to Bertilak and 'hendely hym kysses' – twice.[2] Bertilak responds with his own achievement: the head of a wild boar.

On the third day (and thus the eve of his impending death), Gawain struggles to master himself when the temptation to lust is offered even more forcefully than before, but this time, when he refuses, Lady Bertilak has still more to offer: her girdle. If he wears this, he will come to no harm no matter how fierce the blow. He accepts first the girdle and then the condition attached to the gift: he must not tell her husband.

When Bertilak returns this third time, he gives Gawain the flayed skin of a fox. In return, Gawain gives him three kisses. He has broken his word to his host. He has compromised his honour.

On the morrow, Gawain puts on the girdle, then conceals it beneath his armour, mounts his horse and rides away to the Green Chapel. Sure enough, the Green Knight is there to meet him. Gawain removes his helmet, kneels, and the axe is raised, but his courage fails and he flinches: he moves his head aside as the mighty blade falls. Gawain, ashamed, promises to be still, and again the axe falls, but it is only a feint. A third blow follows, but it is a glancing blow only; it draws blood but leaves his life unharmed. And then, at last, the Green Knight reveals himself. He is the same Bertilak whom Gawain has kissed, whose trophies of the chase Gawain has received, and whose wife he has not enjoyed. But Bertilak knows of the girdle and knows that Gawain has opted to save his own life, but at the cost of his honour (illus. 15).

All is not quite what it seems, though. The Green Knight loses his head but not his life. Gawain keeps his life but not his honour. And yet it is all in play. The Knight is Green withal (but for his golden spurs and the golden threads woven into the mane of his steed); he wields not only a colossal axe but a bough of holly – evergreen and spangled with blood-red berries, emblems of life-blood spilt, but also of the seeds of its own regeneration. Lady Bertilak's prophylactic girdle is green too (but for the gold thread of its embroidery). The Chapel – the place of both baptism and burial, the doorway into and out of life – is Green, even in the deadly grip of winter. Gawain's moral journey from vainglory to self-knowledge covers the ground comprehensively in that it seems to take him to the end of the world in terms of geography and the end of time in terms of the year. It encompasses everything he needs to have the courage to learn, even what it takes to make the heart fail in its course.

In this tale there are seasons to the senses, just as there are to the year. There is despair, and there is turpitude – winter, night, the darkness of the soul without succour or support – just as there is courage, joy and spring. And the whole thing goes round in a circle: a year, a life, a beginning, a middle and an end. Even Gawain's going back to Arthur's court, sadder and wiser but more grateful for life than almost any other man has ever been, is predicated in terms of turning and re-turning. Everything in a completed circle – but with one day more, the clock with thirteen hours (as in *Tom's Midnight Garden*), the thought that is clinched by the afterthought.

What makes *Sir Gawain and the Green Knight* such a magically generous poem is that the extra day – the afterthought, the fifth season of the year (in essence, perhaps, the sense of something above and beyond nature, something *super*natural) – is the perfect complement of Gawain's human nature. He doesn't want to die. And that is a treason to nature and the facts of life, and a treason also to virtue in the context of knightly codes of honour, but it is a truth to himself and to human nature.

There are precedents for much of the iconography, much of the symbolic personifications, of Sir Gawain and the Green Knight.[3] But in terms of the genealogy of recorded myth, Gawain is the original and the Green Knight the Johnny-come-lately. Nevertheless, they are essentially personifications of the same thing, mirrors of each other and of the central issue of knightly honour – they are alter egos, as we might say now. Lady Bertilak also is, in a sense, an aspect of Morgan le Fay (in the libretto by the poet David Harsent of Harrison Birtwistle's 1991 opera, *Gawain*, she is the mouthpiece of Morgan le Fay's plotting), just as she is another of the personifications of the Female Principle that precede her (most vividly the Irish Maeve, one of the great archetypal Earth Mother figures of myth). That said, however, in the case of *Sir Gawain and the Green Knight*, the entire trope hangs upon really just one thing: the fact, the metaphor, of green, and this poem is the *locus classicus* of that.

The entire narrative unfolds in the frame of the natural cycles of the year. The heart of the poem hinges upon kinds of death and kinds of regeneration: biological (botanical death and regeneration) and, precisely in parallel with it, theological matrices of death and resurrection. The Green Chapel is the zone of both endings and beginnings, secular (in terms of natural framings) or religious (if you read the poem strictly on its own terms). Thus, winter is also Christmas, the season of the feast of Jesus' birth, and in any case it marks the end of one year and the beginning of another. Thus, the medieval reader would have remembered that the True Cross was green: that was what authenticated it. Conventionally, traditionally, symbolically, that cross had been idealized always as *green*, even when in reality it may have been gold, silver or ivory. The modern reader is probably more likely to understand the colour simply in terms of something that is natural and organic, and then perhaps in terms of the contemporary challenges to ecological survival: the connection with greenness is carried over, but the tree-ness – geometricized, simplified, into a cross – is lost. The typological connection between God's tree of the knowledge of good and evil (in the Garden of Eden) and the T-shaped wood scaffold at Golgotha upon which Christ atones for Adam and Eve's violation of the fruit of that very tree becomes invisible to the modern, secular mind. Enough remains, however, of magic and mystery and autochthonous connections for the poem to work – and work indeed harder and more urgently upon the beleaguered conscience of our damaged, un-green world.

All of this is interesting in its own right, but Lady Bertilak/Maeve and the Green Knight/Gawain emerge from it mistily but positively as representatives of recognizable patterns, archetypes, personifications, of modern garden deities. We might call these Gaia (the Earth) and the Green Man (the spirit of the wildwood) – or whatever – but these we recognize as the patron saints of the ecological new age. If any of the gods are indeed at large in our gardens these days, they are going to be aliases in one form or another of these. *Sir Gawain*, it seems, can be read as a sort of parable of some of our contemporary preoccupations.

One of the ways in which gardens make sense is that they are seen by some as the Green Chapels in which we can do our bit for nature. There are indeed classic components of quasi-religious affiliation in the psychological profile of the modern apparatchik/votary who tries to live a 'greener' life in harmony with nature. Guilt, and the assuaging of guilt, is certainly there. Self-denial (of peat from wetlands or of chemical pesticides) plays a part. The composting of waste hints at regeneration, and the husbanding of that fertility suggests resurrection (of a sort). There are quasi-religious undertones in the popular lexicon: 'communing' with nature, wildlife 'sanctuaries', 'reverence' for life and so on. Above all, this movement to 'go green' is shot through with a vision – sometimes explicit but much more often only whispered – of Paradise and the recovery of Eden.

In the strictest sense, if you become attracted towards this or even affiliated – to all of it, to some of it – it will be towards a religion of the aesthetic. But there is more praxis than faith, more wish than fulfilment, and perhaps more sentiment than thought. By the most rigorous theological standards, this is not a religion at all, and in any case, most of its adherents would prefer it that way. They prefer gurus to priests, theories to theologies, and intuitions to epiphanies. But it's hard entirely to resist seeing it as a sort of religion if only perhaps in the sense that it is more honoured in the breach than in the observance. And yet, for all of its woolly-headedness, it seems likely that we should welcome this movement towards achieving harmony with nature, reconciliation rather than confrontation.

Commercial buildings – generally anonymous, faceless, pretty characterless – nevertheless sometimes assume, and then embody, the shapes of the ideas which lie behind them. Skyscrapers defy nature and gravity, and then trumpet our conquest of both. They breathe city-ness and metropolitan hubris. Office blocks – the stereotype of them – mirror the activities that go on inside them: identical units of desk, window space, chair and computer screen, from the outside looking like so many stacked racks of battery hens. Housing estates more or less honestly reflect the yearnings for an Arcadia of the people who live in them, but also their unspoken fear of true wilderness. The roads do curve 'naturally', but the walls are straight. The houses seem to be so many apparently sovereign, private realms separated from the next by a gesture of distance, but actually they are connected to, and by, every possible shared amenity. They are nearly perfectly formed reciprocal halls of mirrors where the outsides, the gardens (places often vociferous with style statements intended to differentiate the people who live within from everybody else without), are very visible, but the insides, the spaces where people do most of their living, are not.

That the garden is the more exposed, the much more visible of the two – and its loyalty liminally shared between nature and human nature, culture and wilderness – is one of the factors that make gardens so interesting, make them indices of our own divided nature. But so are some of the less exposed surfaces of the interiors of our houses. The flowers in the vase, the flowers on the curtains and chair covers, the prints of Constable's own seeming Arcadia or van Gogh's sunflowers, the apparently living fire in the grate, the exposed natural wood of the shelves, banisters and dining table, the exposed natural stone of the fireplace, the pine-flavoured aerosol in the lavatory, the house plants on the kitchen windowsill – all these things appear to speak of bringing nature into the home, but also betoken a nostalgia for a lost Arcadia, a yearning for a beauty that we might be able, after all, to see, touch, smell and even hear (the cuckoo clock). Essentially, these places are attempts to bridge the dislocation between nature-out-there and human-nature-inside-ourselves.

Just as the places we have built to house our work and our lives reflect honestly, if unconsciously, what goes on in them, so do the buildings (within the Christian tradition) made to house the god. Historically, the buildings do indeed mirror very faithfully certain perceived aspects of the deity within: power, authority, mystery, magnificence, sublimated suffering and so on. But what those places of worship appear to be, appear to stand for, may actually be at odds with their primitive origins, and with ways of seeing things that faithfully reflect those origins. This chapter is going to argue that that is much less likely to be the case when we consider the Gothic, the churches built in the Middle Ages (or indeed reproduced again in the nineteenth century). Much less likely when we read these buildings carefully. When that is done, a persistent theme emerges, a garden of forked paths . . . bifurcated between the orthodox and the heterodox, the officially approved and the (sometimes) covert, the dissident and the atavistic. What emerges in the Gothic is a consistent, embodied symphonic web of ideas virtually invisible in the Romanesque and the classical, the dominant styles of the first millennium of the Christian faith, the centuries during which this religion tried to consolidate and make an integrity of itself in the form of binding creeds, curricula, dogmas, a systemic theology and an ideology which blended spiritual authority with secular power. This theme, both argument and evidence, is called here – and not lightly or accidentally – the Green Chapel, because it is also reflected, or relocated, in so much of our gardens now, both as the afterglow of the retreating tide of traditional Christianity and as a formative group of ideas that were probably already in place in our minds long, long before the birth of Christ.

In the mainstream, the most familiar of all the patterns of Christian buildings – the style and spirit – is the Gothic. You enter such a place from the west, but even from a long way off you wouldn't fail to have seen that the most conspicuous part of the building points up into the sky. The vertical seems to be as important to the sense of this place as the horizontal. The highest part reaches into the sky and seems to be directing your gaze (and therefore your thoughts) beyond itself. This is very different indeed from the classical dome of the Roman basilica, which from the outside resembles a crown, but inside, instead of pointing to the skies, it traps those very skies within itself. Inside the dome, clouds, stars and endless space are visible – they are painted on to it. The dome is a world in itself, and, indeed, the god is contained within it. Augustus Pugin (1812–1852) noticed that too, and didn't like it: the skyline of a Gothic city (all steeples, pinnacles and belfries) spoke to him of spiring, aspiring, reaching upwards, beyond (illus. 6).

As you go into a Gothic building, you mark the crossing of the threshold – out of the material world and into the transitional

6 Frontispiece to Augustus Pugin's *An Apology for the Revival of Christian Architecture in England* (1843). There is not a single classical dome, architrave or pediment in sight.

world within – by using water from a shallow bowl (a little sea) to purify yourself and to remind yourself of the drowning of the old Adam in you when you were brought here first as an infant. In order to gain admission to the society of people who visit their god here, you had to undergo a ritual drowning: baptism, from the Greek for 'dipping' or 'washing'. This first paradox (water, the killer and the life-giver) makes its mark on you in the form of a cross, a horizontal line bisected by a vertical, the same figure you have noticed already in the ground plan of the building, and then in its tower and spire rising vertically out of the *body* of the church – that itself a telling expression. Already, it suggests an analogy with the linear (horizontal) trajectory of the passage of your life and the way it is interrupted sometimes by stasis, still moments: ongoing time arrested by timeless eternity. An analogy too with a schema of the human body, its arms outstretched.

Once inside, you find yourself within a sacred wood. Beneath your feet there are plants and their flowers everywhere, fixed encaustically into the tiles of the floor. The ends of all the benches flower into huge furled leaves: 'poppyheads', we call them rather misleadingly, but the effect is indeed of some sort of opiate. The exotic, slightly intoxicating whiff of incense (fumes of fragrant resins and gums) reinforces this. In the Christian tradition incense is said to be a symbol of the scent of prayers. Older still, and perhaps one of the antecedents of incense, were the trance-inducing vapours inhaled by the priestess of the Delphic oracle of Apollo. All around you, in a stylized avenue, are the stems of trees frozen in stone. At their tops they branch out, and the canopy, the forest above you, establishes this as a world apart. Walls and vaulted ceiling shut out the rest of the material world and, in doing so, suspend the mere facts of life. Insofar as you are mere matter yourself, this is also true of you. In place of those mere facts (of life or indeed of anything else), you will find yourself offered *meanings*. You notice foliage everywhere, carved into wood and stone. You are walking on and between tomb slabs, they too with a good deal of stylized trees and foliage carved into them. The free-standing tombs are caskets writ large, suggesting something precious within. On some of them lie wooden and stone figures. You are reminded of the similarity between sleep and death. These figures may be sleeping, their deaths only an enchantment, waiting to be broken, to be woken. This stone-frozen forest is a house of the dead – they are stored here – set into the imagery of abundant vegetable life. In the distance, at the east of the building, you can see the largest tomb of all. It has fresh white grave clothes, a winding sheet, laid across it. They call it the altar, the place where things are changed – alterations, othernesses.

You notice other trees, radically stylized, everywhere, some of them reduced to the barest of geometries, one vertical and one horizontal. These are schematically two lines fixed at right angles: crucifixed. They are called 'crosses'. You may be reminded that this is also the old expression for a junction, a choice of directions, a crossroads, a place where things diverge and meet. You remember that signpost, that arrow, that spire pointing into the sky. Especially prominent along the walls, there are fourteen of these crosses, each one set into a different scene. They are tableaux, episodes in the journey of a man himself carrying a large cross. They are called 'stations': pausings, episodes, in this narrative. You too pause to consider them. The man and the cross he is carrying are the same in each station. They confirm what you know already: that this man knows about trees and wood. His father is a carpenter. But even if that weren't so, he is, like us, a descendant of Adam, who was a gardener and a stealer of fruit from trees.

The whole building is laid out in the shape of this cross, this tree reduced to the elements of stem and branch, but you know that the pattern is really only revealed in an aerial perspective. To be sure, it was made to be imagined by you, but it would actually be visible only to God. Inside the building, where the two branches (the transepts) meet the stem – the vertical intersected by the horizontal – you're standing at the axis of the sacred space, and it's two-dimensional: vertical and horizontal. Above you, there is a tower and then a spire, reaching up into the sky. The spire reminds you of the arrow aimed, like Noah's bow-and-arrow, at God, the rainbow, the symbol of the binding contract between the god and his people indeed. It reminds you of Constable's painting of Salisbury Cathedral, where there are indeed both spire and rainbow. You remember that the French for 'spire' (*flèche*) also means arrow and gives us *fletcher*, an arrow maker, in English.

The next steps of your journey west to east through this horizontal space, and immediately after you leave this crossing – this intersection of time and timelessness, of one line intersected and cancelled by another – you pass beneath the largest tree of all, the

Rood, the Rod, the stem. From a mere slip of its wood an arrow could be formed; from another, a longer and tougher piece, that bow could be made. These things – an arrow-straight trajectory contrasting with a concave – remind you of the elemental symbols for the male and female genders and the complementarity of them. The Rood above you reminds you of more trees: the tree of life and the tree of the knowledge of good and evil, which stood in Adam's garden. You think also of the Tree of Jesse, the family tree whose branches map out the lineage of the carpenter's son (depicted stumbling under the weight of his cross, his tree, in the stations that led up to this point). Jesse's Tree you have seen in books or painted on the walls of sacred woods such as the one you're in now. It grows out of his navel, his middle. Or it rises from his loins. The Rod of Jesse indeed.

The great tree above you is vivid with the most important of all the paradoxes of this place. It stands at the axle, the centre of this cruciform space. It is the World Tree, the *axis mundi*, and it is green with life, but on it hangs a dead body, crucified into conformity with the geometry of the tree. This living tree is also a gallows. In the midst of life there is a death. Or the converse. The dead body, stretched across the tree, is wounded by the nails which attach it. The tree, too, bears these wounds. The man's side has been pierced also. This suggests an idea which you recollect from ancient tales of times when the gods still walked the earth. You remember the Earth Tree (Yggdrasil, the ash), which is pierced with a blade no one can draw out. You remember also the wood from the dead tree stacked around the home of the gods, ready to be fired and thus to immolate them. Like water, fire destroys just as it purifies.

You have already noticed all around you foliage, the forest of columns and leafy capitals, leafy bosses at the apex of the vaults above you. Now you look back into the west and you see, set into the wall, definitively the most beautiful of any representation of any flower that you have ever seen. It is vast. It is a rose, lit from without by the sunlight. In a space so far dominated by the upright, masculine vigour of the trees (and the man on the tree), this is a great counterweighting of the feminine, of a circular beauty. It has an equal and opposite which faces it over the vast space of the whole building. Set into the east wall there is an unmistakably male-shaped window of long, narrow lancets. Just as the sun will set in a passion of reds beyond the great rose window in the west, so does it rise in the east, and with it the body of the judicially murdered man they revere here, he who hangs on the tree. This is achieved by the coloured glass and the poetry of place, both of them making bridges between the apparently extreme polarities plotted here: time and eternity, death and life, woman and man, tree and gibbet, light and darkness. A pictorial representation in translucent glass of a man's rising body dominates the east window.

The people in this place use the same language as you. The elements of syntax, vocabulary, grammar and orthography are essentially the same, but it is language whose sound has been enhanced, as it were, by colour. These people are more apt to sing rather than merely to speak, and it is thus that they endeavour to attract, to catch, the ear of their god, and the sound of their ululations rolls round the sacred space like echoes in the forest, like birdsong refined and amplified into the purest abstraction of language made precious, so that every word now glows like a jewel.

Finally, you see that what you took to be the great tomb with the winding sheet has a top like a table. This *mensa* is spread with a gold cloth also, as if it were a throne, yet it serves as the board upon which is spread the ritual meal of bread and wine. Everything about it is thus translated, altered indeed.

If this is the house of a god, to correspond with its immense space you must imagine a very great god indeed, and yet, like the forest, it is an empty place. The emptiness imposes a sense of awe. The god is invisible, but his presence is palpable – the last of the paradoxes: nowhere and everywhere.

In terms of symbolic architecture, these places are impressively coherent, even when we take into the reckoning the fact that Gothic is not the monolith that I have condensed into this sketch but a sequence of stylistic nuances and phases evolved over the span of several centuries. I have offered here only a paradigm, an ideal. Orthodox, educated Christians will argue, however, that the building I have evoked is radically at odds with their theological understanding of the nature of God, and with the purpose and forms of their worship. What I have done is to depict some sort of shrine to nature. It is pagan, heterodox. And heretical.

I agree, because (as I would aver) the correspondences between the Church as a body of ideas (creeds, orthodoxies, theologies) and the buildings in which these ideas were, and still are, ritually played out are often pretty slight, or even entirely absent: football stadia, village halls, hospital wards and fire stations are designed prescriptively to serve their uses, whereas the sacraments can be and indeed are celebrated anywhere. It is easy to overlook this because the two expressions – the Church (the institution) and churches (the buildings) – are so similar and the habit of identification so long-lived. But really the relationship is much more complicated, after centuries of erosion and corrosion now much less symbiotic. Nevertheless, at root, the two are still perhaps essentially only different scions on a single stock. The first, that of the *soi-disant* orthodox institution, is a highly intellectual schema, evolved and involved, one of whose goals was to achieve as much distance as it could between itself and what it perceived as primitive folk religion. The second – the meaning of the buildings in which the institution plays out its rites – is just that: a deeper, older stratum of religious sensibility whose patterns of thought are possibly much less involved (lacking intellectual abstraction, even when they are richer and more developed in metaphor), but which have kept their roots, their power and their meanings in the poetry of the visible, in the tactile. In this more primitive scheme, the great mark of our species and of our human nature – our intelligence – is still rooted in the conditions of life as a whole, in the whole of nature, and not just in human nature.

These two schemata have always run in parallel, albeit with the older stratum keeping its head down, like that archetypal outsider, Robin Hood, forest-lurker, he with his shape-shifting consort, the Maid Marian. This tendency to be invisible is especially likely to be the case when the heresy hunters are at large. But for all the differences between these two, they are still in some respects complementary, and may, in the end, be reconcilable. Yet they are not the same. The myth, the 'folk' religion, is older by far. It is arguably closer both to the 'truth' of nature itself and to the archetypes of the human psyche (and therefore possibly farther away from the 'truth' of *soi-disant* revealed religion), and, as a result, in the end, it may outlive the orthodox.

Perhaps the best place to begin to understand the differences is to note that the Church, the institution, is particularly sensitive to the undertones of sexuality which are evident both in our mythologically informed reading of its buildings and indeed in the fact that if its doctrine of the Incarnation – the idea that God became truly Man in the person of Christ – is to cohere, then there must have been a mother (and maternity) as well as a father (paternity – Latin *pater*, as in 'Pater noster, qui est in caelis'). Mary is impregnated, not by the god in veiled physical form (as in the stories of Leda and the Swan, Europa and the Bull), but asexually by the Holy Spirit, the immaterial, spiritual aspect of his own shape-shifting nature, traditionally represented in the form of a bird in countless *Annunciations*. Mary performs the physical, reproductive function of giving birth to the Son of God, and by so doing she is instrumental in bringing about the third aspect of that divine trinity, but doesn't herself partake of any of the divine. As an intercessor, a go-between with a special purchase on the attention of both God and his Son, she may be approached by the faithful with special petitions and may be expected to lend them some success, but she is not divine. It follows, of course, that whatever happened between her and God was not sex. Thus the orthodox view.

But in practice she has gained entry to that pantheon. She was bound to. Religion is about the reconciliation of antinomies, apparent opposites and apparent contradictions: life and death, degeneration and regeneration, light and darkness, the male and the female.

Another fruitful perspective materializes when you begin to consider how hard and how long Christianity has struggled in order to maintain the idea of the one God, most notably in the doctrine of the Trinity, but – while this may carry at least some conviction intellectually – it is still essentially at odds with the idea of Incarnation. A father predicates a son, and sons must have mothers just as fathers must have had consorts at least once upon a time, if not actually wives. Mary's entry into the pantheon, even after 2,000 years, is still not officially recognized. In the Protestant wing of Christianity, it has been successfully resisted. Judaism, Islam and Protestantism still adhere in principle to the monotheistic ideal. In Catholicism, however (though actually it is quite hard on paper to make serious doctrinal distinctions between it and Protestantism), there is no doubt that in practice the male monopoly of divinity has long been compromised, just as the ideal of a single god has been fractured first by the Trinity, and then by admitting into the pantheon (albeit at a lower register) saints who have been getting their feet through the door opened by the doctrine of Incarnation. Above all, the foundational proposition of monotheism has been fractured, in practice if not in principle, by the attention afforded by the faithful (if not always by the clergy) to Mary.

What we have largely been concerned with are indeed not much more – or less – than architectural and aesthetic translations of the feminine in general, and of Mary in particular, into the fabric of buildings and ritual (as in the whole apparatus of the Rose, the Rosary and so on), but there is no avoiding the creeping institutionalizing of her into the fabric of Catholic doctrine as well. The dogma of the Immaculate Conception was actually promulgated as recently as 1854, but, of course, its popular, informal acceptance had taken place very much earlier indeed. That Mary has been resisted at all is extraordinary too because myth cannot be suppressed as if it were a politics or an ideology. Only a myth, with its own protean energy, could deflect another myth, and here is just such a case. But the principle, the great spine behind the orthodox, the official religion, has always been maleness, the male and the paternity of God, the author of and the authority over all things.

I'm not going to labour very much further this question of the gender of the deities in mainstream Christian observance, and – despite very searching books such as Marina Warner's *Alone of All Her Sex*, now almost fifty years old – there is still a dearth of discussion about it, even by feminists. In some rather interesting way, it remains something of a taboo subject. Nevertheless, over and above theological issues, it also affords a glimpse into the meaning of gardens at a level deeper perhaps than any other we know of. You suspect it as offering more than merely a gloss on, for example, Churchill's bulldog remark that 'war' and 'gardening' were the 'normal occupation of man', or, for that matter, on the famous explanation of himself by Sargon the Great: 'My service as a gardener was pleasing unto Ishtar and I became king.'[4] Ishtar, Isis, Hera, Maeve, Lakshmi, Demeter, Mary: all of them women.

The history of gardens is not identical, interchangeable, with this semi-covert, heterodox cult, but it does run parallel to it, even though it is largely just a forgotten history and not on the surface of popular culture at all. What the *hortus conclusus*, the enclosed garden of earthly delights, meant to the medieval mind is not part of what gardens mean to us now, but it is perhaps evidence of the origins, at least, of some of our contemporary meanings. We should pause to consider the genealogy.

> A garden enclosed is my sister, my spouse: a spring shut
> up, a fountain sealed.
> Thy plants are an orchard of pomegranates, with pleasant
> fruits; camphire, with spikenard,
> Spikenard and saffron; calamus and cinnamon, with all
> trees of frankincense; myrrh and aloes, with all the
> chief spices:
> A fountain of gardens, a well of living waters, and streams
> from Lebanon.[5]

This famous passage from the Song of Solomon is the literary prototype of the enclosed garden, the *hortus conclusus*. There are several other such gardens in Near Eastern (particularly Persian) literature – as indeed, there are examples of the gardens themselves – but for people in the Judaeo-Christian tradition, this is the original. The whole Song is steeped in the sounds, scents and sensuous pleasures of the Near East, not the least of which is a quite explicit eroticism. Scheherazade, the spice road, the gardens of the *Arabian Nights* and the golden road to Samarkand are not far off. Almost certainly, Solomon's garden has a Sumerian model: a walled space enclosing a fountain from which four rills flow, as they do, of course, from the centre of the earth, in the metaphorical *fons et origo* of all gardens – Eden. This was not a garden of forked paths at all, but one in which all paths led directly to the nub, the crux. The Old Iranian word *pairidaeza* grew, morphed and spread versions of itself widely throughout the ancient world. It meant the domain over which a ruler could hunt, in which he could linger, bathe and generate crops – all in safety because he owned it all. The Hebrews got their version of it, their word *pardes*, via the Armenians. The Greeks gave these versions what turned out to be the definitive form of *paradeisos*, perhaps seeing its sense in their own language as a combination of *peri* (encircled) and *toixos* (wall), and the Romans settled for *paradisus*.

For us, the paradigm and finest surviving examples of the Persian/Arabic garden are in Moorish Spain: the gardens of the Generalife and the Alhambra, and it is these places which became, to the European mind, the paragon of heaven on earth, even though these were Islamic, not Christian, places. These were gardens of entirely earthly delights, of sensual rapture as well as sensuous pleasure.

Those Near Eastern models became the pattern of the nunnery, the gardens of the brides of Christ, and the paradigm of the cloister, but insofar as the Church itself (its mystical body made up of men and women) is the bride of Christ, the garden is the *locus* of that mystical marriage, and the churches, the buildings which house the bride as well as the groom, are themselves the mystical gardens, groves, *horti conclusi*. But the trouble with this trope is, self-evidently, that half of the 'brides' – half of the members of the body – are men.

The cult of Our Lady, however, offers to set all to rights, not least because the men are – always have been – among its most fervent devotees. Eithne Wilkins calls her compendious, enormously rich study of prayer beads *The Rose-Garden Game* (1969). The word 'game' is exactly right for the great complex of sexual shadowboxing and sublimation that is going on, at once playful and redolent of unconsummated, abstinent courtship (the whole gamut of medieval courtly love, *Le Roman de la Rose* and so on), but also tense with the *agon* of passion and the intoxicated seriousness of *amour*. In the end, the whole glorious garden trope amounts to a sort of para-religion running more or less in harness with the orthodox. Sometimes it flows underground, as it were (a covert stream of folk religion), but in many respects it has been absorbed into the mainstream, its sexuality sublimated and its passions of worship deftly castrated by a bit of theological sleight of hand, so that what, in practice, is quite obviously worship and adoration (of the Female) is technically authorized by being designated only as Veneration.

In any case, these things have profoundly shaped our perceptions both of gardens and – through the buildings in which we confine and worship them – of our divinities.

The Garden of Last Rites

There is, however, another Green Chapel, a garden in another, distinctly different, mood. Its model is not Eden but Gethsemane. Just as Eve and Adam fell from bliss in, and partly because of, a garden, so also in a garden did Christ suffer his agony and submit to betrayal.

As so often in myth, a polar parallelism occurs; in this case, we encounter both a mirror and an inversion of the Garden of Earthly Delights. It was John Milton (1608–1674) who classically fixed this shadow over our gardens. If gardening is usually (when we stop to think about it) a recovery of Eden, then we do well to remember that that very garden was never itself lost, just our access to it. *Paradise Lost* – Milton's title, which has as much resonance and authority in the map of our minds as any Freudian principle or Jungian avatar – is not about gardens or nature but about us as gardeners and our human nature. Milton's near contemporary John Evelyn (1620–1706) sums up once and for all this way of understanding gardens – and our impulse to make gardens – by shifting their sense away from what actually comprises a garden on to what he sees as their fundamental psychological rationale and analogue: a garden, Evelyn writes, is a 'place of all terrestriall enjoyments the most resembling *Heaven*, and the best representation of our lost felicitie'.[6]

People have made Bible gardens – comprising sometimes cedars of Lebanon, balm of Gilead, lilies of the field and so on – but never a new Gethsemane. Such a place would be a chilling plot in the mind: dark, furnished with the careless sleep of those who should have stayed awake and been loyal, and then the treachery of a kiss. The early modern 'Corpus Christi Carol' fuses almost all the elements we have been discussing and more: sexual love sublimated, passion prefigured and echoed by the Passion, gardens (orchards, forest), the chapel in a clearing of the forest, the sacrificial king/knight (Christ/the Fisher King/Sir Gawain), the predatory bird waiting for its moment in the branches of the tree (the original of which must be the abduction of Ganymede by Zeus in the form of an eagle). 'Make' means 'mate', 'lover', 'consort'; 'faucon' is falcon; and 'may' means 'girl', with resonances of her being virginally fresh in spring. 'Corpus Christi' means the 'body of Christ'.

> Lully, lulley, lully, lulley,
> The faucon hath borne my make away.
> He bare him up, he bare him down,
> He bare him into an orchard brown.
> In that orchard there was an halle,
> That was hanged with purpill and pall.
> And in that hall there was a bede,
> It was hanged with gold so rede.
> And in that bed there lithe a knight,
> His woundes bleding day and night.
> By that bede side kneleth a may,
> And she wepeth both night and day.
> And by that bede side there stondeth a stone,
> Corpus Christi wreten there on.[7]

There is one 'garden' in particular which has achieved iconic status as an Eden in itself but, like Gethsemane, it is also a dark place. The first ever Act of Congress to preserve intact a complete landscape was passed in 1864 almost as an act of redemptive faith, given the preceding years of civil war. What is now Yosemite National Park, in the California mountains, had been discovered by miners greedy for gold (illus. 11). Though bit by bit the gold dwindled, one of the miners – George Gale by name – stumbled upon a grove of trees so tall that he sensed in it another source of wealth, a commercial opportunity. He stripped off a complete 27 metre (90 ft) ring of bark, shipped it back east, reassembled it and had it exhibited. No one believed it had come from a single tree.

Then visitors took photographs of the trees still standing (with people there as staffage by whom the scale of these trees could be seen), and this time the claims made for the bark-circle were believed. A tourist industry sprang up, and in 1890 a national park was declared. Almost from the first, the place was located in the mind by means of religious associations. This was America's Eden. The giant sequoias – their tree rings carefully counted – had been in their prime at the same time that Christ was walking the earth. Early visitors were styled 'pilgrims'. Mountains towering over the valley were dubbed 'Cathedral Rocks'; another was called 'Half Dome'.

All of the enthusiasts and most of the founding fathers of what became the national park went about establishing it in absolute good faith, but from the first there were the seeds of terrible ironies, eventually to mature into our modern realization that we cannot retain our connection with the true wilderness, still less preserve it, unless we separate ourselves from it and – here the bitterest pill of all – keep visitors (tourists, 'pilgrims') out. Communion with nature can only be achieved by divorce. Something profoundly Miltonic was being worked out again: another expulsion.

The very name of the larger area that was about to become the national park encapsulates all the horror of a mistake that cannot be undone. The miners themselves hadn't bothered to dignify the place with a name, and the indigenous inhabitants had been subdued and driven out of their homes violently (the leader of the battalion employed to do this was one Major James Savage), but one item of Native American speech – sounding like *yohhe'meti* – was taken to indicate the local name of the place. It was adopted. The matter settled. Later, too late to change, it was discovered that though this was indeed a transliteration of indigenous speech, what it actually meant was 'They are killers.' Said to be what the nearby Miwok tribe called the supposedly aggressive Ahwahneechee locals, the name ironically captures Yosemite's bloodstained history of dispossession and dislocation.

The American Dream of a new and better world is not over, even now. All may yet be well. But the chances of achieving a New Eden there, we must admit, are not good, any more than they are back in old Europe, new wealthy Asia or anywhere else. Virgil took the cue for his pastoral poetry – some of its subjects, most of its attitudes – from Theocritus, but it was his own *Eclogues* that became the models for the great tradition that has been such a significant part of European literature and such a formative element in the background of garden makers for so long now. It was the *Eclogues* that first mapped out that very special place, newly reminted from the Greek though it was: a place in the mind, a new continent – neither wilderness nor yet a cultivated garden, neither perfectly natural nor yet inexorably moulded by man – Arcadia. Curiously enough, the *Eclogues* were conceived, like the first American Eden, against the backdrop of civil war – in Virgil's case, the internecine struggles following the assassination of Julius Caesar – and, like the national park, Virgil's mind was set far, far away from the centre (of government, of corruption, of nature and human nature corrupted). His imaginative model was Theocritus' Sicily.

The Great Seal of the United States (which appears on the one dollar bill, the great plough that turns wishes into wealth) has on it a paraphrase of a line from the fourth *Eclogue*. Virgil has 'magnus ab integro saeclorum nascitur ordo' (the great order of the ages begins anew).[8] The Great Seal paraphrases this as 'novus ordo seclorum' (new order of the ages). Those founding fathers meant well, very well on the whole, though they formalized, authorized and – several of them – even practised slavery. Like Shelley in the closing chorus of *Hellas* (1822), the spirit of the brave new republic was great with the possibility of history giving us another chance: 'The world's great age begins anew,/ The golden years return . . .'[9] But 250 years on, we are sadder and wiser now. The marriage of Green and Gold – a seemingly beneficent or harmless thing when embroidered into Lady Bertilak's girdle or fixed into the Green Knight's spurs – is a bitter one for us now, the gold of commercial interest and the green of a beleaguered natural world. Now, the fact that our forebears foresaw no irony in forging a union of the two strikes us hard as we struggle to find ways to clean up the ecological mess.

Caspar David Friedrich (1774–1840) was wont to paint frozen scenes with solitary figures (or just a single tree) who are elements in the landscapes depicted but clearly intended to be understood as exiles from Eden and left, as strangers, in this other bleak, inimical world (illus. 12). The images, the sense of dislocation and of hostility, are intensified in the paintings of mountainous wintry landscapes..In more than a few of them there is an impression of a church in the crepuscular distance. Gothic pinnacles chime with the spires of lonely spruces in the foreground. A calvary (a dead tree, as it were) with its burden of the dead god is often and powerfully situated in these desolate places, almost lifeless but for the tentative green of the alpine trees.

Here then is a vision of the Green Chapel at that point where the cycle of the journey to reach it is at its lowest, deadliest ebb. The destination of a *Winterreise* indeed. If you're in any doubt, listen to the final song of Schubert's cycle of that name, 'Der Leiermann':

7, 8 A Victorian copy of *The Poetical Works of John Milton*. Painted onto the fore-edge, and invisible when the book is closed, is somebody's vision of their 'Paradise': the Cambridge Backs.

9 Richard Dadd, *The Fairy Feller's Master-Stroke*, 1855–64, oil on canvas. Through the cage-like frieze of grass stems, a central figure is splitting nuts with an axe. Dadd painted it for the head steward at Bethlem Hospital, where he was confined after murdering his father in 1843.

10 Arthur Rackham, 'He played until the room was entirely filled with gnomes,' illustration for *The Gnome* by the Brothers Grimm, published in 1917. The creatures here are mostly ant-like juveniles, but behind the flautist's right shoulder you can see the familiar pointed hats of conventional adults. Their German allies, the *Kobolde*, have latterly become popular as characters in *Dungeons and Dragons*.

11 Albert Bierstadt, *Yosemite Valley, Glacier Point Trail*, *c.* 1873, oil on canvas. Both literally and metaphorically, the painting projects a golden vision for the American continent.

12 Caspar David Friedrich, *Abbey in the Oak Wood*, 1809–10, oil on canvas. Shadowy figures shuffle across the foreground, a procession burying their dead, but the religious tradition in which they'd hoped for resurrection is in ruins behind them. Only the grim, skeletal oaks – the creatures of nature, not man – go on.

13 Unknown artist, *Sir John Barleycorn, Miss Hop, (and Their Only Child) Master Porter*, 1807–21, hand-coloured etching. Fertility (in the agrarian sense) is underwritten by fecundity (in the sexual sense): the union of Sir John Barleycorn and Miss Hop generates Master Porter, who is himself a sort of infant Bacchus. The hop leaves are botanically erratic but – albeit in parody – Miss Hop could easily be a Roman garden herm, and Sir John a classical cornucopia.

14 Thomas Rowlandson, *Butterfly Hunting*, 1806, hand-coloured etching. The bespectacled, amateur entomologists wreak havoc upon the horticulturalist's flower beds – one pursuit of beauty cancelling another.

15 Sir Gawain and the Green Knight, illustration from a late 14th-century manuscript. In this representation of the story, Gawain is clad in violent red and almost everything else is green: the axe, the phantasmagoric landscape and, of course, the Green Knight.

so bleak, so stoically solitary, the organ-grinder trudges on, ignored by fellow humans, barked at by the dogs. This is the musical equivalent of Emily Dickinson's 'zero at the bone'.[10]

It would not do to leave these matters here, at the point of such desolation. It would be too authentically close to the worst of the prophecies of environmental disaster which inform our daily news, but it would also serve to overlook that other garden event – the Resurrection – which follows hard on the heels of Gethsemane and Golgotha, and during which Mary Magdalene makes the telling mistake, in the Gospel of John, of thinking that the person she is talking to (in fact, the risen Christ) is the gardener.

If there is and always has been this sort of para-religion running alongside the orthodox practices – a tradition which surfaces sometimes in cults asserting the Female Principle but behind the mask of the Handmaid or Mother, Intermediary or Consort, of God – then it too, paradoxically, would appear to have its own male aspect. The Green Knight himself offers us a glimpse of this. More commonly than as the Green Knight, he appears as Jack in the Green, the May King, Puck, the Wild Man of the Woods, or simply as the Green Man. Like any other seemingly archetypal figure, resonances of him can be found almost everywhere: in mythologies ancient and modern, eastern and western. Sometimes he resembles an ecstatic, vine-clad Dionysus. At other times he is, perhaps, John Barleycorn, who loses his life to sustain ours (illus. 13). Dismembered as he often is (very few representations of him show him having anything but a head), he reminds us of Osiris. He is Huwawa (Humbaba), the guardian of the great cedar forests which Gilgamesh and Enkidu want to cut down.

Above all, this Green Man is the figure who peers out at us (quite often when you know how to look) from the foliage of Gothic churches. Usually he does this discreetly, as befits an outlaw. More often than not, he has foliage growing out of his mouth. He breathes, speaks, spits and disgorges leaves and life. The foliage hides him even as it identifies him. Sometimes he (or rather the mason) throws modesty and caution to the wind, emerging quite literally up there in the roof as the overseer of all that we do.

The chapter house at Southwell Minster is the most forested sacred space in Europe. Each of the 36 stalls around the wall has a crocketed tympanum of foliage. Each is separated from the next by stone stems bearing foliage. The capitals and bosses of the vaulted ceiling are richly carved with leaves. The space they surround, the clearing in the forest (the chapter house indeed), is reached by a journey through a much darker passage and vestibule. There are 49 columns in the passage and vestibule and 45 more in the chapter house proper, all of them festooned with leaves.[11] Leaves of the field maple (*Acer campestre*) are the favourite, closely followed by oak, hawthorn, ranunculus and vine, none of them evergreen. They don't need to be because here in this chapter house, situated like an appendix on the side of the big house (the minster) of the dying–rising god of the cross, it is perpetual spring, the walls and roof always in leaf, always in blossom, always bearing fruit, always implicated in song (there are birds there everywhere too) and life. From all this verdure, time and again, a man's face appears. He is glowering, grinning, squinting and pouting. Almost invariably, he is spewing out branches and foliage.

This building – the chapter house – dates from the late thirteenth century. It is one of the great works of medieval art. It is also quite astonishingly and very emphatically at odds with our received notion of Christianity even though it is part of a church.

Now, in our third millennium, the Green Man has become a badge and icon of the environmental movement. He is the secular saint of new agers, eco-warriors, recyclers, bicyclists, morris men, vegetarians, Extinction Rebellion activists, Just Stop Oil veterans and so on. He is not much discussed by the proprietors of the buildings in which his image may be found, but nevertheless he lurks there everywhere, like a fifth column of some fertility cult. His very presence inside spaces which we still respect (at least historically, as having been sacred) offers some purchase on the problem of making sense of ourselves in the context of nature now, even though he still keeps his medieval secrets very close to his chest. I am glad of him as an immensely enduring mask for what I take to be an aspect of the mystery of what we call 'god', and on the grounds of longevity alone, he deserves our attention. As the male mask of the Lady who seems set fair to reach the Christian pantheon at almost any moment, I welcome him too.

16 St Mary's Churchyard, Mundon. Seen here are the north porch and the first storey of the remarkable tower. Both the building and the graveyard are just about hanging on, but the latter will win in the end.

6

INTERLUDE
St Mary's Churchyard, Mundon, Essex

Quite a smart notice stands at the bottom of the rutted track. It says that the church you see before you was leased in 1975 to the Friends of Friendless Churches. Some years earlier, Nikolaus Pevsner – rarely one to wear his heart on his sleeve – seemed to have enjoyed his visit, to judge by his entry in his Essex volume in the *Buildings of England* series, published in 1954. But in the later edition of 1965, something of a pall of doom is spread over the site with the laconic, asterisked addendum: 'Now abandoned.'[1]

This is a Grade I listed building, but it's indeed friendless. If you cast your eye about for some explanation, you can see why. Apart from a farmhouse nearby, it is neighbourless. Level fields stretch all around to a low ridge a mile or two to the south, and to the north and east to marsh and estuary, marsh and sea. Closer to the eye, once proud oaks – now gaunt and leafless – stand along the field boundaries like lines of empty gibbets. A denser clump of them is known locally as the Petrified Forest. The fields are visited now by big machines in spring, and then again for the harvest. Otherwise nothing and no one.

The church is remarkable. There's a late medieval nave and an eighteenth-century chancel – nothing special from the outside, though the porch must have been charming when it was still complete. Inside, however, there are eighteenth-century box pews, a pulpit and tester, and the most curious paintwork on the east wall. It takes the form of a pair of curtains, quite crudely rendered in more or less monochrome brown. The curtains are drawn back and held apart by sashes to reveal – well, it's all so theatrical that you'd expect something rather good, but what is actually revealed is merely the window, and that's nothing special, no stained glass. What's left is a muffled but strong sense of emptiness. From the architectural point of view, the stumpy tower – six-sided at ground level, a latter-day ziggurat, with a skirt of three lean-to aisles – is a gem. From the outside, you see the frame of oak uprights, infilled up to the eaves of the first stage except for two windows, unglazed but shuttered, and then, above, the bell chamber is weatherboarded. Inside, you can see right up and through it, a maze of oak beams and braces. There is little light, but no floors or ceilings either to obstruct your vision up into the bell chamber. If it weren't so ancient, the exposure of its structural anatomy would strike us as very contemporary. The oak members are massive, very close together and grey. Nails have rotted in it, no equals in longevity with the wood. There is a single, heavy door in the west wall.

Outside, there are pools of rank grass, then headstones, a trio of crosses in rusty iron, and one or two rotting wooden kerbs (illus. 16). The badgers have levelled the mounds of the graves and made new ones of their own. A few polished granite slabs, and the words incised on them, are weathering well, but their speech is slurred by the tipsy troughs and swells in the surface of the earth as some shallow graves collapse and the badgers undermine others. One headstone leans out of the wind off the estuary. The windward side sparkles with lichen. On the leeward, the inscription and date are still clear – Edward Sewell, died 1766 – though it must be among the oldest stones here. A puffy-cheeked angel presides over the words – on his right an open book, on his left a skull. His was the last of that tradition of funerary art that left sorrow decently unspoken but death's sting unlanced.

All the things being trusted here – trusted as evidence of certain people having lived and died hereabouts, and trusted as bulwarks against time and decay, against failing memories and the dereliction of the dead by the still living – all these fail in the end to say what they would if only they could: 'Remember me, remember me.' Despite the granite, sooner or later everyone has been levelled here. No one has been able for long to pull rank against the tide of decay.

Yet whatever else it may be, this is no Wasteland. Someone planted a yew here, and not so long ago, for it is not a big thing yet. Elsewhere, on the boundary, is a holm oak, and that's not old either. It looks like a Victorian squatting for a shrubbery – which never happened – at Dunroamin Villa. Someone planted these two, and you wonder who, but hardly why. There are no other trees seeking our attention, just a couple of hollies, an English oak, a chestnut, accidents of wind or birds, just saplings. Ruins of elms that never reached their prime lean or lie, bleached and barkless. 'Tragic trees' someone has aptly written in the unfrequented Visitors' Book. Saplings spring up from the bowls of those old elms, but they'll go the same way. Dutch elm disease allows them to reach perhaps 4.5 metres (15 ft), and then forecloses on them. The hollies make some sort of a living here. Their wood characteristically resists moss and lichen. They shove gravestones out of their way. The dried stems of nettles and the dead spires of rosebay willowherb crackle under foot, rustle or rattle in the wind. Brambles snag at your feet. Somewhere I read that they used deliberately to plant them, and ivy too, to keep the surface of graves safe from animals.

But in February there are snowdrops, four large clumps of them, getting their work done before the larger weeds shade them out. They are doubles – wildings by now, though there's no doubt they were once planted deliberately. There's no telling which clump is the original, and the scattering is wide – a work of those earth-moving badgers, I suppose. In late May there are chest-high massings of cow parsley – Queen Anne's lace – a glorious sight, for all that the lanes are full of it then too. Between the stems and low down, the rude rods of the cuckoo pint will soon be cocking their reddening snooks, like so many randy dogs.

What have we to do with this place? The garden is in ruins, and the impulse to restore it too. To the Christian it must powerfully teach patience – waiting, waiting. But for the rest of us, we'd want to find another sense too. We'd want to be able to think that all this ruin is beautiful in its way, that all this process of reversion and conversion – turning and returning – makes some sense that we can also grasp. It might be so in another place, but not here.

On its own terms, the garden is reverting to wildness, and that's alright. Or better. It is 'natural', right and proper, faithful somehow to the mindlessness of the vegetable world. But just as the names of those buried here escape us, so does the sense. It leaves us out of the scheme of things. In this place, the myosotis – forget-me-not – is just a bit of botany and quite careless of someone having once said: 'Remember me, remember me.' *Viola tricolor* too, the wild pansy, the *pensée*, is as careless of our thoughts as the wind off the sea beyond the coppice, the same wind that carries the gulls who follow the plough. But those white rags are not the souls of dead sailors after all; they are just birds eating the worms eating us and shitting it all out again. Even the lords-and-ladies, the Jack-in-the-pulpit, lose their cheeky poise. Here are no lovers to pollinate their sense for them, but only flies. Here are no priests or prudes to blush at their phallic rods stuck up like so many disrespectful fingers.

I think of all those other literary visitors to graveyards and the places they fixed in their words: Thomas Gray at Stoke Poges, Robert Lowell at Nantucket, Thomas Hardy at Weatherbury, Robert Frost 'In a Disused Graveyard', T. S. Eliot at Little Gidding, W. G. Sebald at Dunwich.

The making of gardens is a fitting way to locate our own memories, our own memorials and perhaps even our own memoirs. Certainly, there are august classical precedents for this last, and many people have followed their pattern. Like memory, gardens have a life of their own. There the analogy ends, however, because though their forms and appearance change, the energy of gardens is essentially indestructible. Memory, too, is wonderfully porous to impression and metamorphosis. But it is not impervious to decay: sooner or later it dies.

Melancholy, the special gift of ruins, is an achievement too, though, and it is a sad irony that, though we have become now so accomplished at ruin ourselves, we hold our emotional response to it as suspect. We have become shy of the shadow that melancholy casts, and think ourselves fit only for the psychiatrist's couch if we entertain it. For his part, Sir Thomas Browne, physician though he was, reckoned not the consulting room but looked further: 'For the world, I count it, not an inn, but an hospital, and a place not to live but to die in.'[2] Let Robert Frost close our contemplation of this melancholic place:

> Wind goes from farm to farm in wave on wave,
> But carries no cry of what is hoped to be.
> There may be little or much beyond the grave,
> But the strong are saying nothing until they see.[3]

7

The Green Study

Cicero knew his Homer. He knew Homer's description of the Garden of Alcinous in Book VII of *The Odyssey*. He would have known that Plato's Academy was conducted often enough not indoors but in a garden (probably just outside Athens, a mile or two from the Acropolis). But Cicero himself worked not in a retired, leafy place, but in the noisy, dusty, smelly and often ugly city of Rome. So he took to his garden as often as he could. Tusculum became the solace and refuge of the man of affairs, the study of the political philosopher and the hospital of his soul.

Pliny, the other great Roman gardener to have come down to us, had at least three gardens. He often remarks in his letters that Cicero is his model for the dignity of his prose, the acuity of his oratory and the probity of his conduct in law. It probably follows also that Cicero's example in respect of gardens goes some way towards accounting for Pliny's affection for his own and for the ways in which he conducted his life there when he was not in the city. Between them, these two people consolidated the idea implicit in Plato's Academy, Theocritus' poetry and even Homer that the garden is a place of refuge from business and bustle, a place instead to read, write and hold intelligent conversation with like-minded friends. They set the pattern for what Horace was the first perhaps actually to fix in words: almost a vocation to 'seek truth in the groves of Academe' ('inter silvas Academi quaerere verum').[1]

The images we get from these classical originals and other later literary recoveries are various. Sometimes, it is a picture of places set apart in gardens for solitary study; at others it is of spaces for coteries of scholars occasionally convening to listen, learn and discuss. Thus, these gardens were to accommodate the solitary scholar but also places for the association of like minds: the academy.

Aristotle's Lyceum and Plato's Grove, when they appear on the scene long, long after Homer, sound suburban in the very best sense. They are just out of the mainstreams of civic and commercial life, but not detached from them. The shade cast by what seem to have been the trees of old orchards there would have been a boon. We can imagine freshened air, the murmur of a breeze and perhaps that of water too – things conducive to relaxed private study or engaging debate with others – but the word *academy* was appropriated for the place only because Plato's premises were hard by the grove of a certain Academus, and the latter's fame rested not upon anything scholarly at all, but upon his revelation of the teenage Helen's whereabouts after Theseus' abduction of her. The association of the word with study was Plato's doing, but only by accident of local geography.

Pliny's villa at Laurentum was quite easily reached from Rome. He could travel back there comfortably after a day's work. But the villa had no extensive grounds, so he kept what there was to himself, his beloved wife, Calpurnia, and his friends. We have his own words for his attitude to the place: 'there I do most of my writing, and, instead of the land I lack, I work to cultivate myself.'[2]

He prizes the villa and garden for the views they afford over the sea, for the sea breezes and for the intensity of the reflected light. There is an apsidal room with windows to catch the light and warmth as the sun moves round during the day. One wall is fitted with shelves for his library. The bedroom wing has heating, if necessary, by hot steam. There is a heated swimming pool, but because you can see the sea while you are in it, you enjoy the illusion of an infinite warm-water space. Around the house (or possibly even around the entire garden) there is a circular drive lined with box and rosemary. A vine-clad pergola, a well-stocked kitchen garden and plantings of figs and mulberries flourish here.

Then he describes a covered arcade 'nearly as large as a public building', in front of which is a terrace planted with violets.[3] At the end of this arcade, and furthest from the house, is his pride and joy: a suite of rooms built to his own specifications. There is a sun parlour, then two bedrooms, one 'built out to face the sun and catch its rays the moment it rises'.[4] This last is his sanctum, his retreat from noise and business. Always a decent fellow, he remarks that during the Saturnalia he can retire there while everyone else is free to make as much noise as they like without having to be anxious about disturbing him. There was no piped water when he wrote all this in a letter to Gallus (the purpose of which was to induce him to visit), but there was abundant spring water.[5]

Much less frequently was Pliny able to visit his other estates, but they were where his Roman thoughts often wandered. Comum was his birthplace. He inherited large properties from his father, and on the death of his uncle (Pliny the Elder, the naturalist, who famously died because he went too close to the erupting Vesuvius in AD 79), he gained even more.

In a letter to Voconius Romanus, Pliny explains that he has two villas in Lombardy which give him 'a lot of pleasure but a corresponding amount of work'. One he playfully calls Tragedy because it is set high up on a hillside over Lake Como, as if on the tall heels worn by actors in tragedy; the other, closer to the shore, he calls Comedy.[6] In another letter to Domitius Apollinaris, he evokes his Tuscan villa. He describes a long colonnade and in front of it a terrace. Then there's a bed of acanthus. The whole oval space is enclosed by a drystone wall masked by tiered box hedges. Behind this is a meadow 'as well worth seeing for its natural beauty as the formal garden'. This formality seems to consist of that oval geometry and, within it, concentric (but elliptical) paths and beds: regular and geometrical, but not emphatically regimented. Apart from the acanthus, Pliny mentions plantings of box and 'bushes' 'clipped into different shapes', 'figures of animals cut out of box facing each other', 'various box figures' and 'clipped dwarf shrubs'. It seems to have been a topiary garden. This would have made it typical of Roman gardens as a whole.[7]

At the upper end of the cursus – the riding ground – is an arbour shaded by a vine trained over four marble columns. Beneath is a curved seat of white marble from which water flows as if 'pressed out by the weight' of the sitter. The water fills 'a finely worked marble basin' around whose edge the main dishes of an al fresco meal are placed, for this arbour is an open-air dining room. The hors d'oeuvres and lighter confections float on the water 'in vessels shaped like birds or little boats'. There is a separate fountain which throws up jets of water high into the air to complete the playfully aqueous mood of the place. Opening on to this space, through folding doors, is a bedroom of white marble but covered – walls and roof – by a vine. 'There you can lie and imagine you are in a wood, but without the risk of rain.'[8]

Pliny closes this particularly expansive letter with a sort of apologia for its length. Such epistolary weight, he seems to be thinking, ought to have belonged properly to some appropriately ponderous matter (he cites Homer's very developed description of the arms borne by Achilles as example) rather than being expended simply upon a garden, but clearly he is immensely proud, immensely fond, of the place and considers it worth as much trouble to read as it is to write about it. He counts its blessings one by one in the closing sentences. Here, he says, he finds a 'profounder peace', 'more comfort' and 'fewer cares' than anywhere else he knows. He doesn't have to wear a 'formal toga' here. No neighbours disturb him. The air and opportunities for exercise and relaxation are healthy and benefit both body and mind.[9] Both body and mind are occupied here, as he writes in another letter: 'I am in my home in Tuscany, hunting and studying, either in turn or both at once, but I'm not yet ready to pronounce judgement on which I find it harder to do – catch something or to write it.'[10] Always the careful master, Pliny remarks that no servants have ever died on him here; in celebrating the advantages of the place, this comes last, as if it were his proudest boast of all.[11]

Individual elements of Pliny's Tuscan garden became models for later gardens. This is particularly true of the watery elements (thus, the Cardinal's Table at the Villa Lante, the water jokes at the Villa d'Este and elsewhere). The idea of fountains and water setting the scene for musing, and thus for the Muses themselves, developed into the grottoes and nymphaea which became obbligato features of every Italian Renaissance garden. But perhaps it is the general character of topiary which has been most often repeated, and indeed still is in our current infatuation with clipped box.

A keyword in the recreation of early Renaissance gardens and their spirit is *exedra*. The literal sense of the word is straightforward enough. It means 'seating outside', but it came to mean 'a courtyard with seating for purposes of philosophizing'. It also accrued an architectural character, perhaps from Pliny's garden rooms: an exedra was eventually taken to be apsidal in shape, almost a semicircle. Whether later reproductions were faithful or not to the real history of the word – if only we could definitively recover it – it is images of Cicero in his garden at Tusculum and of Pliny in his at Tusci that have become paradigms for the idea and practice of the garden as a *green study*. The model (the ancient original) was endlessly reproduced. It still is. For example, the crescent with its famous Lutyens bench at Sissinghurst in Kent is simply but perfectly an exedra.

Somewhere during its history, the word went on to gain a developed sense of meaning not only of an apsidal shape but of a theatre: whether in the sense of a lecture theatre or as a venue for dramatic arts, it is very hard to tell. Burlington, Kent and Pope (and all the other high-minded gardeners of the English eighteenth century) seem to have treated it as a geometrical abstract, but when exedrae occur in Italian gardens of the previous two centuries (as they do very often indeed), there is something much more theatrical about them. They are settings for sculpture – stages, as it were, for extravagantly dramatic (even though immobile) figures. Given the lightness of spirit of so many Italian gardens, it may not be very far from the truth to imagine also that they were venues for more conventional kinds of theatre: masques – scripted by playwrights and then spoken, acted and sung by aristocratic amateurs – or, if not that, at least the unscripted theatres of dalliance, of showing off fine clothes and manners, and of the dissembling and shadow-boxing worlds of masquerade. But all of this is to anticipate.

Horace too is, in part, responsible for the ideas of the garden as exedra and the gardener as philosopher, though Horace's thinker is a homespun Sabine farmer rather than a patrician Roman (illus. 17). His name is Ofellus. He is part mouthpiece for Horace himself, part rustic wiseacre and part hands-on farmer. It is his detachment from the hurly-burly of the city, from the fickleness of academic fashions and from the political interests of self-promoting careerists that gives his voice its authority. It is his attachment to the earth and the seasonal rhythms of farming and his vulnerable exposure to the vagaries of nature and weather that lend him credibility. He is the original of every homespun philosopher with dirt beneath his nails, the sceptic of abstraction and, in some respects, the leveller of the posturings of academics in ivory towers.

And then there is Virgil (the recoverer of the pastoral vision of Theocritus), for whom rural Sicily – rather than Sabine farm, Tuscan idyll or Roman garden – is recast as Arcadia. Virgil, in the *Eclogues*, fixes the pastoral milieu and that voice of seemingly natural wisdom for every poet and every philosophically posturing gardener

17 Horace at Tivoli, illustration from Volpi, *Vetus Latium profanum* (1745), vol. x, part 1. The Tiber flows in the bottom of a deep valley; Rome and signature cypress trees stand far off; the poet, quill pen in hand, sits on the left.

thereafter, but his influence was still more deeply significant than ever he could have foreseen because the medieval mind read him as a sort of proto-Christian. As a result, he became the religiously acceptable, culturally adoptable, precognizant voice of pagan classicism. It is the fourth *Eclogue* particularly, written around 42 BCE, which gave his reputation this pre-Christian gloss. In the poem, Virgil hails the imminent birth of a child who will recover for us all the Age of Gold. While not going so far as to claim that his epic *The Aeneid* was actually presciently Christian, medieval scholars were eventually to realize, and then to exploit, the parallel between Aeneas the founder of Rome and Peter the founder of the See of Rome.

For these reasons, Virgil is important for the idea of the garden as *grove of scholarship*. He doesn't himself suggest it in so many words (unlike Pliny, Cicero and Horace), but he does supply, first, a confirmation of that whole pastoral frame of mind and, second, a legitimation for Christian scholars to conduct their work and deliberations in a self-consciously pagan milieu if they so wished.

Petrarch supplies, I believe, a third element, and this, compounded with the foregoing, completes the frame of ideas which still gives us, hundreds of years later, the notion of the garden as green study. We see Petrarch now as one of the fathers of literature in Italian, but by his contemporaries he was celebrated as an exponent of classical antiquity revived rather than of their own modernity. Most of his work (though not the parts that we read much now) was written in Latin, not Italian. He was a champion in the 1340s of Roman republicanism. He was one of the exemplars of what happened to the mind when modern scholarship was fertilized by ancient ideas. In Vaucluse, where he lived in exile, he framed his work as a writer inside the context of a garden.

That contextualizing, that *mise en scène*, is a frame of mind which is central to what we see four hundred years later in eighteenth-century England: not so much attitude as attitudinizing, not so much stance as pose. If what Petrarch furnished his mind with was not so much the presence and fact of Rome as a memory of these things, then how much more true was that of Burlington, Kent, Pope and their circle, even more distanced by time and place from classical originals and precedents? If they made the Grand Tour, what they saw was ruin, moss-clad decay, an echo of former glories to be sure, but only a residual, faded echo nevertheless. Petrarch's distance – and then that of everyone who followed him in the making of gardens down through the High Renaissance, through Pope in Augustan England, and to us now – was the necessary opportunity and authority for poetic licence: not only to recover and recreate (as memory will), but to extrapolate, develop and create something almost new. From the really quite small seeds of a handful of classical authors, the idea of the garden as scholar's study grew, reconstructively through recovered fact and recreatively through imagination and memory.

The year 1719 saw three events of peculiar interest to the history of gardens and the history of what gardens mean. The Prince of Wales (having fallen out with his father, but later himself to become George II) and his consort, Caroline, began to establish their own court at Richmond. In retrospect, we think principally of the event as a milestone in the history of Kew, but at the time it meant something quite different: a powerful arbiter of taste striking out in new directions of style.

Lord Burlington – essentially the apostle of the new Palladianism – returned that same year from a Grand Tour, and returned moreover in the company of the young painter who was to put into graphic form the ideas Burlington was espousing. This young man was William Kent (1685–1748), he who famously 'leapt the fence' into nature.

The third seminal event of 1719 was Alexander Pope's settling at Twickenham. Pope (1688–1744) had achieved financial independence largely through sales of his *Iliad* translation (1715–20; his *Odyssey* was still to come), and was bent on making a home and garden of his own to match the temper of his mind. The tone of the place was suggested from the outset by a classical precedent: Tusculum. The spirit of Cicero, and all that he stood for, was to be recovered on the banks of the Thames.

Pope's garden there – down to the river in the front (with its famous weeping willow), and much more extensively in the plot of land he leased on the other side of the road from Hampton Court to London – was to become the work of the remainder of his life. He did a great deal of the labouring himself. He was never wealthy enough to be able to employ more than one faithful gardener. We know his name. It was John Serle, the same 'John' whom Pope addressed at the beginning of the *Epistle to Dr Arbuthnot* (1735): 'Shut, shut the Door, good *John*! fatigu'd I said,/ Tye up the knocker, say I'm sick, I'm dead . . .'[12] But the relatively modest extent of the garden – somewhat less than 2 hectares (5 ac) – meant that there was always enough to do, in a spirit of pleasure rather than duty and obligation, and rarely so much that it became a burden. Lord Bathurst, a good friend whom Pope helped to plant hundreds of trees on his estate near Cirencester, quipped that he could send one of his 'wood carts' to pick up Pope's house and garden in one fell swoop.[13] The garden is all gone now; so is the house. But the tunnel Pope excavated under the road to give access to the larger part of the garden from the house remains. In some ways, because incrementally it matured into a grotto, this was the heart of the place, and we are lucky to have it still. As for the garden itself, we have Serle's plan (illus. 18, published after Pope's death),[14] drawings and paintings, the recollections of visitors and friends, and (most impressively but hardest to grasp) the sheer volume of the reputation that both garden and gardener enjoyed.

Much has been written reconstructively about this garden. It is indeed one of the great landmarks of English cultural history,

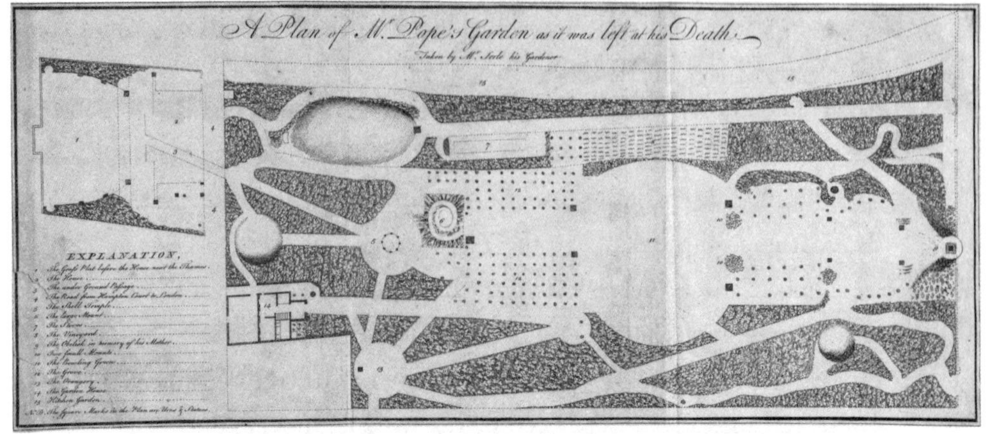

18 John Serle's plan of Pope's garden at Twickenham, 1745. The celebrated grotto is at fig. 3 (on the left, the 'under ground passage'). The obelisk in memory of the poet's mother is on the extreme right at fig. 9. The central oval space is the bowling green.

but of the history of English ideas I think there is still room for a few more remarks. First of all, Pope's garden, however fine it was and however influential it has been, was always going to have been different from most other gardens – its antecedents and its descendants – in one very important respect: it never was the setting for a house. The garden was set apart from the house (by the road, by the tunnel under the road), and the house was apparently more or less invisible from the garden. (I mean, of course, the main garden and not the small riverbank lawn in Turner's painting of 1808, where the house is already partly demolished.) While all the other elements – the grotto, mounts, shell temple, stoves, vineyard, lawn, grove, orangery, kitchen garden, monuments and sculptures, little 'theatre' (an exedra, really, made for Pope by Charles Bridgeman and a team of workers in the 1720s), and even the element of memorializing evidenced by the obelisk in memory of his mother (d. 1733) – can be found in other gardens both earlier and later, it is the absence of a house to be framed by a garden which makes Pope's English Tusculum special: a free spirit, as it were, among gardens. The only other important garden where the house was intentionally obscured from view is

Stourhead in Wiltshire. This – with Pope's villa – is the exception that proves the rule.

The second respect in which this Twickenham garden deserves even more attention than it has already received is that what the place meant was (and is) much more important than what it looked like, what it contained or how it was gardened, even though its meaning is self-evidently conditional upon those very things. What this garden produced far in excess of its beauty or size or contents was an *idea*. Or rather, the recovery and then the development of an idea: the garden as green study.

Much evidence of this can be found in Pope's letters and in the writings of other people in his circle. Thus: 'gardening is near akin to Philosophy,' he told Jonathan Swift in 1736.[15] Or this in 1740, when he wrote to Lord Bolingbroke: 'I hope yet to live to philosophise with you in this museum [he meant the grotto at Twickenham], which is now a study for Virtuosi, and a scene for Contemplation.'[16] Pope's literary exposition of Alcinous' garden, in an essay of 1713 for *The Guardian*, is informed by that same frame of mind (and it's also one of the several places where he excoriates topiary, a strange opinion for the classical recoverer to hold). When he uses the new word 'picturesque' in the postscript to his translation of *The Odyssey* (1725–6), it is in the literary context of those 'imaging and picturesque parts' of Milton, but we cannot help noticing that his usage prefigures not only a style but a purpose of gardening: the inducement of thought by the contemplation of scenery.[17] When William Shenstone (1714–1763), another poet and fine gardener, writes thoughtfully about 'picturesque-gardening', he glosses it as the practice of 'pleasing the imagination by scenes of grandeur, beauty, or variety'.[18] He alludes to Pope, he refers to Joseph Addison, but rather interestingly, he does not mention William Kent, a name that crops up almost everywhere else. So much so that it must seem sometimes as if it had been Kent from whom the whole landscape gardening movement had very largely sprung. The reality, however, was that both the new nuance attached to the word 'picturesque' and a very great deal of Kent's practice stemmed from Pope. The *Epistle to Lord Burlington* (1731), Pope's ideas on perspective, and the famous and fundamental idea that 'All gardening is landscape painting', were, to be sure, Kent's meat and drink, but from the table of Pope.[19]

The theme – topos and praxis of 'picturesque' gardening – is taken up by virtually everyone else who was even remotely sensitive to Pope's achievement. It became a cliché of garden discourse, and quite possibly most people lost sight of its origins in Horace's famous declaration 'ut pictura poesis' in the *Ars Poetica*, translated as something like 'just as it is with the work of a painter, so it is with that of the poet.'[20] One example only will have to suffice to make the point (because this is a much-tilled field already, and because, commonplace though the idea is now, it was new then and it is as clearly expressed here as if it were a proverb). This is Pope's friend Gilbert West in his poem *Stowe* (1732), intended to extol his uncle Lord Cobham's garden as a 'Landskip' – a painting, as it were – but also simultaneously as the product and the inspiration of poetic sensibility and plantsmanship:

> The same presiding Muse alike inspires
> The *Planter*'s Spirit and the *Poet*'s Fires.[21]

There is, however, more than just recovery and reproduction in Pope's idea of the garden. To the classical ideals passed on to them through Petrarch, Pope and his friends added something else, something which quietly but enormously fortified the idea of the garden as green study. Thomas More (1478–1535), in his *Utopia*, had set essentially the same familiar scene; he is worth quoting for the evidence of the green study extending away from the classical south and into the Protestant north even as early as 1516. This, the garden where the very word 'utopia' began, is placed in Antwerp; the English translation (from the Latin) is Ralph Robinson's (1551):

> And there wyth I turned me to Raphaell; and when we hadde haylsede [greeted] thone thother, and hadde spoken thies comen wordes, that be customably spoken at the fyrste metynge and acquentaunce of straungers, we wente thens to my house, and there in my gardeyne, vpon a benche coueryd [covered] wyth grene torues [turf], we satte downe talking togethers.[22]

But Pope's garden means more than this. The new Tusculum in Twickenham – and indeed the house, the *villa*, the fashionable Latin word everyone adopted for their classicized house – was not just the fit scene and posture (the theatre, in effect) for noble thoughts; it was intended as an agent in the production of those very thoughts. Pope, for all the hints of proto-Romanticism we think we can see in him, stops far short of implying that gardens (or nature) could be the *author* of our thoughts, but his frame of mind does quite loudly suggest that he saw gardens and the natural as what we would now call catalysts for thought, even if by the 'natural' he really meant very little more than bushes spared the disfigurement of shearing.

The difference between Petrarch and Pope is accountable for not only by the passage of time and altered tastes in gardening styles but by thinking styles, and the new element is the thought of John Locke (1632–1704). Locke appears in the pantheon of British Worthies at Stowe, as sober a garden building as you could wish for (and, indeed, an exedra). Though not a gardener by any manner of means, Locke's thought might as well be the parent of another kind of cultivation: that of the mind. Against Descartes, he argued that sense-perception, ratiocination and/or a combination of the two are the only sources of knowledge. It followed that clarity and variety of perception were critical for clarity and variety of understanding. As classes of experience available to sense-perception, both wilderness on the one hand and culture on the other confuse because at the same time as they individually and then consecutively make themselves available to experience, so do they each condition (*re*-condition) the experience of the other. The form and meaning of the one reciprocally reconfigures, alters the perception of the other.

Locke has the reputation of being first among the great empiricists, but he also deserves credit for having been among the first to take some account of what we'd now call 'cultural psychology' or something of that sort. Thought is conditional on who we are, on where we are and, critically, on who our thinking neighbours, both in space and time, are. Locke spent much time establishing what he understood as the grounds of personal identity. Most interestingly, he characterized this as a continuity of consciousness and memory. Though he never explicitly makes the connection, it is only a short step forward to our modern view of cultural conditioning, or backwards for that matter to the Platonic ideal of educating the mind by surrounding it (conditioning it) with wholesome, beautiful, indeed edifying things. It is the shift away from Cartesian pure reason and towards empiricist experience which makes clarity and variety of experience so important, and which renders solitary reasoning less absolutely dependable.

Locke is an apostle of the ideal university, a place which offers two kinds of milieux: libraries (massed resources of information and discussion for solitary digestion) and societies of learned people who have time, opportunity and place to debate, discuss and try ideas in the furnace and crucible of a community of experience. A library. Or it might as well be a garden, a place full of opportunity for sensory perception, for solitary observation and contemplation, or for concentrated debate with other scholarly minds. It is no accident whatsoever that virtually all our Oxbridge colleges have – indeed, often boast of – gardens.

What Pope meant by 'nature' was absolutely not what William Wordsworth would feel his way towards half a century later. Nature, to Pope, did not itself educate, but it did provide the proper milieu for education. Moreover, when he speaks of nature, he means natural philosophy. Thus, he looks the new world of Newton full in the face. There is no nostalgia in Pope, and yet the context of this world, as far as he was concerned, was always the recovery of the classical. He went on and on sealing his letters with an image of Homer's head, and he was wont to remark that 'I cough like *Horace*.'[23] He renders Horace's 'Beatus ille' thus:

> Happy the man, who to the shade retires,
> But doubly happy, if the Muse inspires!
> Blest whom the sweets of home-felt quiet please;
> But far more blest, who study joins with ease.[24]

Pope's identity is the thrust of the modern driven by the accumulated memory of the past, and this must lead us back to the matter of memory and its formal location in the grotto. That word comes from the Greek *krupte*, meaning 'vault'. It also gives us our word 'crypt'. Latin has *crypta*, meaning 'subterranean vault' or 'grotto'.

Grottoes were high-minded Platonic caves of memory, or they were excuses for sculptures of fetching girls having a bath. Actually, there's impeccable classical authority for nude bathing. After the ancients themselves, it was Petrarch who, by explicitly reinvoking the Castalian springs of Parnassus where these ablutions originally took place, recovered the idea for the second millennium. Grottoes – and never mind sometimes the skinny-dipping – were opportunities for geological exposition (Pope encrusted his with special minerals collected by him or given to him by friends from multiple sources). They were places sometimes to get unwittingly squirted with water. Always, however, it was the spirit of Mnemosyne that presided. She, Memory, consort of Zeus, and mother of the nine Muses – those begetters and patrons of all arts and sciences – guided and directed the thought and work of all that we do, all that we've done already. Memory, that quintessential component of identity as Locke saw it, governed all our lives. The Muses specialized each in their discrete departments of knowledge: Clio for history, Urania for astronomy, Terpsichore for lyric poetry and dancing, and so on. But over them all it was Mnemosyne – Memory – who presided. The grotto became, for all its frivolous sexiness, the locus of life itself as our university.

The Grand Tourists saw not the continuing living presence of ancient Rome, but its ruins – that moss-upholstered, dust-crusted, dilapidated memory, as it were, of former things – and what they brought back were memories of these memories, souvenirs indeed (*souvenir*, 'to remember'). Time and looters had inexorably rendered incomplete what they saw, but that very incompleteness was critically formative when the travellers came to reflect upon what their experiences meant. The lacunae left the door open, not to memory as mere recall of the past, but to memory as the faculty of constructive recreativity.

As we have seen, one of these recoveries-cum-recreations was the whole idea of Arcadia, a never-never land of pastoral bliss, but this constructive process could equally well generate something fearful. There are, for example, Piranesi's drawings of frighteningly labyrinthine chambers, of Henry Fuseli's impossibly vast fragments broken out of their original contexts and separated from those completed wholes which would have made sense of them: a severed foot or a colossal hand. Shelley's vision of 'Ozymandias' (1818) translates the cultural experience of ancient Rome to pharaonic Egypt, but it is in the same vein: memory generating memento mori, emblems of the vanity of human endeavour.

19 Giovanni Battista Piranesi, *Veduta della fonte e delle spelonche d'Egeria fuor della Porta Capena*, *c.* 1766, etching. People such as Piranesi, Fuseli and Hubert Robert ('Robert des Ruines') specialized in such scenes of vanitas three hundred years ago, but that chilling emptiness occurs again in the ghostly cityscapes of Giorgio de Chirico painted in the 1920s.

Piranesi's mid-eighteenth-century view of the Grotto of Egeria (part of his *Vedute di Roma*) will usefully serve to make the point (illus. 19). There are two collapsed figures – one leaning against a crumbling wall, the other lying almost indistinguishable from the rubble on the ground, both dishevelled and half-naked. Their poses strongly echo the (headless) effigy supine on an altar-like shelf above the outflows of the spring. Two more people – seemingly visitors – furtively, gingerly creep about the site, which colossally dwarfs them. A fifth – also ragged – gestures while seeming to read an inscription: learn well the lesson of this place. Stumps of trees litter the ground, inversions of once-proud Corinthian capitals. One or two bits of detritus hint at skulls. The legend at the bottom is from Juvenal's third satire, which speaks of a shrine and a sacred grove here, but this place now is a cavern of gloom and sinister decay. The artless swags of vegetation hanging down like a tattered curtain from the lip of the precipice above take the form of a pair of sightless eyes staring at the tiny figures below. Everything evokes the mysterious and the awful, the ruined and the vain. The scale is the great thing: the people are so tiny and the space so great. That distance, that implied gap, is what lifts the curtain on the theatre of memory. Weeds sprout from the crevices. The grandeur is unmistakable, but the tone is tragic. It is not awe or vicariously transferred pride in achievement, nor even antiquarian curiosity, that can make sense of this place. Only memory can do that.

Piranesi exemplified all this with his characteristically disturbing clarity, but Pope was equally sure of *his* ground. For him there were no tensions, no frictions or fractures between past and present, then and now, the ideal and the real. Pope had, however, a very special advantage (over Piranesi, over almost everyone else) in that he had never actually seen Rome for himself. There are long-standing controversies about how much Pope was actually physically disabled. Certainly, he would travel to the estates of his friends in southern England, but he was never fit enough to make that journey to Italy except through his reading, through his reconstructive imagination.

However, his close friend Joseph Spence, professor of poetry at Oxford, did make the journey in the flesh several times, as mentor (or cicerone, or Bear Leader) to rich young men. His *Polymetis* (1747) is a series of dialogues (thus, the ghost of Plato determines its form) discussing the relationship between classical literature and art. Almost never read now, the book was enormously influential in its time, not least because the dialogues take place – of course they do – in a garden.

How much, though, of all this is really just posture, just attitude and theatre? How much is really only antiquarianism or reconstructive fantasy, nostalgia? A lot of it. But the rest truly is the result of this strange business of creative memory which we have been observing and discussing. After all, proposing in a garden to the person you wish to marry is not all theatre either. It is also a gesture towards locating what you think and feel in *where* and *why* you think and feel it, an attempt to place bliss in a physical as well as emotional, intellectual, metaphysical – even theological – context. And that (almost paradigmatic) locus is a garden, a recovery of Eden. Writing letters or books and reading the same in a garden is not all posture, and not just a matter of seeking out a quiet place; it is also a framing of the mind by appropriate, sympathetic, perhaps creatively impelling circumstances. Andrew Marvell's 'green Thought in a green Shade' predicates some sort of psychological truth for all of us.[25] Placing a book or a life in a garden tends to provoke nostalgia – that especially creative aspect of memory itself – but it also affords an opportunity quite literally to make sense of experience which might otherwise be inchoate. It wouldn't work for everyone, but some lives, some experiences, are hard to imagine framed by any other circumstance.

In any case, the tradition and practice of the garden as green study, as venue for private contemplation and communal discussion, are alive and well – and have been for years – on the allotment. The shed as reclusive den (with books, kettle and armchair) is the quiet, green heart of a lot of people's lives, just as conversations with the proprietors of adjacent plots – discussing the finer points of brassica cultivation or putting the great affairs of the world to rights – have always been its most satisfying complement.

And – accidental though it almost certainly is – there may be a sort of pre-echo of this reclusive, contemplative, occasionally conversational life in the eighteenth-century vogue for hermitages. Caught up in this enthusiasm, you built (or recovered) a modest, chapel-like structure on your estate. It might be stone-built, a monkish cell. It might be a root house, something of an ossuary crossed with a chantry, and crossed again with a burrow. There might be a little garden for the growing of medicinal herbs in the manner of

Friar Laurence in Romeo and Juliet's Verona. Inside, there would be a bookshelf, a rude table and stool (leather bottle, candlestick, wooden platter, inkwell and quill) and a rough couch to sleep on. On the wall a crucifix or possibly an image of a tutelary 'Druid' (the religious complexions of these places tended to be syncretist, to say the least). Ideally, you would have a resident 'hermit' who would conduct himself in a suitably ascetic manner: celibate, sober, scholarly – a wild pet for the super-cultivated. He would be visible to visitors through a chink in the wall. Not quite celibate but genuinely bookish was Stephen Duck (*c.* 1705–1756). He was an agricultural labourer who wrote pious poetry. Taken up by (among others) Pope's friend Joseph Spence, he was eventually installed by Queen Caroline in her Merlin's Cave, a companion building to the Hermitage that William Kent had made for her at Richmond. Most of the other 'hermits' were predictably disqualified sooner or later for sundry immodesties. One or two were replaced by automata. Whatever the case, it is not difficult to see how having a hermitage – with its connotations of a simple, decent life – both counterbalanced and complemented the installation of a grotto, a cavern, a semi-ruinous folly and so on.

The apparently modest designation 'hermitage' is itself curious and prone to ironies: think of the vast hermitage built for Louis XIV at Marly or the gorgeous museum with that same name in Saint Petersburg. But the misty analogue with the modern allotment site – the refugee camp of bruised urban souls and organic foodies – lingers on too, curiously proleptic now of 'the good life' and a strangely attractive blueprint of a utopian, cooperative, supportive and self-supporting better world.

But if we should want to persist in a sceptical view of the eighteenth-century green study, suspecting it of posturing only, then we must also reckon with that special skill the age had to debunk its own imposters. It was a golden age for their own contemporary polemicists, cartoonists and lampoonists: William Hogarth (1697–1764), James Gillray (1756–1815), Thomas Rowlandson (1756–1827), George Cruikshank (1792–1878) and Pope himself in his satire *The Rape of the Lock* (illus. 14).

John Boyle (1707–1762), 5th Earl of Orreryand friend of Swift and Pope, arm's-length acquaintance of Samuel Johnson, exemplifies the same interconnected literary and gardening worlds and this spirit of self-mockery. His translation of the *Letters of Pliny the Younger* was published in 1751. He gardened famously at Caledon in County Tyrone and carried at least some of it off with characteristic Swiftian panache and wit. Here are his plans for a house built of bones in 1747: 'We intend to strike the Caledonians with wonder and amazement, by fixing an ivory palace before their view. We have already gathered together great numbers of bones. Our friends the butchers and tanners of Tyrone have promised to encrease [*sic*] the number.'[26]

Having said that, for every Augustan or modern gardener sensitive to the idea of these places as green studies, there must have been just as many people who found the whole thing a bore, or an artifice, or both. The complaint that life in the country, even when it approached Arcadian bliss, was 'like sleeping with your eyes open' was voiced originally in Rome, repeated remorselessly in eighteenth-century London, and is commonly enough said (or at least implied) now. And yet a garden that means nothing at all is probably as inconceivable as the proposition that a person to whom gardens mean nothing is necessarily a bore. And the person who would prefer to eat their lunchtime sandwich at the same office desk that they've been working at all morning, rather than in the little garden round the corner on the site of a bombed-out London church, spangled once a year with the petals falling from a beautiful cherry tree, is even more unlikely still.

8

INTERLUDE
Green Thoughts

In Cambridge, the novelist Henry James (1843–1916) was easily persuaded by his guide that the garden of Trinity Hall was 'the most beautiful *small* garden in Europe'.[1] I think I can agree with him sometimes. It is a beautiful, small, intense garden. But why 'in Europe'? It is that which dates and places it for us, that limiting of the view only to the old world which colours it with something of the hue of a lost era. James is entranced, and his pen rises to the occasion – perhaps a little too much: the venerable horse chestnuts, for example, are 'heart-shaking'.[2] It's odd how he comes through as the very pattern of an old-fashioned, impeccably mannered English gentleman. It takes an American and the passage of a hundred years to show us what we've lost.

The University Botanic Garden in Cambridge, too, is a lovely place in almost any season. It feels spacious, but it's really quite modest in its size: it doesn't wear you out. It also reminds me of one of my favourite Cambridge stories (along with Thomas Hobson, the Elizabethan livery stable proprietor who gave us the expression 'Hobson's choice', and along with stories of the feats of those mythical Cambridge night climbers). This story has a botanical slant, and it runs like this. The university's first botanic garden was sited near Trumpington Street, as indeed is its modern successor, but closer in to the city then, on what is now the New Museums Site. Workmen clearing a blocked chimney in the adjacent Free School Lane sometime in the eighteenth century found that the offending obstruction was an accumulation of wooden plant labels – over two hundred of them, in fact. They had been stolen from the garden by jackdaws. (And was this the inspiration – the germinal idea – of Tom Sharpe's hilarious Cambridge novel *Porterhouse Blue* (1974), where another chimney has got blocked, but not with plant labels? This time it's condoms inflated with inflammable gas.)

As with many people, however, my favourite garden of all in Cambridge is that of Clare College. Year after year, come droughty springs and damp summers, come lousy, chilly English Aprils and Mays, come flooding sometimes from the Cam, the double herbaceous borders strike me as the finest thing the skills of a gardener can achieve anywhere, even down to the seeming artlessness of it all. As an undergraduate, my heart didn't quite shake, but it did settle into the happiest of all its rhythms when I passed through the gate, climbed carefully down the steep steps to the riverbank, touched again the old Judas tree as it stumbled into its dotage, and looked once more upon the garden. The tree fell – and no one was surprised – in a winter more than two decades ago. It's much missed though: something about its old stooping slant, its steadfastness in adversity?

Another very great favourite is the churchyard behind Little St Mary's: old roses and self-seeded foxgloves everywhere in summer, hellebores and windflowers in spring, comfrey, bluebells and cow parsley in April and May. They don't so much clamour for attention as linger. So does everything else – the easy poise of the trees, the rambling gait of clematis and roses, the gentlemanly shuffle of the woodland carpeters – lingering long after you've left. Sometimes there's someone playing in Peterhouse's music room a few feet away from you. Brahms's Piano Intermezzi when I was last there. Rich, rich music.

But we must go on. The real purpose of our visit is to be in Trinity College Fellows' Garden somewhere near twilight. The shadows will help not only to prevent us from being observed (the garden is private) but to allow our imaginations to supply the missing trees. They all succumbed to Dutch elm disease, and their successors – London planes – are not mature enough yet to allow us to see the garden more or less as it was in May 1873, when the people we have come to eavesdrop upon were holding their conversation. The young Frederic Myers, author of a highly regarded volume of poetry – *St Paul* (1867) – and joint author-to-be of *Phantoms of the Living* (1886), the first published findings of the Society for Psychical Research, was listening awestruck, appalled and almost convinced as the 53-year-old George Eliot took

> as her text the three words which have been used so often as the inspiring trumpet-calls of men, – the words *God*, *Immortality*, *Duty*, – pronounced, with terrible earnestness, how inconceivable was the *first*, how unbelievable the *second*, and yet how peremptory and absolute the *third*. Never, perhaps, have sterner accents affirmed the sovereignty of impersonal and unrecompensing Law. I listened, and night fell; her grave, majestic countenance turned toward me like a Sibyl's in the gloom; it was as though she withdrew from my grasp, one by one, the two scrolls of promise, and left me the third scroll only, awful with inevitable fates. And when we stood at length and parted, amid that columnar circuit of the forest-trees, beneath the last twilight of starless skies, I seemed to be gazing, like Titus at Jerusalem, on vacant seats and empty halls, – on a sanctuary with no Presence to hallow it, and heaven left lonely of a God.[3]

Thus a veritable *Götterdämmerung*. And other comparable texts begin to crowd in. Not far off, I'm imagining a smouldering pile of couch-grass (as in 'In Time of "The Breaking of Nations"') – the last of Thomas Hardy's twilit faith that nods across the ages to a once vigorously Burning Bush. And then Graham Greene's play of 1957, *The Potting Shed*, a place full of the ghosts of gods past, catching the last of the light with its shabby door snatched shut by the wind.

Myers – and his interest in the paranormal – seems to have survived this demolition of his grounds for faith, this awful exposition of the Categorical Imperative. He went on, for example, to coin the word *telepathy* in 1882. I wish that he had gardened, that he had been given the opportunity to begin to understand something about why some people do it – another aspect of imperative perhaps: the impulse first to make a new world or, failing that, to be a guest at least, if not a dweller, in a better.

9

Garden Follies

The English have a soft spot for eccentrics. Or they like to think that they do. The Official Monster Raving Loony Party brings no shame upon the nation. On the contrary, it contributes a certain lustre to our reputation for tolerance, a reputation we cultivate sometimes when it suits us, even if we don't quite deserve it. But I do believe there are two particular areas of eccentricity which, while not being exclusive to the British Isles, nevertheless constitute a rather special characteristic of national life. One of these is allotments and their buildings: places that are fiercely careless of what other people think, doggedly improvisatory, whimsically gimcrack. Allotments and their sheds are castles against conformity, snooks cocked against the good sense of sound construction, against the improvidence of throwing anything away. They are one of the great silver linings to the dismal cloud of our often pretty grotty cities. But they must bide their time (for another book all to themselves perhaps), and this chapter will concern itself with a different manifestation of English oddness.

The second of these species of indigenous eccentricity is an extension of the old adage that 'the English love a lord' and, by further extension still, we love (some of) their creations. To wit, their follies. The names of these people (the prolix accumulation of toffee in their titles) often amuse us and tickle our anticipation of absurdity. Quite often we are rewarded. William John Cavendish-Scott-Bentinck's (1800–1879) passion for digging tunnels – miles and miles of them, and underground stables, and a ballroom – beneath his Nottinghamshire estate combines the lunatic, the grandiose, the profligate, the absurd and the essentially harmless on a noble scale, so we're not uncomfortable with him also being 5th Duke of Portland. The contemporary case of Alexander Boris de Pfeffel Johnson – certainly an aspirant to affluence and luxury – mines the same vein, even if his essential absurdity eventually proves to be neither loveable nor amusing. Or there was 'Mad Jack' Fuller (1757–1834), who was offered a peerage but – in the time-honoured way – went one better by turning it down.

Jack (we register the name, the familiarity, the common touch of the true aristocrat) was a man after the zaniest corners of our own hearts. Or he had been until he was recently identified as a slave owner. In pursuit of the better reputation as an eccentric, he invited his dinner guests one evening to imagine and applaud the views from his house (Rose Hill in Brightling, East Sussex) and expatiated upon the same to the effect that they were so comprehensive that you could even see the steeple of a church obscured to everyone else's view (and well known to be so by reason of its situation in a hollow). The guests suspected some hyperbole. Jack bridled and offered a wager that, should they come to lunch the next day (when daylight would permit), they would see the steeple for themselves. The next morning – so the story goes – he gazed out to confirm his own good opinion of the view and to enjoy anticipation of the bet won, but the steeple let him down. It wasn't visible. Nothing daunted, he had a simulacrum built – very summarily and in the space of only a few hours: no mortar between the stones but just mud – on the hill where the steeple would have been visible had not the same hill obscured the real thing. It still stands: a cheeky cone of stone with no tower or church beneath it.

But Jack, having acquired a taste for the sassy, enjoyed cocking a snook at pretentiousness as well as indulging in pretences himself. He had Sir Robert Smirke, that most unsmiling of severe

20 William Bernard Cooke, after J.M.W. Turner, *Brightling Observatory*, 1816, etching and line engraving. Turner was invited by 'Mad Jack' to come and paint in Sussex. Smirke's Observatory is visible on the horizon. The restoration of nearby Bodiam Castle was initiated by 'Mad Jack'.

neo-Classicists best known for designing the British Museum, make him first a rotunda, then an observatory and finally a mausoleum (illus. 20). The first Jack is plausibly thought to have used for orgiastic parties, the second just possibly for astronomical observation, and the third most certainly for his own long wait in anticipation of the resurrection of the dead. It's a hollow pyramid. Inside, Jack is said to be comfortably seated, fully dressed and supported by a bottle of port and a ready-roasted chicken on the table in front of him. As a precaution, the floor is strewn with broken glass should the Devil arrive to try to claim his soul.[1] Jack Fuller died in 1834. Had he consulted James Barclay's *Complete and Universal English Dictionary*, he would have encountered the following, and snorted, no doubt: 'FOLLY, *s.* [*folie*, Fr.] the act of drawing false conclusions from just principles; a weakness or want of understanding; an act of negligence or passion, unbecoming the gravity of wisdom, or the dictates of cool and unbiassed reflection.'[2] Was it not rather a question of conviction, or commitment, or even of breeding? It was only the dullard who conformed, wasn't it? Instead, 'Mad Jack' Fuller would have preferred to subscribe to Blake's more encouraging axiom in *The Marriage of Heaven and Hell*: 'If the fool would persist in his folly he would become wise.'[3] And anyway, *pace* Goldsmith, is folly necessarily a stooping? Why not rather a rising above the common herd?

Perhaps he reasoned thus. Almost certainly, he recognized the indulgence of folly as generally the particular privilege of the rich, but overlooked the disaster it would usually spell for the poor if given its head. Indeed, as we shall see, there is often an intimate and ironic connection between rural poverty and these rich men's toys. Whatever the case with 'Mad Jack' Fuller, however, we are more or less seduced into gratitude to him for colouring our own lives, like his, with a little bit of absurdity.

The word *folly* is slippery. Erasmus was playing with the idea as early as 1511 in his book *Moriae Encomium*, translated for the English market as *The Praise of Folly*. Now, actually to finger contemporary perpetrators of folly and to deplore them (as Swift does in *Gulliver's Travels*, where the Big-Endians – those who opened their boiled eggs at the wide end rather than at the narrow end – conducted their immemorially absurd and bloody quarrel with Little-Endians) is bad form. These days, people are entitled to their Big or Little Ends, just as they are to their own opinions, vouchsafed and rendered irreproachable by the imprimatur, no less, of social media.

Folly seems to have come to us through French, fending off with the one hand (censorious thumb turned down) a sense of the stupid. With the other hand (thumb cheerfully raised) it greets a spirit of light-heartedness – as in the famous place and name the

Folies Bergère. As for the peculiar association of the word with garden buildings, it seems to be trailing both connotations (opprobrium and applause) as far as we are concerned now, but in the first place the word itself may well have come about as a corruption of *feuillée*, suggesting a rustic building, a retreat, a place of leafy connotations. Thus, in the first place, the word meant perhaps no more or less than a house in the country, and was no laughing matter at all. And that leads us on to the next problem: most so-called follies aren't funny or even slightly daft, bizarre or incongruous. If they are dubbed a 'Gothic folly', then we know (or think we do) that we're in for a medieval sham, and we behave accordingly with a mixture of witheringly tolerant condescension and an indulgent pretence at being amused. If it's a 'classical folly', however, we approach it quite differently. Condescension gives way to serious meditation on themes of grandeur, vainglory, cultural heritage abiding even in its ruin, and we nod gravely as we scan its Latin motto: *sic transit gloria mundi*. But neither of these behaviours is quite fair, let alone logical.

The more one thinks about it, the less satisfactory is the term *folly*. If we try seriously to use it to embrace the whole gamut of things to which it has traditionally been applied, it becomes even less so, but the alternatives – 'sham ruin', 'garden building', 'absurd structure' and so on – are too restrictively specific, or they miss the mark by overlooking the *spirit* of these things.

What about a building like the Royal Pavilion in Brighton? Or Strawberry Hill in Twickenham? As pastiches of particular styles, both of them offer not too little conviction but too much. And was this deliberate too? That Brighton protests the Mughal and Strawberry Hill the Gothic – but both of them egregiously – is quite good fun, I think, but were they supposed to be seen like that?

An awful lot of so-called follies do not deserve the classification at all. They are fantasies (of geography), but they are not absurd or funny. They are not evidence of dottiness in the builders or wackiness in their fans. I'm thinking of the Pagoda at Kew or the Chinese Dairy at Woburn. Except for their scale, they are really no more or less odd than the architectural features and/or bric-à-brac with which so many people sprinkle their patios to induce a bit of flavour into their back gardens now: a fat buddha from Thailand or a bamboo deer-scarer from Japan. It's really only the geographical displacement which makes them seem odd or exotic. Much the same goes for Swiss cottages, Palladian bridges and those Alhambra palaces which used to grace every high street in the heyday of the cinema. These are not the self-conscious, self-debunking jokes which mark out a certain strain in the true spirit of folly.

Mausolea and memorial columns, obelisks and even chapels are often classified as 'follies' – though probably not by their originators, who were often in deadly earnest. Nevertheless, some of them deserve the accolade. That we should dub them 'follies' at all is rather unsettling, I think. But perhaps that is the explanation: the impulse to jest in the face of death is essentially a defensive, nervous reflex?

Another species of 'folly' brings us back to the winningly fantastic, if not the thoroughgoingly absurd. Mock medieval military buildings are opportunities for clever builders to play tricks on us. There are so many examples of the real thing still extant that patterns to copy have always been easily accessible. On the other hand, the eye of the visitor is now correspondingly quite well educated, and the fraud, while in principle easier to accomplish, can all the more easily be detected. 'Mad Jack' Fuller patched up and renovated the shell of the real but very battered Bodiam Castle so that it would grace the view from his estate, and he did it very well indeed. Windsor Castle, on the other hand, is a dog's dinner – not just architecturally inept sometimes (the ratio of windows to wall space, for example, is, in credible military terms, ridiculous), but daft in its trying too hard to be Gothic. It's probably not a coincidence that the most dubious of the 'improvements', the least respectful of the originally Norman and medieval buildings at Windsor – the Waterloo Chamber, St George's Hall, the new towers and much of the battlements along the outside walls – were commissioned by the same man, George IV (1762–1830), responsible for the Brighton Pavilion, the king himself a bit of a folly, a laughing stock (his vast bulk and profligate expenditures), and mockingly but not affectionately known as 'Prinny'.

Reproductions of styles more ancient than the Gothic are somewhat different. Their stylistic characteristics are less specifically imprinted in our critical eyes. The further back into the past they seem to be projected, the more ruinous we expect them to be, the less precise, the less coherently complete, the more gestural. The Leptis Magna columns at Virginia Water in Surrey are a celebrated case in point. The components of this folly are authentically Roman and ancient. They were the gift of the Bey of Tripoli to the Prince Regent, later George IV. The British took some of the stones from the site. Shipped back, the spoils were piled up in the yard of the British Museum and stayed there for eight years. No one really wanted them. They weren't even very good of their kind – and certainly not coherent, taken as they were from a single site but from several different buildings. But something had to be done if a diplomatic incident were to be avoided. One of George IV's architects, Jeffry Wyatville, was commissioned to do that. His re-erection of them in 1828 and his carefully conceived air of abandonment about the occasional fallen shaft and the slightly dislodged architrave are actually very convincing. Perhaps he had been reading Shelley's 'Ozymandias' and had caught the knack of insouciant decay. Only the English light gives the game away if, indeed, game it is at all.

But 'ruins' more ancient still – prehistoric henges and so on – tend to revert to form, that is to say, to the risible. The Druid's Sideboard at Alton Towers is engagingly clumsy to be sure, and seemingly all the more authentic as a consequence, but the clumsiness is overdone. The Druid's Temple at Ilton in North Yorkshire might almost have been convincing if its author, William Danby (1752–1833), had left it at that, but he didn't. There is not just one altar but a whole grove of them – and cromlechs, menhirs, dolmens and, most suspiciously of all, an awful lot of archly phallic sarsens.

In another respect, Danby's caprices draw our attention to a common origin of many follies in the British Isles and in Ireland. Like his Shamhenge, follies were often conceived as philanthropic schemes to provide work for the poor: the unskilled and the unfed. Many a homespun ruin betrays an excess of enthusiasm over technical skill in its builders. Remembering by whom they were actually made may account for the clumsiness of so many of them. I have seen some fine workmanship too, though, particularly in Ireland, where famine relief works also quite often took the form of folly building, but your heart sinks to think of undernourished people manhandling great lumps of masonry.

English and Irish follies – the best of them – hint at absurdity. German and Austrian follies are much less successful at absurdity, but sometimes have a baroque theatricality that is almost all their own. They go in for quite a lot of the exotic too – chinoiserie and so on – but rarely something actually to smile at. There's the Garden Theatre at Herrenhausen, where the trapezoidal stage is defined by hornbeam hedges and lined with life-sized gold-plated lead statues – male and female – of august figures, all in magnificent classical poses. And all in the buff. So there's snow in winter on private parts, flies examining nostril cavities, wet leaves trapped in armpits. It's absurd, but I don't think we are expected to find this even faintly amusing. We're supposed to take it seriously.

There's the wonderful assembly of pavilions, sculpture, aviary, mosque, bath house, fountains and the Temple of Botany (in the form of a massive faux tree trunk) at Schwetzingen, but nothing tongue-in-cheek about any of it. Apparently, when the sculptor of the god commemorated in Schwetzingen's Temple of Apollo was mocked (by Schiller, among others) for having made the lyre-playing god left-handed, instead of pretending that it was a deliberate joke, he would have it that any god worth his salt would naturally be ambidextrous.[4] Which might be true of the hands of the immortals, but certainly isn't of lyres, which would have had to be completely restrung. And then someone painted the whole place shocking pink. But still we aren't supposed to smile.

Italian follies, however, restore the playfulness while tending sometimes to cultivate the grotesque. The expression *scherzi d'acqua* – water jests – defines the spirit in which you are invited to take the soaking you get from hidden jets triggered by the pressure of your footsteps, or there are the spewing stone monsters, dragons and fantastic fish in the fountains and – wittiest of all perhaps – the stone boats that still appear to float. The *catena d'acqua* at the Villa Lante – the water chain in the form of vomiting crayfish – plays on the name of its proprietor, Cardinal Gambara (*gambero* means 'crayfish'). The Mouth of Hell at the Villa Aldobrandini is grotesque indeed: a great gob of carious, leering teeth waiting to

21 Amey Aldrich's photograph of Bomarzo, *c.* 1930–39. Similar in spirit to a medieval gargoyle – both comic and grotesque – sculptures like this invest the garden with the spirit of an early theme park.

swallow you down into its Lethean maw. And there's something quite similar at Bomarzo – both comical and terrifying, until you get close enough to see a welcoming picnic which might be set out for you on the table that could rest on its awful tongue (illus. 21).

The Italians also seem to have had a penchant for animals in gardens. It had always been in Italy that zoos had found their best expressions, and where the zoomorphic had first become an almost obbligato part of the spirit of follies in gardens. The taste for animals – live and terrible, or sculpted and caricatured – seems to have been so deeply rooted that, with an eye on how to ingratiate himself into the affections of a reluctantly subject people, Napoleon Bonaparte (1769–1821) catered for this especially Italian fondness when he incorporated a large collection of exotic animals into the public gardens, the Giardini Napoleonici, he had laid out for them in La Serenissima, his newly annexed Venetian Republic. What is now the hothouse in the Boboli Gardens, behind the Pitti Palace in Florence, was originally the zoo (and its keeper's house), and the grotto at the nearby Villa di Castello is carved with life-sized and very lifelike horses, stags, a rhinoceros, a camel, a giraffe, ibex, boars, cattle and, for good measure, a unicorn.

The childishness of the water jokes, the clumsy exaggeration of the grotesques and the voyeurism of the zoos (then as now) can breathe a sort of unabashed vulgarity which – to the open-minded, the modern sophisticate – is sometimes quite hard to enter into. The English eventually mimicked elements of this unreformed tastelessness but failed often to grasp it wholeheartedly – and more's the pity perhaps. Even now, when the English see peacocks on an English lawn, they're expected to be impressed: these birds represent money, hauteur and something classy. However, the Italians in the eighteenth century, and perhaps still now, saw the matter more clearly. To them a peacock's mincing stride was seen for the preposterous strutting it really is, its plumage as not so much avian splendour as tastelessly gaudy puffing, and the whole ensemble all of a piece with the appallingly raucous noise the bird makes when it opens its mouth.

There's an awful lot of snobbery, suppressed sometimes or flaunted at others, in some English perceptions of gardens. Latterly, only the French and Italians seem to have got the true spirit of folly and follies nearly right. They saw it not so much in terms of buildings or garden features, but as something entailed in their own particular humanity, a frame of mind, an attitude – a holiday from the stiff formality of a lot of French gardens to be sure, but also a truth to themselves: a necessary burlesque of manners which endorses received forms and conventions even as it pokes fun at them.

In 1670, when Isola Bella in Lake Maggiore was virtually finished, there was a fantastic water-borne party to inaugurate it: a mock sea battle, fireworks, choruses of beautiful voices heard but not seen, feasting and, for a few hours, a visa to visit a certain kind of paradise, a world taking its cues from poetry and theatre, childhood and imagination, the absurdly unreal and the ideal almost realized. In France (and generally on a smaller scale), you'd call these bits of theatre 'bagatelles' – trifles, *petits riens*, sweet nothings. Sometimes, they were made only of short-lived laths and cardboard, sometimes of more durable stone, but almost always painted with *trompe-l'œil* trelliswork, trees, birds and flowers to bring the natural into collusion with the sensuous and, as often as not, the sensual. The settings were pure theatre. The mood was *folie* – living, frolicking, eating *en plein air*, dancing, masquerades, music, bathing – but the essence of the plot was indulgence: fashionable coffee drinking in the afternoon perhaps, amorous seduction in the evening as likely as not. Is it any wonder that so many men's preferred mistresses were also actresses, people adept and fluent in masks literal or metaphoric?

By trick of inversion, the outside – the garden – becomes the 'real' world. By dint of its both matching and stimulating the covert desires within us – things which we normally mask to the everyday world in performances of the dissimulation of rectitude, level-headedness and propriety – the garden seems to become our natural milieu. The pretence to be carefree, or immortal, or solicitous of other people – or is it to dare to be our real selves? – is given temporary licence because it is invested with the natural. In *L'Invention de la liberté, 1700–1789* (1964), Jean Starobinski thinks that pleasure in these places took on a life of its own and generated a sort of parallel world, where gardens used the discipline of art to suggest the freedom of nature, where places dubbed 'temples' – but which actually were *folies*, bagatelles – played a game that seemed to invite worship but actually apotheosized pleasure.

But before we concede an absolute monopoly of all this frivolity to those Continentals, let us climb aboard a thoroughly English pea-green boat and sail back home in time for supper at Faringdon House, home of the Right Honourable Sir Gerald Hugh Tyrwhitt-Wilson, painter, poet, bon viveur and rather considerable composer, whom we probably remember best as just plain Lord Berners. He was born in 1883 and died in 1950. Berners may yet turn out to be the last of the possibly loveable lords we like to think we can still keep as national pets.

Our vessel delivers us appropriately enough to the large, formal garden pool at Berners's country house in Oxfordshire. We tie up on the only thing which conveniently offers itself. It is the head and shoulders of that Victorian worthy Sir Henry Havelock, whose bust is emerging from the surface of the water for all the world like the head and shoulders of a puffed-out swimmer. You suppress the urge to paint on to him the whiskers of a walrus, but you wouldn't be surprised if the estate handyman, suspiciously festooned with wood shavings, who helped you out of the boat into the twilit garden, were actually that celebrated other joiner, moonlighting from Lewis Carroll's 'The Walrus and the Carpenter' (1871). A dog jumps out of the dusk to greet you. The creature has been harmlessly dyed blue with woad and may be keen to rub some of his colour off on to your legs. From the dovecote comes the soothing coo of peaceable birds. They are pretending to be useful in the manner of liveried carrier pigeons. They are temporarily coloured Royal Mail red.

Caution is advised during dinner on the terrace and later inside. There may be duck in the soup. The horse of Penelope Betjeman has been invited to partake of the collation and enters the room through the French windows. There's a beer mug in amongst all the other clutter on the grand piano. It doubles as a music box and takes the form of the Duke of Windsor playing the national anthem, a morceau of exquisitely vulgar kitsch. But you can be pretty sure that Berners keeps the very best of his follies for the dessert trolley – Knickerbocker Glories for the squeamish, Mamelles de Venus for the gluttons and connoisseurs of the voluptuous and the vulgar – and something about him and his life makes you think that he may be pointing a half-serious lesson in our direction: about taste certainly, but also about rank, about life's fragility and brevity, about make-believe in a fact-stunned, data-stupefied world.[5]

And they sailed away for a year (or a day), *au Pèlerinage à l'île de Cythère*, perhaps – but if you don't take it (or yourself) too seriously, why not 'To the land where the Bong-tree grows' (this tree surely Edward Lear's own caricature of that Victorian favourite, the monkey puzzle), where you can dine on quince with runcible spoons and sing to the moon above with the sound of a small guitar.[6]

The absurd has a place in our hearts, so it may as well be enjoyed in our gardens too. Gardens, by their very nature, are tropes, illusions, fantasies. We, being the only terrestrial creatures who are not really part of nature any more, create these places to act out the fiction that we are. Gardens are the places we have devised to persuade ourselves that nature is on our side after all, that we are not indifferent to it and it is not indifferent to us – probably wishful thinking in the first instance and delusion certainly in the second, but there we are.

Given this essential fiction underwriting the very nature of gardens, it seems only right somehow that follies belong there too.

22 Gingerbread house crossed with Stratford-upon-Avon, the toolshed in London's Soho Square is cunningly only just unconvincing.

10

INTERLUDE
Some Favourite Follies

Soho Square is not one of London's best. It lacks that sense of being a place apart. The streets and the traffic around it are still visible, still audible. The premises on all four sides go on competitively staring at each other across the space. But in the very middle of this modest square stands one of the most delightful buildings in the entire city: a sham Tudor toolshed (illus. 22). Sham it certainly is, but its slightly irregular black timbers – and something about the dudgeon of the pigeons who find themselves resisted by the steepness of the roof – make it very nearly convincing. This is no mere dog kennel writ large but a shovel house to end them all: a grand two-decker of a toolshed. Even the roof is big enough to house an attic. A veritable argosy of every sort of engine for mowing, clipping, delving or potting could be contained within its capacious walls.

The building is a narrow rectangle to begin with, and then there's a second storey, which is octagonal and overhangs. There are windows snugly tucked under the eaves of this upper storey, and something about this snugness suggests a gingerbread house of yore, though unless you were Alice, magically grown more than 2.75 metres (9 ft) tall, you wouldn't be able to peep inside. The windows are mysteriously boarded up – from the inside. The projections of the upper room are supported on free-standing wooden stilts. The whole thing looks something like a bird's nest (but with avian legs dangling out the bottom), something like an afterthought of a Stratford-upon-Avonian caprice, something like the precarious towers of pans, pots and plates that as children we made of the tea things after the meal was over and when nobody was looking, and something like a gingerbread house indeed, complete with tea-cosy on top.

Rumour has several explanations for the building: (a) it is the disguised entrance to a nuclear bunker; (b) it's there because someone couldn't bear to waste the bits and pieces left over after the building of Liberty's, that splendid half-timbered pile round the corner in Great Marlborough Street; (c) it is the prototype for the Millennium Dome (now the O2) in that its real purpose is to mask the ventilation shaft for a subterranean tunnel.

At any rate, the reputation of the place is that no one has ever been seen either to go into it or to come out of it bearing tools, tea flasks or anything else. I can attest, however, that on 20 April in the two thousandth year of our lord, the door was not locked but ever so slightly ajar. There was a gap of half an inch, and a horrible glare from fluorescent lights within, but no sound – either of whetstone on sickle or of cheerfully chinking teacups. No voices. No petrol fumes from motor mowers. And no flick of the pages while Martians were having their entrance or exit visas checked. The trepidation that prevented me from knocking and entering will dog me for the rest of my days.

At Pitchford in Shropshire stands the broad-leaved lime with the largest known girth in the British Isles.[1] It is probably also the oldest, though it isn't the tallest by any means because at some time in its history it was pollarded some 3.7 metres (12 ft) above the ground and then left to throw out branches, huge branches now, more or less horizontal to the ground to begin with, but then arching up to form a massive cradle perched on top of the stumpy trunk. Some of these branches are now as much as 2.5 metres (8 ft) thick. They are cracked and ribbed. As protection from the weather, they have been draped with huge sheets of lead. It is an awesome sight.

In the rough bowl formed by the pollarding, a tree-house was built probably during the seventeenth century (and it underwent a major restoration around 1760). You climb a flight of wide stairs up to a square, half-timbered room. It has a door and windows with matching Gothic ogees. Inside, the walls and ceiling are covered with plasterwork: columns in four corners, frieze all around and an arcaded dome above. The capitals and frieze are leafy. This is indeed a *cottage feuillé*, a true exemplar of the true folly.

The present house – charming and venerable though it is – suggests what should have been the world of a child usurped by the sensibilities of adults. It is too self-consciously pretty for children to enjoy, too big, too accessible and too well behaved as well. What we see now probably dates from the eighteenth century – the style is a sort of Batty Langley flummery of Chinese, Rococo and Gothic – but the tree and the opportunity its open cradle of branches provides for climbing is much, much older.

There's no local stone hereabouts where I live in Essex. For church building, castle building, it all had to be imported. But there still stands, two fields away from us, a very imposing arch – all that is left of an Augustinian priory. What remains is the west arch of the crossing of what must have been a substantial cruciform church.[2] As a child I was convinced that excavations in our garden (we lived closer to the ruin then) must reveal foundations of monastic outbuildings and, of course, buried treasure.

As it happened, when I moved, in the 1980s, into my current garden, there was a good deal of loose stone. Someone was said to have imported it here once upon a time – perhaps from a bombed-out London church. They may have intended a rockery. It was in confused piles covered, like everything else then, with brambles and

23 Visitors to the author's own folly are regularly duped into believing that it may be the ruins of a chapel-of-ease belonging originally to a real monastic site half a mile away.

bonded together with the roots of sapling elms and weedy blackthorn. Some of it had been dressed. There were one or two sections of arches, deeply shaped and carved. There was one fairly long slab of an oak-leaved frieze. Most of it, though, was just roughly broken.

I set about squaring up sufficient pieces to enable me to build enough of a wall to set a window in: a cast-stone copy of an Irish Cistercian light I'd brought home a few years earlier. The stone dust was prodigious. So was the heaving about of heavy lumps. But soon enough, there was sufficient to build a bit of wall, and so it was constructed. For stability, I made enough of the stump of another wall – almost a buttress – set at right angles. And away from this proud, upright corner, the wall tapered off into deliberately fractured ruin, but not before I'd set the window into it and laid the bit of the oak-leaved frieze above it as a lintel (illus. 23).

The whole thing is quite small, and the window is low in the wall, which itself is only 1.8 metres (6 ft) or so high, so it seems to rise out of the surrounding vegetation rather than to have been stooped and crushed by time into it. Something about this small scale tempts you to discredit its plausibility as an honest-to-goodness Gothic survivor, but something about the planting – right up to it and reaching in summer more than halfway up it – suggests that it has sunk, the soil level having risen over the centuries, and that it really has always been there.

Children warm straight away to its scale, and never doubt that it's a bit of a castle. Adults look, miss it, look again, and then they are charmed, I believe, by the way it fooled them for a moment, but then only to find that the plants around it seem to authenticate it after all. It's a folly that doesn't labour to make a joke either of itself, or of me its maker, or of visitors to the garden who see it for the first time. I'm glad of its being there.

The spirit of folly seems to be enjoying something of a contemporary revival. It won't be long perhaps before the Royal Horticultural Society shows at Chelsea and Malvern begin to have a Fringe in the manner of the Edinburgh Festival where folly can make a new start, can begin again to chip away at the preposterous presumptions and tyranny of good taste elsewhere. I hope so.

11

The Garden of England

Not just England but other countries too have their 'gardens'. In France, it is Amboise; in India, Awadh; for Italy it's Sicily; for Spain it's the Vega of Granada; in the USA it's New Jersey. England has its own local garden too: the Weald of Kent with its orchards and hop fields (or some prefer the Vale of Evesham). In the early nineteenth century, it was reckoned to be the Isle of Wight; in the 1770s it was Herefordshire. Our perception of where this 'garden' lies has changed with the march of taste, agricultural use and time. Some territories could reasonably lay claim, in a literal sense, to being entire gardens in themselves: Nepal perhaps; Taiwan with its extraordinarily rich flora and varied terrains; Ireland, especially in its far southwestern counties; Holland with its tulip fields; Japan at the time of cherry blossom; Shangri-La mythically (probably). But only of England is it a part of the national myth that the whole place is, in some idealistic as well as realistic sense, a garden.

It is an ironic paradox that at the very moment when this may be becoming 'true', we are also witnessing what looks very like the end, more or less, of the English countryside. The myth is becoming true in the sense that making and keeping private gardens seems to have become a national obsession; putting up hanging baskets in streets, planting up roundabouts and avenues, and generally gardening public spaces in our towns seem to have become a civic obligation. Retailing plants, gardening gadgets and books, along with television programmes offering every species of advice, seems also to have become very big business indeed. But changes in agricultural practices, warmer and stormier weather, and pressures of traffic and population in an overcrowded island have relentlessly shrunk the countryside, altering the character of what remains, and rendering the myth virtually untenable.

Why England should ever have been thought of as a garden is interesting. Modern historians of the landscape (W. G. Hoskins, Oliver Rackham and several others) have taught us that most of what we see now – groves of mature (un-coppiced, un-farmed) trees, neat hedges, gates and walls, enclosed fields, all those elements which look 'gardened' – date only from the eighteenth century. Being so late on the scene and, indeed, so man-made, our vision of a 'timeless' English landscape must therefore allow of some scope for ongoing revision, even to the extent of our coming to terms with the possibility that, being so recent, it may also have to be treated as temporary and transitory. The very essence of what we now know about the English landscape is that it is not 'natural' at all, and that being so, it is both more vulnerable to change and more capable of being preserved for the artifice that it is.

Nevertheless, some elements of what we perceive as the quintessentially English landscape really are natural. I'm thinking particularly of the closeness of the horizon, which is the result of the natural undulations and folding of the land. While not often steeply hilly, it is rarely flat. Another natural element is the prevailing greenness, the consequence of the famously benign English climate. A third is the remarkable variety of shapes and sizes which make up the units of the landscape – the fields, woods and copses – along with the (relative) lack of straight lines in roads, boundaries and water courses.

The character implicit in this natural countryside garden is, of course, that of the English landscape style. 'Capability' Brown's (1716–1783) achievement – he the style's chief disseminator – was to distil, intensify and clarify (but really only quite slightly) the new, modern, enclosed landscape of eighteenth-century England, and then to blur the edges so that where park ended and countryside began could not certainly be discerned. Significantly, neither park nor farmland (unless it were orchard) had much evidence of flower.

What Brown and the English landscape movement were deliberately obscuring was the 'natural' tendency of the countryside towards that other peculiarly English gardening style, the cottage garden. But there is really no contradiction here; it is simply a question of perspective. Seen in the appropriate way, England naturally suggests both styles. To read the landscape as a 'landscape garden', you have (had) to take a broader, more distanced view, and then you see (saw) it quite plainly. To read it as a 'cottage garden' (albeit writ large), you have (had) only to take a closer, more local view of hedgerows, meadows and verges, especially in spring. That natural characteristic of the English landscape noticed earlier – the relative closeness of the horizon, the never-too-open-ness about it – enables this. Translated into garden styles, both the cottage garden and the landscape manner can be seen as idiomatic because they both derive fairly closely from 'natural' originals. Such tensions as exist between the two have rather more to do with artificial canons of taste than because they are in any way incompatible.

Paintings such as Samuel Palmer's (1805–1881) *The Magic Apple Tree* (1830) and *In a Shoreham Garden* (*c.* 1829) capture perfectly the essence and origins of the cottage garden style lying in the English orchard, and were they better known, I think they would have become images iconic of both Englishness and English gardens (illus. 28). As it is, the role and rank of 'national painter' has fallen largely to John Constable (1776–1837). His landscapes make Claude Lorrain (the consciously studied model of many an English landscape garden) speak English, and he – Constable, that is – does this essentially by moving his horizons a little closer, by making his figures and human incidents slightly larger in physical stature but smaller, much smaller, in the scales of heroic significance, and

24 Myles Birket Foster's cottage scene, from *Pictures of English Landscape* (1863), with 'Pictures in Words' by Tom Taylor. Taylor's poem 'Old Cottages', which this image illustrates, is alert to the contradictions here of which Birket Foster, friend though he was of the socialist William Morris, seems oblivious. Taylor is aware of 'the foul miasma of their crowded rooms . . . the rank ditch that stagnates by the door'.

by allowing the light to play on the surface of trees to suggest the chromatic equivalent of subtle, undemonstrative blossom – the light blooms even when the trees and bushes themselves do not. A typical painting by Constable is both landscape garden and cottage garden – and has a strong tendency towards the blending of the two garden styles which bear those names. Paintings such as *The Cornfield* (1826) or *Dedham Vale* (1828) fix in the national imagination what we like to think of as the quintessence of England. Both paintings (and indeed the greater proportion of all Constable's works, both well known and obscure) have nurtured and contributed to the myth of England as a garden. A myth, moreover, in which a great many people have made an emotional investment.

In these paintings it is the apparent realism – the hairs on the back of the dog in *The Hay Wain* (1821), the damp patch on the wall of Willy Lott's Cottage – that invites both literal credence in the myth and the admiration of the man in the street who willingly gives Constable his vote as the 'national painter'. However, the (much less literal) poetry of the paintings is more easily overlooked. The fact that there is something valedictory about even these apparently fresh, real and emotionally uncomplicated images is not what endears them to the public eye, and not what makes their reproduction on chocolate boxes or placemats sell those items on sight. But it is there. Constable, in suburban Hampstead, was painting his heart out in representations of another, better, lost place – the valley of the shadows of his past, his childhood, the countryside where he had pined for the woman he loved but was forbidden for so long to marry. The Stour Valley was both the land of his heart's desire and the land of lost content. Consciously or subconsciously, we may be recognizing in Constable the same soft ache, the same sense of exile from Eden that so many gardeners have felt at some point in their lives.

For more idealized images of the cottage garden ethos, we'd have to look to other painters and illustrators, people such as

Myles Birket Foster (1825–1899), Helen Allingham (1848–1926) and Arthur Claude Strachan (1865–1954) (illus. 24). Though very different painters indeed from Constable, their images are both as popular and almost as iconic as his. But these painters don't so much edit and refine their vision of a real landscape as manufacture a fantasy. They are the visual equivalent of the literary sentimentality epitomized climactically in the 1930s in Agatha Christie's Miss Marple bicycling down her bowery English lanes, or in 1959 in Laurie Lee's Rosie quaffing her cider in the hazy afternoon shade of a Gloucestershire haystack. A comparison with the unsentimentality of, say, Flora Thompson's *Lark Rise to Candleford* (1945) would make the point. Strachan's paintings are the staple of a certain kind of greetings card. Typically, there'll be a cottage embowered with hollyhocks, a hedge sparkling with dog roses and a gate half open to lead your eye in. The lane outside is the sunny playground of a girl in a smock and of barefooted boys. Though one blushes slightly to admit it, Foster, Strachan, Allingham and their ilk are, in a way, also 'national painters'. They too supply the myth of England as a garden.

Two centuries on from Constable, one hundred years on from Allingham and her kindred idealists, many people (the consumers, as it were, of this myth) live now neither in the city exactly – that is to say, the commercial hub – nor really in the country, but in those suburban regions, places that are neither here nor there, places whose residents look to the city for their livelihoods but also, perhaps wistfully, to the countryside for their life and soul. It is these people and the gardens they make that are the subject of this chapter. More particularly, they are viewed in the light of the proposition that somewhere around the end of the nineteenth century, and then in the first two decades of the twentieth, before people like Lowry (1887–1976) spoiled the view, as it were, and before nationalism became a reproachable point of view, a remarkable solution to the problem was begun.

The problem identified by reformers and visionaries around the turn of the century was not quite the same as the earlier, simpler, appalled recognition of Blake's Albion and its 'dark Satanic Mills', the living conditions in industrial England's manufacturing towns that later evangelists for reform, such as Dickens, did so much to make the common property of the reluctant Victorian conscience.[1] Half a century after the publication of *Hard Times* (1854), the problem was seen in a peculiarly different way. It ran something like this: if England – self-evidently by then the beating, manufacturing, cash-counting heart of a great empire – was no longer a country in the sense of having a predominantly rural way of life, how could the great ideal (or, in our terms now, the myth) of England as a garden be maintained? The solution was the Garden City. Though, as a formal movement, this is pretty well a dead letter now, as a self-sustaining, voluntarily contracted modus vivendi, paradoxically it is probably even more alive than ever in the twenty-first century – alive as an idea/ideal because we are in the process of making a radical shift in our conception of what a garden is and of what gardens mean. Whether we have realized it or not, in the first instance we still think of gardens (at least when we think of them in the abstract) as occasional incidents in the country rather than in the city. What we are shifting towards now is the idea that, after streets, buildings and car parks, gardens are the essential, identifying component of towns (the engrossed city centres and suburbs: the entire built-up area) – and the desire for gardens a frequently identifying feature of the minds of town dwellers. It is not a mere coincidence that both the National Trust and the magazine *Country Life* were founded during the last decade of the nineteenth century (1895 and 1897, respectively), the same critical period during which both the problem of the end of England as a garden and its solution as the garden city began to take effect.

It was the Romans who gave us the antithesis of town versus country (and, indeed, the words *urbs* and *rus*, and thus *urban* and *rural*), but an even older axis still haunts us: not country versus town, but country (cultivated, humanized, productive and safe territory) versus wilderness. Ironically, this is an axis which dropped out of our consciousness for something like 1,500 years but is beginning to revisit us now, and with a vengeance, the country remaining the safe zone of health and wholesome well-being, but the town as the new wilderness, the urban jungle, the dangerous city, the concrete, soulless wasteland.

All these nuances – nationality, nostalgia and exile, proprietorial pride in territorial possession, safe haven and sanatorium – underwrite the meanings of what now constitute the vast majority of gardens. And if there is any justice in a residual sense of England as a garden, it will lie with them, but these are not gardens in the country. They are the now much smaller plots behind houses in towns. Smaller they may be, but – and partly as a consequence of that same straitened scale – their significance to their owners would seem to be growing (illus. 29).

House and garden – what the estate agents call a 'property' – represent the biggest single investment of money most people ever make, after bringing up their children, that is. If you live in such a place but don't own it, you'd call it a 'house'. It's property but not yours. Once you own it, it becomes a 'home', and then the investment involves so much more than just money. Not just tenancy but custody. Not just a matter of your occupying it, it is your possession, your own stake in the linguistic, cultural, geographical (and financial) collective that makes up the country. It represents both possession and belonging. It's yours to do with it more or less what you like, but it's also a projection of a little bit of England: a corner of the national field of self-consciousness expressed not very much in political (let alone nationalistic) terms these days, but strongly resonant of cultural terms – and this most especially in the garden. This is the space that is at once your own and yet also a part of, and harmonizing with, the larger world outside, the space that belongs, however anonymously, to everyone. The sum of all those houses and gardens – their public frontages, I mean, especially their front gardens – is the necessary visual living space of all of us.

But umbilical with this appearance of seemingly inclusive collectivity is the idea of the Englishman's home being his castle, his quasi-autonomous state-within-a-state, where he can enjoy freedoms unavailable in the shared spaces outside. In short, there is an equal and opposite will to exclusion and exclusivity, and therein lies tension.

When Pip – striding out now in discharge of his *Great Expectations* of 1861 – in the company of Mr Wemmick (he of the frayed bachelor's linen and mouth like a postbox) reached the district of Walworth, the former observed what appeared to be a collection of back lanes, ditches and little gardens, and to present the aspect of a rather dull retirement. Wemmick's house was a little wooden cottage in the midst of plots of garden, and the top of it was cut out and painted like a battery mounted with guns. 'My own doing,' said Wemmick. 'Looks pretty; don't it?'[2]

Pip continued:

> I think it was the smallest house I ever saw; with the queerest gothic windows (by far the greater part of them sham), and a gothic door, almost too small to get in at. 'That's a real flagstaff, you see,' said Wemmick, 'and on Sundays I run up a real flag.'[3]

They passed over the plank which constituted the drawbridge, and Wemmick put into motion the mechanism for drawing it up and thus for declaring a state of independence from the rest of

Walworth, London and the world. Wemmick showed Pip the only piece of real ordnance (as opposed to sham) and explained how he treated his almost deaf father – the 'aged parent' who is the object of Wemmick's affectionate care just as Wemmick himself is the object of the old man's greatest pride – to a very loud bang at 'nine o'clock every night, Greenwich time'.[4]

But then, at the back and out of sight so as not to compromise the embattled spirit declared at the front of the property, we find Wemmick's true living space, the world refashioned in the image of his imagined paradise. There are chickens, rabbits and a pig, a cucumber frame and a salad garden. And there's pride in the anticipation of the homegrown meal Pip is soon to be offered. Wemmick explains that, by dint of this horticultural self-sufficiency (should it ever be necessary), a siege of considerable length could be withstood.

'I am my own engineer, and my own carpenter, and my own plumber, and my own gardener, and my own Jack of all Trades,' declares Wemmick;[5] and we intuitively recognize, perhaps for the first time in English literature, the now familiar figure of the man who – self-made – is master and maker of all he surveys, the prophetic archetype of the man who grows out of the toyshop and into the DIY centre, the self-sufficient, self-making author of his own Little England. And at least the half of this new Principality has the unmistakable features of a kitchen garden, of horticulture.

When it comes, Wemmick's explanation of its meaning is no surprise, as if we hadn't already seen in him the pattern of the thousands of grey-faced, grey-suited, sandwich-packed briefcase bearers who endure the commuter trains in and out of London every day. 'Well; it's a good thing, you know. It brushes the Newgate cobwebs away, and pleases the Aged.'[6]

Of course it does, and of course this counterpointing of the private world with the world outside, this Little England with the Large, makes sense of what would otherwise be unbearable.

The briefcase may be light – indeed, almost empty of anything that actually matters – but what it signals in terms of lives scrabbling for meaning in the Wasteland of the World in Pursuit of Paper is not, even when by habit and by conviction of its being necessary we become inured to it (convicts, as it were, in the Newgates of Life-in-the-Office). Wemmick is our familiar, our contemporary. He is where B&Q pitch their sales, where the garden centre rigs its tent, and where Constable (though this time it is not Wemmick's sham Gothic but the noble ruins of *Hadleigh Castle*) meets the English city.

Later, when he introduces Pip to his work in the city as the criminal lawyer Jaggers's factotum, Pip remarks to himself: 'It struck me that Wemmick walked among the prisoners, much as a gardener might walk among his plants . . . Thus, we walked through Wemmick's greenhouse' (Newgate Gaol). The felons, approaching now their trial, conviction and hanging, are likened to ripening fruit and vegetables. Characteristically, Wemmick, with 'his post office [mouth] in an immovable state, looked at them . . . as if he were taking particular notice of the advance they had made, since last observed, towards coming out in full blow [blossom, fruit] at their trial.'[7]

Constable in Hampstead in the 1820s and '30s, the last two decades of his life and after the achievement of that long-deferred marriage to the unattainable Maria Bicknell in 1816, was a Little Englander too of a sort. There he was, in exile as it were, recovering on canvas his vision of a little patch of English earth – the Stour Valley – worlds away in effect, but real for all that. Samuel Palmer too, born as he was in Wemmick's Walworth, made a fateful visit to Shoreham in Kent in 1824, and though for the sake of his career he was settled in London by 1833, he never really left Shoreham in his imagination for the rest of his life. And it shows in his lack of material, metropolitan success, in the powerful enchantment of the dream-like rural world he committed to canvas, and in the disenchantment of his unhappy life.

These people had lost their Edens. They were technically still in England, but not that part of it where biologically they began, or where psychologically they lived and belonged. In effect, they too were expatriated, deracinated exiles. And while the impulse to recover we are quite likely to call (and dismiss as) mere nostalgia, the reality is not quite so simple. What we make of our sense of loss – in our paintings, our novels, our gardens – is artifice to be sure, but the need to have made these things in the first place, and then to go on remaking them throughout our lives, is real: a spiritual and psychological imperative which entirely undoes the caricature of the neurotic, soft-headed, foolish fantasist.

The English suburban garden is all of those things we might smile at, not only because we recognize in it a tendency to self-parody, to exaggeration and to the sentimentalizing of the myths that underwrite it, but also because we enjoy a sense of home-coming. These places are the independent states in which we enjoy at least some immunity from the taxes (of conformity to everybody else) levied upon us whether we wish it or no. These gardens are the real parts of Englishness which make up the artificial construct of what we call England.

Heaven, the New Jerusalem, is significantly a city, and it is in cities – their residential parts especially – rather than in the country that gardens now are really justified, really necessary and, somehow, really 'natural'. It is an irony that even Oscar Wilde (1854–1900) himself cannot have imagined that Gwendolen's famously fatuous remark that she 'had no idea there were any flowers in the country' actually resonates now with a kind of truth.[8] The Garden City movement of the early twentieth century – a gentle species of utopian millenarianism really – caught the imagination of people then because it represented a far better way of life than the back-to-back terraces of the Victorian slums. That much was obvious to almost everybody. Some reconciliation had to be found (or, more likely, had to be forged) between England's traditional view of itself as a garden and the dark, satanic mills of the Industrial Revolution – between mythical Albion and all-too-real Acton Town.

But the idea had been in the air for a very long time before. Benjamin Disraeli (1804–1881), in *Sybil* (1845), has his Mr Trafford found a model village. Titus Salt (1803–1876), the Victorian tycoon of alpaca, began Saltaire outside Bradford in 1851. A *cité ouvrière* was built in Alsace in 1853. And in very much the same vein, Llewellyn Park in West Orange, New Jersey, was begun in 1857.

It wasn't until 1903 and 1907, respectively, that Letchworth Garden City and Hampstead Garden Suburb were founded, and they are seen now as the great exemplars in terms of both principle and practice. They took their reformist zeal from consciences and their funds from investors and philanthropists. Hampstead was founded by Henrietta Barnett. With her husband, Samuel, she had already co-founded Toynbee Hall, the East London settlement house, in 1884. Their social conscience – and that of other people like them – was growing at the same time as that national self-consciousness that spawned *Country Life* and the National Trust. The cross-fertilization which took place between individual consciences and collective thinking is one of the formative influences of the early twentieth century. As was also the wider reading of Wordsworth and Ruskin, the de facto godfathers of these later reformers. Canon Hardwicke Drummond Rawnsley (1851–1920), one of the three founders of the National Trust, was nothing if not a disciple of the poet, whom he enormously revered.

These places – Hampstead and Letchworth, as well as Brentham and Bedford Park – are pleasant, leafy quarters, but they achieve this not by reconciling workplace with living space; rather, it is by divorcing them. In the cases of the mill towns of the 1860s, the whole ensemble – factory and satellite slums – was unspeakably ugly, but it was, at least, an integrity. There was a continuity of social, economic and architectural style and function, grim, exploitative and insanitary though these places were. In the case of the early garden cities, the mills and factories remained, but the housing, though far better, was emphatically set further apart from its economic *raison d'être*. This was not so much a matter of reconciliation and general improvement as the simple expedient of spatially separating them. In retrospect we can see in this the seeds of our own characteristically modern problems – social, architectural and environmental – which have come about as a result of mass commuter travel: the blighting of not just one zone (the workplace) but of another too: the associated residential dormitory towns and suburbs to which the commuters return every evening after work.

It was Ebenezer Howard (1850–1928), George Cadbury (1839–1922), Joseph Rowntree (1836–1925) and Seebohm Rowntree (1871–1954) – all of them social reformers and three of them Quakers – who turned the idea of a garden city away from what had happened in Bedford Park (a redoubt of progressive but still essentially middle-class trendies) and towards the people who needed it most: factory workers whose lungs were clogged by dust, ears confounded by the noise of machinery and spirits smudged by drudgery.

The title of Howard's book *Garden Cities of To-morrow* (or *To-morrow: A Peaceful Path to Real Reform* when it was first published in 1898) catches the millenarian flavour of the movement. The Rowntrees had their New Earswick built to designs by Barry Parker and Raymond Unwin, the architects of Letchworth. Cadbury built for his workers the model village of Bournville. Each cottage there carried a lease with all the usual clauses (obligations, penalties for default, et cetera), but the charges were modest and the amenities – in terms of open spaces, clean air and comfortable, attractive housing – were irresistible. So was the obligation to cultivate your garden. Cadbury believed not just that it was unneighbourly to allow your neglected patch to infect others with weed seeds, and not just that an unsightly front garden was a trespass upon the rights of everyone else to enjoy the view of the street even when it didn't belong to them, but that gardening was virtuous. It was good for you, wholesome, recuperative, thrifty and soul-cleansing. So, framing each house was a garden of something in the region of 500 square metres (600 sq. yd), which was what Cadbury reckoned was as much as an average man could cultivate. Each tenant was supplied with eight apple and eight pear trees, twelve gooseberry bushes, one Victoria plum tree, six climbing plants to clothe the house walls, as well as 'one or two forest trees'.[9] No one could really fault the principles, but there was a streak of zealous, improving paternalism in Cadbury that strikes us now as unreasonably interfering. The rules he supplied to his tenants were full of precepts about domestic economy, plant husbandry, clean, wholesome living and so on, in such variety and quantity that they amount to a textbook on how to live. Indeed, there are even instructions on how to breathe: 'through the nostrils with the mouth closed, especially at night'.[10]

The Garden City movement grew, but very slowly. Welwyn Garden City was begun in 1920, and other, partial developments of already existing settlements followed, such as Wythenshawe. Harlow, Basildon and Stevenage were all begun in the later 1940s. But in the aftermath of the Second World War, the need for new houses to be built quickly proved the greatest obstacle for the movement; given the urgency and scale of the problem, the shortage of available funds and the war-weariness of spirits generally, it largely fell short of meeting the challenge. The original social ideal is more or less a dead letter now, and the evidence of its quondam achievements has become social and architectural curiosities.

Yet people have now begun to use again the expression 'garden village', though cautiously and, it must be said, often rather disingenuously. Occasionally, it's the selling point of some new housing development. And there may be at least a fraction of truth in it. Where the new access road meets the old thoroughfare, a lot of money (and sometimes even some skill) will have been expended upon setting up an eye-catching garden. There will have been a bit of earth moving and landscaping, the planting of a grove of semi-mature birches, the installation of life-sized sculptures of a family of deer (faux bronze or pre-rusted steel), a pond and a frieze of box hedges – two or three parallel, but not straight, ranks of them, planted close but not touching, and cut low in waves, gently succeeding into the shallow distance – up and down, up and down. It has a sense not so much of nostalgia as of a tentatively Brave New World. If you were inclined to mock, you might hear strains of that Second World War song:

> There'll always be an England
> While there's a country lane,
> Wherever there's a cottage small
> Beside a field of grain.[11]

But with a wave of the semantic wand, the word *home* has changed its valency. What you'll be buying from the developers now is a ready-made 'home' – if you believe the sales pitch.

Posh or not so posh, relentlessly gardens have shrunk, both in the city and in the country. They have kept pace then with our shrinking language. But probably the craving for a sense of space has correspondingly not shrunk at all but grown, and the need for a space of our own – one moreover that lives – has grown too, possibly because so much else around us seems to make only for difficulty.

Once again, it is language itself that gives the game away. In this case, it is the word *growth*. Economies, we are told and almost believe, must grow; incomes must grow and grow; businesses must grow or fail; cities have a manifest destiny to grow. But we also know by now – and almost incontrovertibly – that all of these 'growths' are simultaneously at the expense of the life chances of every other living thing on our planet and, indeed, of ourselves sooner or later. In the middle and long term, 'growth' actually predicates its opposite: contraction.

The word *wen*, with its double meaning, comes to mind as perhaps a useful, possibly sobering, truly grown-up, reintroduction. It too means 'growth', but this time it is both 'a suppurating boil invading the surface of the skin' and 'a great city, ever-increasing its size'. The expression was used most memorably by William Cobbett in 1821: 'these unnatural embossments; these white-swellings, these odious wens, produced by *Corruption* and engendering crime and misery and slavery', with London being 'the *great wen* of all'.[12] Sixty years later, Richard Jefferies's strange, futuristic, apocalyptic novel *After London* (1885) doesn't use it, but perhaps it should. In this book, London – and everything it stood for – has been overtaken by inundation. Flooded, drowned. And then naturally rewilded. The idea of a pustulating, evil-smelling growth might still be useful in certain circumstances, not least as a corrective to some of the semantic sleights of hand we are befuddled by: 'development' (meaning overdevelopment), 'growth' (meaning self-imploding swelling).

In the United States as things stand now, 'By square footage, there is more housing for each car . . . than there is housing for each person.'[13] Every car – anywhere – demands at least two parking spaces: one at home and one for each of its destinations (the place of the driver's work, shops, a theatre, a leisure centre and so on). The home-parking space is exclusive, the others shared more or less, but – all told, in terms of space – these will amount to several times over the car's size. The consequences upon land usage have been profound: suburban public roads have become in effect parking spaces; city centres have evolved into spaces contested between businesses seeking customers and people seeking access to them, and then into revenue streams for local authorities capitalizing upon parking charges. The visual litter of car parking has crept up on us for years, but now amounts to the single biggest blight on our landscapes. An RHS-commissioned survey conducted in 2015 revealed that during the previous ten years three times as many front gardens had been entirely paved over, compared with ten years earlier, presumably to provide space for car parking. The aggregate was 4.5 million (one in four in the UK). In sum, over 5 million front gardens had no plants growing in them.[14] It's morbidly fascinating to watch how we strive to counter this drift towards inert, impervious, flood-facilitating, oxygen-squeezing, hard surfaces even as we press on with more of the same.

London's Garden Bridge (abandoned in 2017) is probably the most interesting – and absurd – of all of the putatively mitigating schemes so far. What is more, the location of this project was not the periphery – the suburbs – but the very heart of the metropolis. Most of the attention has been drawn to the astronomical costs of the venture (£53.5 million in planning expenses alone), but it is the very concept – its garden character – which is more thought-provoking, in the sense that it is an index of how gardens in cities are simultaneously perceived as necessities and as impossible to achieve. At once, the project conceded victory to the march, the oozings, of concrete: this new garden (on a purpose-built Thames-spanning bridge) would not be rooted in the earth, it would not take up terrestrial space, competing with cars, new houses or people. And it was bidding to create a new green lung, a new sacred space, for the asphyxiated chests and souls of Londoners expatriated from the real, the natural world. But it was also almost straight out of the dystopian world of Swift's *Gulliver's Travels* (1726), specifically the third of his voyages: it is uncannily similar to the flying island of Laputa, not just in absurdity but also because bridges are often now glossed as flyovers. Thinking upon possible etymologies for this strange word 'Laputa', Gulliver observed that '*Lap* in the old obsolete Language signifieth *High*, and *Untuh* a Governour.'[15] But actually it is nothing of the sort (and Swift knew this, of course); to his more judicious, more polyglot readers, then and now, *puta* (in Spanish) is simultaneously a low word for 'whore' and the common expletive 'motherfucker'. Nevertheless, Laputa is – the Swiftian version of it, at least superficially – a beautiful place, replete with gardens, an Astronomer's Cave and a very great many musical instruments. Because of its literal detachment from the rest of the busy, money-making world (it is a *flying* island), it affords a special freedom to inventive, inquisitive people. But everyone there is nevertheless racked by anxiety about the sun. Does it still shine today? Will it go on doing so indefinitely? These inhabitants are of a scientific, investigative, entrepreneurial cast of mind. So far so good, but they are also arguably deranged. And deformed. One of their eyes turns 'inward', the other 'directly up to the Zenith', the disquieting sun.[16] This reads like an eighteenth-century equivalent of us now, one eye engaged looking at our phone and the other (sometimes) at our interlocutor. Elsewhere, the scientists in Laputa are busy conducting research into 'extracting Sun-Beams out of Cucumbers',[17] turning turds back into the edible food they came from, that sort of thing.

The most interesting aspect of this Garden in the Air – the London Garden Bridge – is revealed in the way that the once visionary, the once impossibly exotic, fantasies of 160 years ago (in a children's book), and again sixty years ago (in a popular song by the Beatles, with its illicit, narcotic overtones), might have become a realized, entirely licit eventuality. The magic mushrooms of Lewis Carroll's *Alice's Adventures in Wonderland* (1865), and then the hobby-horsing equestrians of the nursery (the trees looking and tasting like lollipops, a diet of pies made from squishy confectionary) in John Lennon's 'Lucy in the Sky with Diamonds' (1967), might have been realized in a garden indeed. Not quite a real one, but a flying garden situated, like the fantastic *mise en scène* of Lennon's song, on a bridge, looking down over a river. This was indeed *rus in urbe* for the twenty-first century. Conclusively (perhaps), the similarity between the character of the proposed bridge and the diet in the song puts a new gloss on the expression 'pie in the sky'.

It wasn't the only such project either. Only a few years after the Garden Bridge scheme collapsed into its own funding fantasies, Londoners were regaled with the Marble Arch Hill installation in 2021. At 25 metres (82 ft) high, this scaffolding and plywood mound (planted with turf and trees through which you took an ascending, winding path to the top) would simultaneously afford you views of your city and look back to the belvederes of the Renaissance gardens of yore. It was a pitch both backwards into nostalgia and forwards into a futuristic horticultural, tokenistic, greened city. And it convinced no one.

These projects were not a matter any longer just of greening an environment – that is to say, of gardening a city – but of reinventing green itself so that a new word could come out of the wings (as, indeed, did the new verb *to green* only a few years ago). And perhaps we should anticipate more of the same: new mantras, new expressions, such as *to environ*, such as *environing* (to live *with* concrete and *without* soul/soil, but to imagine that it's okay anyway?).

The children's area of Kew Gardens now has fake, plastic grass, and the greatest horticultural authority in the land has declared that it's okay when what they really mean is that we give in, we give up, we've lost touch with the word *hortus* (Latin for 'garden') not just physically and literally but semantically. We must go now with an irresistible tide, with the 'culture' of trying to accommodate too many people in too small a place, itself a parable perhaps in miniature of the present human condition vis-à-vis planet Earth. And what has happened at Kew gradually becomes the pattern for everywhere. Cities seem to have run out of aesthetic, horticultural and 'environmental' options. Residual moral and philosophical scruples are often perceived as luxuries we can no longer afford or indulge. In any case, we no longer have any access to them.

Listen to Edward Thomas (1878–1917) in 1914. He wrote a book ostensibly about cycling west out of London, but mistily, mysteriously, drawing connections and parallels between a songbird trapped in a cage in a London pet shop and the condition of the souls of the citizens of that same great, modern city. There's a misty chronology too, remembering, revisiting streets and the once-open spaces of twenty years earlier: a pub called the Sultan, a funfair on Garratt Green, where coconut shies provided excitement and revenue for itinerant showmen.

In the present, 1914, it begins to rain. Thomas shelters in the doorway of a shop selling caged birds and doomed goldfish 'squirm-[ing] about a globe with a diameter of six inches, in the most complete exile imaginable'. A man – Thomas's doppelganger, perhaps, 'the other man' who appears and reappears throughout *In Pursuit of Spring* – buys one of the birds, 'a dingy cock chaffinch', and cycles off with it frantically fluttering in a paper bag. And then he releases it. But the idea of incarceration has already coloured what Thomas sees as he makes his way through the suburbs, out of the city. It is not just people and the songbird about to be liberated, but the gardens he passes and the trees in them that speak of loss. The gardens of Burntwood Lane become a microcosm of this universal forfeit: 'The almond, the mulberry, the apple trees in these gardens have a menaced or actually caged loveliness, as of a creature detained from some world far from ours, if they are not, as in some cases they are, the lost angels of ruined paradises.' On De Burgh Street, a memory of gypsies in the past blurs into a place mythed now by virtual speech marks: 'The monotony of the tiny front gardens is broken by a dark pine tree in one, and by an inn called the "Sultan" – not "Sweet Sultan", which is a flower, but "Sultan", a dusky king.' *Amberboa moschata* – the cheerful, cornflower-like bedding plant – is morphed into a drinking hole, and the 'dusky king' is blurred into a dark-skinned gypsy Thomas remembers encountering those years ago on Garratt Green and now emerging again from the pub to deliver a spiel, 'exquisitely finished in its mechanical servility', about becoming separated from his family. Thomas falls for it and gives him the price of a drink; the Romany – the once epitomous free spirit – is now reduced to begging.[18]

The compulsion to recover our Edens, again to build 'Jerusalem,/ In England's green & pleasant Land' is very real, and when expressed as well as this (by Edward Thomas, by William Blake), the image is powerfully poignant, the centuries and oceans between us falling away, the hopelessness of our ambition and vain attempts closing in.[19]

12

Gardens and Painting

When life appears to be imitating art we generally express surprise, and the occasion ('It was just like a scene out of Chekhov!') gets marked down as a curiosity, something to mention over supper, something perhaps which is useful in showing how well the observer knows their Chekhov even if the rest of us have to take their word for it. At bottom, however, it is no more than a curiosity. It was a curious coincidence only. Life doesn't imitate art; it just happens to look as if it does sometimes.

And yet we do, we *do* imitate art – sometimes. People sometimes model themselves upon a character in a book or a play. This used to be noticed by a clever, bookish detective, and, recognizing the plot of the book, he (or Miss Marple) would be able to predict the villain's next move. But it was fiction feeding off fiction itself, and though it was fun, it wasn't true. There was nothing in this literary device to disturb our sure conviction that life must be primary and art secondary.

When, on the other hand, art imitates life, we tend to find at least some of it somewhat dull: plodding photo-journalism sometimes, representational painting, music that imitates the cuckoo. When art imitates *low* life, the public is apt to be roused from its traditional indifference to art to express indignation. An unmade bed with dirty linen exhibited at the Tate is mischievously pilloried by the popular press (but equally mischievously perhaps, scrutinized seriously by the broadsheets) as possibly offending against our sense of what a work of art should be.

The ancient issues behind all of this, originally and right up to the present day, are these. Is art mimetic (and secondary) or is it creative (and primary)? Do we see something new in looking at a picture, or do we see something familiar anew? Does art create and we see for the first time, or does it recreate and we recognize? People have chewed over those philosophical bones for a very long time, and this chapter gnaws at them again, but in respect of gardens and paintings of gardens.

A famous dictum established in the eighteenth century a certain modern way of thinking and speaking about gardens. It runs thus: 'All gardening is landscape painting.'[1] Now, some 250 years later, all our literature and thinking are saturated with the idea. So much so that to suggest that the art of gardening (if indeed it is an art, but we'll call it that for the moment) is actually very far removed from that of painting may come as something of a surprise, something of a blasphemy. But to demonstrate the truth of this is quite a simple matter. Painting is two-dimensional, static and (literally speaking) lifeless. A garden is three-dimensional, almost always changing and, in any case, invariably subject to movement through time, through variations of light and variations of air and wind pressure, and it changes too because of the vagaries of the weather, because of the attention (or neglect) it receives. In addition, gardens are accessible not only through sight but by touch and scent and, to a degree, through the ear. If we are to make analogies and correspondences at all, it is perhaps to Joseph Addison (1672–1719) that we should look: 'a Man might make a pretty Landskip of his own Possessions.'[2] And yet because there remain so many intimations of painterliness in gardens, it is indeed to painting that we reach first. And because it is by reference to painting that we make so many apparently useful analogies, it is hard after all to resist for very long that primary impulse to compare the two.

Historical precedents, and contemporary examples too, are as manifold as they are compelling. They are the stuff of posh garden journalism and popular art criticism, and have been for years. There's Monet (1840–1926), gardener and painter at Giverny; Gertrude Jekyll (1843–1932), painter then gardener at Munstead Wood; there is Stourhead as a Claude made flesh, and the largely overlooked fact that Richard Colt Hoare (1758–1838) – the third in the generations of garden makers at Stourhead and the one who essentially refined it to what we see now – was himself a painter. Most fundamental of all is that very word 'landscape': Milton in the 1660s has it as 'lantskip',[3] Addison fifty years later as 'landskip', Pope as 'landscape' – all of them betraying an origin in the Dutch language, specifically in the lexis of painting and painters, denoting not primarily the prospect of a scene being apprehended by the eye, but a painting of a prospect constructed by an artist.

We go on to talk about composition, tonal relationships, colour harmonies, background and foreground, in language which is interchangeable between paintings and gardens. Both arts 'frame' views, articulate 'perspective' and modulate 'textures'. Most tellingly of all, perhaps, is how pleasing and how apposite it seems when someone compliments our own patch and declares that 'the garden looks a picture.' But a lot of this is misleading. The garden that seeks to reproduce in the flesh a Claude (or a Poussin or even a Monet for that matter) must choose its painterly moment very carefully. It must select the scene with the least shadow-casting verticals possible, because by the time that sun and shadows have moved round, you'd be looking at something very different indeed from that with which you began. The results, when the project is pursued, tend to have to be minimalist if they're going to be successful at all: the essence of the painterliness of 'bonsai', as it were. The experience of seeing the garden picture at the wrong time of day can be as disconcerting as listening to familiar music played on the wrong instrument. If and when they do work, they are only as convincing as a show garden at Chelsea: here for a moment and then gone.

In short, it is possible to transfer something about a garden on to canvas (or, better still, a sequence of canvases), but it is very much more difficult to do the reverse: to translate a painting into a garden. Painterly principles move easily and so, to a degree, do painterly moods and styles, but the reproduction of particular scenes is fraught with difficulty.

It would probably be useful here to examine the very word 'memory'. There are broadly two approaches to this branch of psychology. The first – the Aristotelian – sees memory as a library of experience, a storeroom of impressions more or less objectively laid down and more or less objectively recoverable. If there really is such a thing, then that's what so much of formal education is predicated upon, even now in an age sceptical of the value of the regurgitation of merely factual information. If there really is such a thing – moot point though it certainly is – then it is clearly of critical importance to the conduct of criminal law. The very idea of being called as a witness to something presupposes the involvement of memory. It also assumes that – at least in principle – there can be such a thing as fidelity in its recall. The likelihood that there is no such thing – neither a simple, unqualified objective recall nor a faithfulness that easily equates with the good intentions of the witness's sworn oath – is the faultline that a cunning barrister mines.

The other model sees memory as a shaping power less concerned with objective recovery of the past than with projecting its sense on to the way we construe the present, and perhaps even the future. It is not historical accuracy which is its principal constituent, but the memorability of the thing remembered. Considered thus, the recovered image would be inseparable from the imagination which recovered it. In Jungian terms, there would indeed be a storehouse of 'facts', but only in the sense that these archetypes were the unrefined ore of what we know. In Platonic terms, such 'memories' would look very much like shadows cast on to the walls of the mind, but whose originals were forever irrecoverable. In both analogies (and there are others too), it is the extraordinary power of these memories, rather than whether or not they are accurate, that makes them a force to be reckoned with. Regardless of cultural background, for most people the fundamental components of their perception of landscapes will be essentially the same: the dialogue between horizontals and verticals (flat water and rising mountains, level meadow and upright hedge), intensities of light competing with degrees of darkness (representing freedom but also exposure, or danger but also refuge), and then the contrast between openness and enclosure (savannah-like expanses but local glades of trees, distant horizons as opposed to nearness or confinement). The 'habitat' theorists of the New Geography reckon that what we are expressing in our preferences sometimes for open spaces, and sometimes for refuges (summer houses, closed-off valleys and so on), are primal instincts. This kind of memory – the sort that selects and preserves not by historicity but by memorability – is exercised easily. So easily, and often with so much relish and pleasure, that it seems somehow more natural than the struggle involved in the other sort: recalling facts for an examination or witnessing in a court of law. We remember facts, but we memorialize experience. Memory leaks, it makes mistakes, but there are no accidents of memory – ever.

However all that may be, it is by the workings of memory and imagination that we construct the myths of our own lives, and those myths are the realities of the places in our minds in which we conduct our lives. In turn, this bears upon the character of the gardens we make, the locations in which – even more than the hard surfaces of our houses – we can construct and reconstruct our own places. The construction will come from textbooks, from TV makeover programmes, from the examples of other people's gardens. The *re*-construction, however, is the work of private memories, recollections of the places we played in as children perhaps, places seen on holidays, and then – most formatively of all – atavistic intuitions of our own Edens, our own perfected worlds.

Part of our difficulty comes about as a result of the taint that adheres to the word *nostalgia*. We can date both the word and the taint to the late seventeenth century: Johannes Hofer's *Dissertatio medica de Nostalgia, oder Heimwehe* appeared in Basel in 1688 (illus. 25). The word meant, from the outset, 'homesickness'; it has a clearly pathological etymology: *nostos* ('return home') + *algos* ('pain'). The condition was considered a disease, and its disabling symptoms became the serious concern of those who ran the sort of organizations whose members were particularly prone to it: the military, navies, far-flung empires. It impinged upon business and commerce too. Slave traders – people who deracinated living, sentient people from their homes and transported them to alien places – had a clear vested interest in understanding and dealing with the pathology of pining away.

Serious concerns gave rise to seriously expounded cures. In 1790 a French textbook of military medicine discoursed on a disease of the spirit ('maladie de l'ame [*sic*]'), identified as a compellingly intense and melancholic desire to return to one's native country. As a corrective cure for this condition, it cited the instance in 1733 of a Russian general said to have treated his ailing army to the example of burying alive a number of sufferers and found, as a result, that the incidence of the 'malady' markedly declined. Jourdan Le Cointe, the author of this book, recommended a similarly psychological approach to the cure of this sickness. In the event of the failure of milder therapies – persuasion, distractions, et cetera – sufferers should be warned that red-hot irons ('fer rouge') would

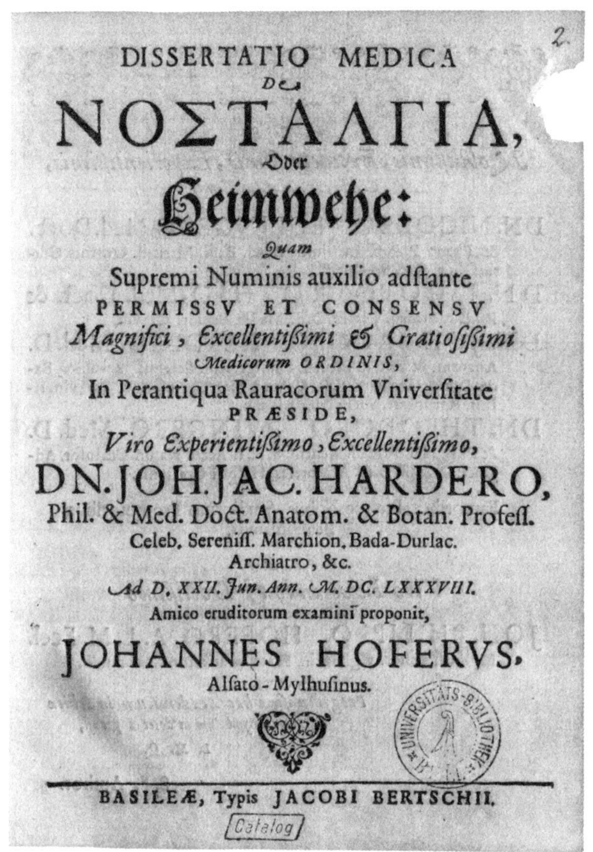

DISSERTATIO MEDICA

De

ΝΟΣΤΑΛΓΙΑ,

Oder

Heimwehe:

Quam

Supremi Numinis auxilio adſtante

PERMISSV ET CONSENSV

Magnifici, Excellentiſſimi & Gratioſiſſimi

Medicorum ORDINIS,

In Perantiqua Rauracorum Vniverſitate

PRÆSIDE,

Viro Experientiſſimo, Excellentiſſimo,

DN. JOH. JAC. HARDERO,

Phil. & Med. Doct. Anatom. & Botan. Profeſſ.

Celeb. Sereniſſ. Marchion. Bada-Durlac.

Archiatro, &c.

Ad D. XXII. Jun. Ann. M. DC. LXXXVIII.

Amico eruditorum examini proponit,

JOHANNES HOFERVS.

Alſato-Mylhuſinus.

BASILEÆ, Typis JACOBI BERTSCHII.

25 The macaronic title page of Johannes Hofer's word-coining book *Nostalgia* (1688) is loud with a hyperbolic plethora of superlatives: 'Excellentissimi', 'Experientissimo', etc.

be applied to the abdomen.[4] Shock therapy, we would call it now. There's a nice irony there too, insofar as there's something psychologically authentic about it. We naturally associate the branding of people (whether it be with a prison number, a criminal conviction, a slave owner's stamp, a Star of David or just an identity tag) with the marking out of displaced persons – transported felons, reviled Jews, everyone who's been violently taken from their home and cast into a diaspora of exile. Given the earlier discussion of exile from our own personal Edens, it comes as no shock to remember that the first recorded branding was the biblical mark of Cain. But given that the will to make gardens (as remakings, recoveries, of Edens) is so compulsive, so ubiquitous, we are far more likely to see nostalgia now not as an illness but as the remedy to other contemporary pathologies generated by the way we live.

Because it corroded valour, morale, industry and profit, nostalgia was identified in the seventeenth and eighteenth centuries as a pathological condition. We take it somewhat less seriously now. We tend only to dismiss it as a lapse from good sense, a self-indulging in the past at the expense of engagement with the present. We counter it with mantras such as 'moving on from . . .', but one of the consequences of this is that because nostalgia is associated with feeble-mindedness, it lays open an exposed flank of gardens to attack by the aphids of psychological hygiene. Nostalgia is regarded often as an embarrassment, as something almost synonymous with regression. What is more, observant critics have not been slow to notice that while a 'postmodernist garden' seems a very fruitful idea indeed, a 'modernist garden' is almost a contradiction in terms: almost by definition, gardens are retrospective, reactionary, nostalgic.

In the 1750s, Charles Wyndham, 2nd Earl of Egremont (1710–1763), commissioned 'Capability' Brown to remodel his park at Petworth. The damage wrought by the 1987 storm apart, Petworth is perhaps the best-preserved Brownian landscape we have. The surviving plans and memoranda are astonishingly detailed in respect of plantings, but unclear as to exactly what would have been necessary in terms of earth moving and what was the source of the water.[5] Certainly, there was already a canal. It seems likely that Brown connected existing ponds and the canal, and then formed the large serpentine lake we see now. Some of the spoil would have been used in the dam, and the rest was possibly moved to form the low ridge to the north, which frames the view from the house. Then he cleared trees which obstructed the view, planted others which enhanced it, characteristically thinning lower slopes and thickening upper ones. A rotunda was built; a Doric temple already in existence was moved to a better position. Other planned buildings – among them a 'sham bridge' and a grotto – either were never actually realized or have not survived.

By the time J.M.W. Turner (1775–1851) visited Petworth in 1809, the Brownian landscape would have been mature. Twenty years later, the third Lord Egremont (1751–1837) – philanthropist, prodigal patron of the beau monde, the turf, the arts and the celebrated courtesan Mademoiselle Duthé – was in his closing decade and more or less domestically settled at Petworth. He is known to have fathered more than forty illegitimate children, among whom was probably the future Lord Melbourne, Queen Victoria's first prime minister. Most of them lived at Petworth (and a sprinkling of their mothers too). It was a lively, populous place.

Egremont, who had given Turner a studio in his house, commissioned the painter to provide four pictures. They were to be views of Petworth Park and its environs. They were required to fit into unusually proportioned spaces in the panelling (with carvings by Grinling Gibbons) of Petworth's Carved Room: the paintings are all quite narrow and, relative to their height, very long (*The Lake, Petworth: Sunset, a Stag Drinking* measures 53.5 × 132 cm/25 × 52 in.). Two of them are of the park itself, seen more or less directly from the house (the others are of the Chain Pier at Brighton and the Chichester Canal). In principle, then, the viewer had only to gaze out of the windows of the room in which the paintings were hung to compare life with art. It's a singularly interesting circumstance and one that reveals a good deal, but not so much about what gardens *are* as about how we see them, how vision informs sight, and perhaps about how memory models both.

Turner's Petworth studies represent an accommodation between the way things were (what the camera – neutrally, objectively – would have seen) and the way the painter saw them. The finest of them – the painting known as *Petworth Park, Tillington*

Church in the Distance (*c.* 1828) – is very much in the proto-Impressionist manner of the Norham Castle paintings (illus. 26, 27). In the most literal of senses, the scene is like nowhere else on earth . . . but how you wish you were there. There's very little concession to accuracy of topography. It's almost all light tempered by low mist, and there's only a perfunctory distinction between air and earth, each a mirror of the other. By a considerable stretch of the imagination (and that, after all, is what it's for: to enlarge, to exercise vision), you could just about concede that on an extremely fortunate autumn evening, if you were to stand in the park an hour or so before sunset, if the meteorological conditions were absolutely propitious, you might see the very same thing. You might.

But for all that, there's no doubt whatsoever that this picture is *true*, that you recognize a faithful rendering of the way you would see the world (if only you had Turner's eyes, and not just a blink of them from time to time), and that this is indeed the visible world – not some invisible ideal, not some dialectic between *is* and *should be* – being offered to and believed in by a perfectly normal pair of eyes. Unimpeachably normal, because they're yours.

It's not just that the picture is individually and intrinsically beautiful. Here the particular is dissolved into the essential. The exemplary resolves into the essence. It both minds and reminds us that memory is finally inseparable from whatever had been the originating thing seen, process inseparable from product. Whatever is going on in the mind is simultaneously active and reactive, creative and recreative. What might have been that Platonic dialectic between the real and the ideal has been elided: what we know is being reconciled (instead of being in dispute) with what we know *better*.

It seems likely that Egremont saw the picture evolve (Turner was said to have painted at Petworth 'with his door locked against everybody but the master of the house').[6] But it also seems more

26, 27 J.M.W. Turner, *Petworth Park, Tillington Church in the Distance*, *c.* 1828, oil on canvas (*bottom*) and the scene out of the window as it is now (*top*). Both the actual blandness of the Brownian landscape and Turner's capturing of its hidden spirit are evident in this comparison of the real with the imagined, to the manifest advantage of the latter over the former.

28 Samuel Palmer, *In a Shoreham Garden*, *c.* 1829, watercolour. Like almost nowhere on earth, this garden, and the mysterious figure that leads the eye in, speak of an achievable Eden . . . if only in the mind. Palmer's son described the likely model for this place as 'clotted' with blossom.

29 Chloë Cheese, *My Urban Front Garden*, n.d., etching. The density and integration of people and plants, coupled with a bustling informality, expresses a spirit of gardening almost completely decoupled from the old idea of rolling rural acres.

30 Cedric Morris, *Benton End*, 1947, oil on canvas. Unsentimental but nevertheless projecting a powerful sense of place, Morris typically employs a strong ochre colour to make the farmhouse glow warmly. The colour is now a cliché of fashionably chic exterior decoration.

31 Vincent van Gogh, *The Poet's Garden*, 1888, oil on canvas. The transfiguration of the real into the ideal – the natural trajectory of centuries of so much art – reaches a new intensity here and a new density of identification between poetry, painting and gardens.

32 Ivon Hitchens, *Lavington Common*, 1938, oil on canvas. As with the tree in the ballad 'The Wife of Usher's Well', the birches here grow 'fair enough', 'at the gates of paradise' perhaps.

33 The Friedsam *Annunciation*, *c.* 1445, oil on wood. Scholarly debate about who painted it has tended to distract from this painting's sheer beauty. Details go on delighting even after the painting overall has made its impact: the adventitious weeds here and there, for example – wild carnations perhaps (on the left-hand buttress), the tuft of grass where no one treads at the foot of the door.

34 James Abbott McNeill Whistler, *Nocturne in Black and Gold*, *c.* 1875, oil on panel. The pyrotechnics here would not have been for 5 November, but for the regular firework display at Cremorne Gardens.

35 John Singer Sargent, *Carnation, Lily, Lily, Rose*, 1885–6, oil on canvas. The lilies and roses are evident enough, but carnations are less obvious. There are however splashes of white ones beneath the girls' feet and taller ruby blossoms leaning against their smocks.

than likely that he was disappointed with what he would have seen. Hung in the Carved Room in 1828, this oil study was later replaced by a more 'finished' painting – *The Lake, Petworth: Sunset, Fighting Bucks* (1827–31).[7]

That 'preliminary' study, *Petworth Park, Tillington Church in the Distance*, is the more enjoyable painting by a very large margin indeed. In it the park stretches away into the most valedictory of sunsets. The lake is invisible (as, in fact, it is from the terrace of the house), and in its place there's a veritable field of cloth of gold painted on to its surface by the dying sun. Several stags stare alertly towards where the painter must have stood. An irregular group of fawns and their mothers graze the turf. On the right, 'Capability' Brown's knoll rises but more steeply than it does in reality. Turner suggests perhaps a quite massive ancient tumulus where Brown meant only a swelling of the tides of landscape. A human figure (probably Lord Egremont himself) is walking towards the terrace from halfway across the field of gold, the field of vision. Numerous dogs are scampering out to meet him. An empty, untenanted chair on the terrace rhymes with the emptying light. A curtain blows into the left of the picture. Everything is drenched in this diluvium of draining gold light.

But this is also a disturbing picture, full of the sense of an ending. The golden light is rich and filled to the brim of experience, but it is an old, old gold. The solitary, diminutive figure in the painting is leaving behind him the light, just as the light itself is leaving the world. The chair is fixed there in the painting, empty. The curtain moved by the light breeze makes us think of autumn, of the American painter Andrew Wyeth's empty rooms, empty homesteads.

Part of the conviction the painting gives out is authenticated by the optical truth of the perspective which curls elliptically round. The terrace bends in a concave arc, just as the eye actually construes it. Thus, the entire park becomes a bowl, a golden bowl.

It seems that Egremont – this somewhat attractively unconventional man – fell at the hurdle of Turner's unconventional, Hesperidean, elliptical vision. So another picture was essayed: the same view, but beginning further away from the terrace and further into the park so that the lake is visible. Brown's knoll becomes steeper still. So does the rising ground into the west. The trees in the grove on the left have their lower branches cleared and, as a result, display a more Claudean profile and poise. Two bucks are fighting. Man and dogs, chair and terrace, have gone, but in the distance a cricket match is playing its final overs. The golden, red-scarred sunset is still authentically Turneresque, but a darker, old-masterish patina of browner pigment, darker varnish, has been made to cover the whole painting, even when grass, trees and leaves have already been forced to revert from the gold of the earlier painting and to assume their more 'natural' tones of green.

The 'finished' scene is more topographically, more explicitly, identifiable. It is much more full of incident. And it's much less interesting. It is also faintly absurd: Venetian light and English cricket seem an implausible combination. Crucially, the viewer is relegated from the position of imaginative participant to merely admiring spectator. Whereas the first picture gives rise simultaneously to a sense of having been here before (in the life of that mythic memory) but of never, ever, being able to go there again (and thus becoming so much more valuable because it is the evidence, to which you can return again and again, of an unrepeatable experience), the new painting requires complicity in a farce – albeit a very refined one. As a visitor to Petworth, gazing on the painting in its original, intended position, turn your head through 180 degrees and there, out of the window, you see the same thing . . . except that you missed the day of the cricket match, the bucks aren't banging away at each other just at the moment, and the sunset is not playing to the gallery quite as it should in Petworth, the best of all possible worlds – where the rutting season improbably coincides with the cricket season.

William Hazlitt (1778–1830) wrote in 1816 that Turner's pictures are 'too much abstractions of aerial perspective, and representations not so properly of the objects of nature as of the medium through which they are seen . . . The artist delights to go back to the first chaos of the world . . . Some one said of his landscapes that they were *pictures of nothing, and very like*.'[8] Exactly. Turner, at his greatest, does *not* paint objects. His paintings are themselves their own subjects. They are not similes (facsimiles); they are not *like* anything. Rather, they are their own metaphors. They simply *are*. Why we feel cheated by the later painting, *The Lake, Petworth: Sunset, Fighting Bucks*, is because we are given a reproduction of optical experience where we looked for an original.

Something of the same distinction marks our apprehension of a good garden. Something of the difference between mere spectatorship and imaginative involvement occurs too. Some principles (and paradoxes) about paintings, as about gardens, seem to emerge from all this. The degree to which a painting veers towards or deviates away from strict adherence to the physical contours and volumes of its putative subject (the garden, the landscape – the painting's objective correlative) has a significant influence upon the degree and nature of our involvement as we look at it. The more the painting 'faithfully' reproduces (as in much reportage photography), the less we may be encouraged to respond, to invest ourselves and our imagination in it, though of course there are exceptions: for example, photography of the character of Bill Brandt's, and the almost objective images of Goya's *The Disasters of War*.

In part, this is simply to say that some element of mystery is as welcome in paintings whose subject is gardens as it is in the gardens themselves. In the space left open (Proust's *absences*, I suppose), we find ourselves; we remember as it were that we've been here before. In a good painting, as in a good garden, there is always some element of being reminded – of memory, in effect – both of ourselves and of the mythic landscapes we make for ourselves in our dreams. It is through the gaps and understatements, the lacunae and the conscientious omissions, of our sensory experience that 'the weather in [the] soul' penetrates (in George Santayana's memorable, and very Wordsworthian, phrase).[9] In both gardens and paintings, it is the *virtual* reality of imagined and imaginary places that is often the source, the measure and the yardstick of our approach to the real.

Turner himself was never a gardener. Nor did he claim any particular place or region as his own. There's no Turner Country as there is for Constable or Palmer, Spencer or Hitchens. The nearest he ever came to settling himself and his vision in a particular place was when he bought a Thameside plot at Twickenham and began to build a house – Sandycombe Lodge – there. It was partly in reverence to Pope that he settled there. He began by deploring the demolition of Pope's villa in 1807. At the very moment he had decided to settle in Twickenham, Baroness Howe, tired of all the visitors to this shrine to Pope's memory (and to her property), had the villa demolished. For this act of vandalism she has gone down in history as 'Queen of the Goths and Vandals'.[10] Turner stayed put, however, to enjoy the melancholy of its absence. His oil painting *Pope's Villa at Twickenham* (1808) has, for its background, the house, its windows knocked out, a hint of the demolition contractors' scaffolding leaning up against it; in the foreground, a group is gathered around the trunk of a fallen tree and gesturing towards the ruined building. But the tone of the painting is really of Thames in Arcadia, and it is very beautiful, somewhat melancholic and suggestively Claudean. It was to provide the subject for the first mass-produced engraving of a topographical view with which Turner was entirely satisfied.

In part, Turner's plan to settle there reflected allegiance to his other métier. He had always been a poet, or at least a versifier. A lot of his finished Academy paintings had verses attached to them. Or perhaps it was that a lot of the poems had paintings attached to *them*. The precedence is often unclear. The issue seems to me central to an understanding of Turner's art, though actually it is a very simple thing. His natural procedure was to begin a painting as if it were an illustration, as if it had a programme, as if it were a secondary reproduction of something primary and extraneous to itself. And then at some point (but generally quite early on) he would forget, he would overlook as it were what he had begun to do and would see instead his own vision on the canvas in front of him. Object is relegated, or even abandoned, in favour of subject. But it is odd that memory should serve him not only by inclusion but by occlusion.

It was John Ruskin (1819–1900) who made the famous distinction between two kinds of response to a painting: *aesthesis* (the visceral response to sensuous pleasure) and *theoria* (response of the whole moral being to beauty).[11] What he meant was to distinguish between a painting as an object and a response to it as both subject *and* object. He would agree if we were to apply the principle not only to the processes of responding to painting but to the processes of making it – and then, indeed, to the matter of gardens, both the making and then the viewing of them.

At any rate, I think it was Turner the poet rather than Turner the painter who decided to settle on the Thames. His Thomson-like verses, with their pastoral attitudinizing (and stilted diction and tottering scansion), sought their locus there. Here, for example, are the verses he composed on the demolition of Pope's villa:

Dear Sister Isis tis thy Thames that calls
See desolation hovers o'er those walls
The scatterd timbers on my margin lays
Where glimmering Evening's ray yet lingering plays.[12]

But Turner the painter didn't actually belong at Twickenham, or indeed almost anywhere else, with the faint and interesting possibility of the exception of Petworth. The best of his paintings are visionary rather than visual, in the same way that so much of his landscape is an inflexion of his way of seeing, of his eyes and his mind, rather than a reflection of the objective spaces and incidents outside them.

We come back to that famous remark with which we began: 'All gardening is landscape painting.' That is also where so much other writing in the history of gardens begins, and indeed sometimes ends. As a pendant to this, it is sometimes remembered that Pope's friend William Kent, he of Walpole's equally famous remark about gardens 'leaping the fence') was originally a painter. He was an illustrator too. And among a lot of other books, he made the plates for James Thomson's *The Seasons*, which, as it happens, was Turner's favourite reading.

The two art forms – painting and gardens – are not in the end by any means completely interchangeable. Direct translation from painting into garden is not really possible, and the procedure in reverse – making paintings of gardens – while seeming simple enough (and it's often been done) is actually more difficult still to pull off successfully. Nevertheless, there is a good deal of traffic between the two, sharing as they often do common origins (elements of a common language, and patrons in common) and sharing essentially the same processes: a revision – thus literally, and tellingly, a *seeing again* – of the real world through the dual lenses of memory and of the ideal, media which are, in any case, so close to each other as sometimes to be impossible to tell apart.

On 19 February 1818, John Keats (1795–1821) wrote to his friend John Reynolds:

> Memory should not be called knowledge – Many have original Minds who do not think it – they are led away by Custom – Now it appears to me that almost any Man may like the Spider spin from his own inwards his own airy Citadel – the points of leaves and twigs on which the Spider begins her work are few and she fills the Air with a beautiful circuiting: man should be content with as few points to tip with the fine Webb of his Soul and weave a tapestry empyrean – full of Symbols for his spiritual eye, of softness for his spiritual touch, of space for his wandering of distinctness for his Luxury.[13]

Here is the familiar drawing of a distinction between memory as objective recall and memory as creative, revisioning process, but here also is the germ of an idea whose day may finally have come in our own time. Keats says: 'Many have original Minds who do not think it – they are led away by Custom.' Later, in the same letter, and having allowed the image of the spider to have been taken over completely by something else, something explicitly vegetable, he goes on: 'thus by every germ of Spirit sucking the Sap from mould ethereal every human might become great, and Humanity instead of being a wide heath of Furse and Briars with here and there a remote Oak or Pine, would become a grand democracy of Forest Trees.'[14]

That, in a sense, is what we do when we garden. That, possibly, is why tower blocks fail . . . even after some of the people who live in them may be filling their balconies with pots of tomatoes, troughs growing herbs and baskets of petunias and geraniums. Roof gardens are not as rare as once they were. Occasionally you see whole walls of high-rise buildings almost smothered with greenery. The Bosco Verticale in Milan calls to mind straightaway visions of modern Hanging Gardens of Babylon. But most cities, most urban residential districts, are not like that.

Perhaps it is that something in us may wither a little when our feet (and eyes and hands) make no contact with the earth, when we have no plot of our own to realize another, better world. That, perhaps, is why more and more people make of their gardens – big or small, fifteen storeys up or at ground level – the places where the wasteland is kept at bay, and why I would hazard a guess that it is the Wasteland – of T. S. Eliot's poem (about our souls), or South Dakota's Dust Bowl, or the Gulag, Gaza, or all those refugees from loneliness and meaninglessness we see about us all the time (or even in the mirror), or just the economics and politics that have sown and reaped so much insane history everywhere – which will become the dominant image in our reading of the twentieth century, the age when humankind finally effected the divorce between themselves and nature.

13

INTERLUDE
Essex and Suffolk, Giverny and Arles

Thomas Gainsborough (1727–1788) was born in Sudbury. That's just inside Suffolk. Throw a stone over the Stour that runs south of the town, and it'll land in Essex. The estate over which his Mr and Mrs Andrews proprietorily gaze – in that icon of English art – was at nearby Bulmer. None of the poor people who were dispossessed to form those rolling acres are the least bit in evidence, but the painter has managed to record the ghost of a sneer in the couple's faces and in their postures, even though they were his patrons. John Constable lived in these regions too: in the flesh and then in spirit up and down the Stour Valley. The painters and sculptors Edward Bawden (1903–1989), John Aldridge (1905–1983), Michael Rothenstein (1908–1993) and Michael Ayrton (1921–1975) all lived in or near Great Bardfield. So did Eric Ravilious (1903–1942), Tirzah Garwood (1908–1951) and Bernard Cheese (1925–2013). The original of Gainsborough's *Cornard Wood* (1748) is just over the hills.

Cedric Morris (1889–1982) – painter, teacher, gardener – lived not far away at Benton End, an outlier of Hadleigh. First at Dedham and then at Benton End, he made of his hospitable house and garden the East Anglian School of Painting and Drawing – among his students Maggi Hambling (b. 1945) and Lucian Freud (1922–2011). He is remembered now for his paintings, of course, but also for his plants. Irises were his special favourites. He was the first to breed a pink one. His most celebrated introduction, however, was the poppy *Papaver orientale* 'Cedric Morris', but there were other fine plants too, sought after as much now as ever among people for whom his name is a byword for something special in the way of soft colours: *Dianthus* 'Cedric's Oldest', *Ferula tingitana* 'Cedric Morris', *Rosa* 'Sir Cedric Morris', *Narcissus minor* 'Cedric Morris', the snowdrop *Galanthus* 'Cedric's Prolific' and so on. All his irises bear in their names the prefix Benton (Benton Cordelia, Benton Arundel, Benton Deidre). The *Papaver rhoeas* marketed now as 'Fairy Wings' originated from Morris's breeding. Characteristically, it is variable, but a proportion of the seedlings always turn out to be in his most prized colour: a light, luminous grey with the same texture, oddly enough, as Mrs Andrews's satin dress. Both are very slightly, very beautifully crumpled and puckered.

The garden at Benton End was more or less informal. It occupied the site of an old walled garden, and there were box hedges along narrow paths, but the former were eventually taken out, and the latter were apt to disappear too beneath the exuberant growth of summer. There was a grand old medlar, and other venerable fruit trees besides. *Yucca gloriosa* was one of Morris's favourites, and so were old-fashioned roses.[1] Once the hedges were gone and the paths invisible, some visitors reckoned the garden was informal to the point of seeming formless or even a downright mess, but sooner or later they'd learnt to replace the apparent absence (either of form or of distinctive style of gardening) with what they felt as a very strong sense of place. Benton End, as Tony Venison remembers, 'was not tidy in the conventional sense'.[2] It was a question not so much of matter but of mood. It was a plantsman's garden, where abundance and freedom, variety and generosity, set the tone (illus. 30).

Morris (and everybody else) painted in the garden often. He recorded the forms of his plants more or less faithfully, but never with the punctilious accuracy of a botanical artist. He was far more interested in their spirits, and in what they did to his own. He tended to paint from low down, as if he were looking up through stems towards the light, towards the flowers, and perhaps towards a hill, a sky or a wall, or sometimes all three, in the aerial distance. The effect is Rousseauesque sometimes because by looking up so much he makes the viewer feel like a child again. His characteristic colours are brooding bruised greys, blues, smoky pinks and mauves. 'Muddy colours' are said to have been 'anathema' to him.[3]

In the paintings, his irises flutter like so much cheerful bunting, often with an abandonment of any self-conscious colour scheming, as if the flowers were so many disparate articles of clothing, jumbled up in the laundry and hung out, hugger-mugger, to dry in a playful wind. Somewhere there is an undertone of the erotic – and perhaps that's endemic to irises anyway – and there's something priapic in the buds and gladiatorial leaves. In full flower they flourish ruffs like the great scarves of bison. Yet the effect is lightly done, even when you sense some rude power in the image.

Iris, the messenger of the gods, radiates her prismatic pigments in Morris's world, but a less mythic painter would be hard to imagine, and certainly he makes no place for that story of her rainbow being the bridge between heaven and earth. Morris's paintings celebrate an Elysium in the here and now. That's the point of them: it's as if he is saying that this is only a little bit of England, but it's all of heaven he could ever know or want.

A bit of England, brushed with heaven perhaps, but literally daubed on to the canvas. The paint is thick; the brush digs into it sometimes like a spade. Morris was earthy and territorial, local and parochial, a champion of weeds and cultivars alike, and his imagination worked with the indiscriminate freedom (but biological imperative) of a fertilizing insect. He was very informed and skilled in the natural sciences – botany, of course, as well as what we now call ecology – and extremely hostile to what he thought of as the enemies of life: agribusiness, chemical poisons and so on. One quite late painting – *Landscape of Shame* (*c.* 1960) – is of an endless prairie of withered grass. Burnt out, it might be (if not by fire, you can still sense smouldering anger). All over this treeless, monochromatically hopeless desert, the corpses of songbirds lie dumped like so many piles of excrement. Perhaps there's a grim pun intended: *Turdus ericetorum* is the song thrush.

Not far away, at the bottom of an unmade, winter-miry lane, in a house called Bottengoms, lived John Nash (1893–1977), whom we remember now as among the finest of the official war artists. In 1926 he was commissioned to make illustrations for the Six Hills Nursery catalogue. It must have seemed like a natural extension of the paintings he was doing then of the countryside he lived in, and some gesture at least towards answering the pressing contemporary problem of what, exactly, was meant by the slogan 'a land fit for heroes'. The landscapes Nash painted – even though in a very different style – evoked the same sort of integral vision that Morris achieved. Their little bit of England *was* fit to live in not only because it was prospering but – and necessarily so – because it was beautiful. Quietly, comfortably, domestically beautiful. Nash once remarked that if he could choose his life again, he would have been a musician first and a gardener second, neither of which surprises us, or strikes us now, as somehow incompatible.[4] He never, however, wished to have lived anywhere other than here.

A useful place to ponder on the association of gardens with paintings may be the experience of the modern visitor to Giverny in northern France. The garden fell into decay after Claude Monet's death, but restoration (of a kind and on a very lavish scale) was complete by 1980, since when it has become doubly celebrated as a fine garden in its own right and as a shrine to Monet (1840–1926). The visitor is almost bound to be impressed by the latter but, at the same time (and strangely), confused and disappointed by the former, the garden. For all Monet's fidelity to his principle of retinal sensation, the truth of a seemingly contradictory assertion – 'the motif is something secondary; what I want to reproduce is what exists between the motif and me'[5] – is brought home to the visitor with a conviction which the paintings did little to prepare you for.

It's not that you don't recognize the characteristic colours in the cleomes, the irises, the water lilies and so on, or their blending, or the sheer opulence of their volume. All that is familiar. So too are one or two particular features: the six flattened arches of the *grande allée* and, of course, the bridge. But other things – both presences and absences – you cannot help noticing as well, and they certainly do not conform to what the paintings have led you to expect. On the contrary, they contradict. There is nothing in the paintings whatsoever to prepare you for the quite visibly intrusive adjacent houses, contemporary though they are with Monet. Nor did you expect the road (railway) which separates the water garden from the flower garden. Above all, perhaps, you had no prior inkling that Monet, the self-styled rebel against the rules of academic painting, would have made a garden of such unchallenging conformity to the horticultural conventions of French formality. The flower garden is actually very geometric and structurally very formal indeed. Taken all together, the tone (like the context) of the garden is incontrovertibly suburban – and not just in the literal sense of the word.

You might begin to formulate an interesting idea: Monet gardened like a Frenchman and painted in a manner we retrospectively think of as quintessentially French, but what actually appears in the paintings – for all that the light is more intense – looks very much like moments (impressions indeed) of an English garden. On the canvases, the garden appears to be informal, the sort of place where plants naturally set the tone for themselves, rather than where they are used, in the French manner, essentially as decorative components in a formal, man-made scheme. The paintings speak English whereas the garden, which is their putative subject, speaks French. The vision, though faithful to the moment, is partisan. Impression – the word suggesting, now that you come to think about it, something glib as well as fleeting – turns out to exclude the contexts, the very things which would literally as well as metaphorically have given the paintings the integrity you always thought they had a just claim to.

The water garden (the site bought in 1893, three years after the purchase of the freehold of the house and flower garden, and ten years after Monet originally occupied the latter as tenant) had a fascinating and pioneering genesis. Monet knew very little about Japanese gardens – their spirit, their spiritual and social functions, even their minimalist planting – but he knew more than most people about Japanese prints of gardens and Japanese prints of garden plants. Thus, the water garden at Giverny was modelled not on the actuality of Japanese gardens on the ground, but on the vision of them seen through the eyes of Japanese artists. Monet's imitation is thus at one remove from the facts, but surely none the worse and possibly somewhat the better for it.

Monet's planting has little oriental authenticity but a great deal of vaguely evocative flavour – the wisteria (but that is Chinese), the peonies (and so are they, mostly), Japanese anemones, chrysanthemums, weeping trees, cherries and so on. Many of the *impressions* – the local moments – one gains at Giverny (and which Monet captures in the paintings), however, come about through the abundant use of *non*-Japanese plants, particularly cleomes (American) and drifts of poppies (European and Near Eastern). Everyone remarks of the paintings that they contain a sort of documentary truth to nature. As much as in a Dutch flower piece, you can clearly recognize and identify the particular species and variety of plant, though part of Monet's magic is that this process is never brought about by the obvious expedient of singling them out (as in a botanical illustration and, to some degree, in a Dutch painting). What we also recognize and enjoy is the way the flowers in the paintings look naturally comfortable – as indeed they do outside in the garden – grouped and partially obscuring each other. This you notice sometimes also in their poise, and even

– paradoxically – in a characteristic occasional shyness. Above all, of course, it is the way the flowers in the paintings absorb and reflect light that convinces us of their truth to nature. The very moment at which they are about to become abstractions of light is the same instant that their specific identity is registered – an extraordinary thing and the touchstone of the Impressionist claim to visual, retinal authenticity.

And yet there is a colossal forfeit: truth to retinal function occludes truth to what we actually do experience when the experience matters to us. The visual forfeits the visionary. A painting by Monet is decorative – and I mean that in the best of all possible senses – but if you look at it to learn something not only about the visual events of a garden but about the *nature* of gardens, you'll be disappointed.

For all that from the 1880s he would adopt the pose of a man of the people – as if moving out of Paris and a little bit into the country made him confederate with the earth – and for all that he had indeed been impecunious in his time, he was able to employ six gardeners at Giverny, and we should not allow the passage of time, admiration for the paintings or anything else to obscure the fact that Monet's perceived market for his paintings was the emerging urban middle class. It was with that social class that so much in Monet's life – as with the essentially decorative character and subject of his paintings – was allied.

You can rarely, for example, tell from Impressionist paintings (without their titles) whether the subjects are private gardens or corners of public parks, as you almost invariably can when you visit one in the flesh – and this is true though there are plenty of examples of paintings of both, and though the actual styles of those two classes of garden were (and still are) really very different. The women in the paintings are often very slightly self-consciously decorative too, but at the same time they are almost always equally anonymous. These are not so much individuals as exemplars of society. The children – the languorous but unconvincingly pretty images of implausible children – represent some of the least compelling kitsch in all of western art. By and large, Impressionist paintings are about and for the bourgeoisie, and that goes a long way towards identifying and explaining their great qualities – best of which, I think, is their lightness of intellectual touch – but also their weaknesses.

Once again, the paradox of hanging pictures on the interior walls of houses as if they were windows on to the garden outside raises teasing questions about representation and illusion. But in the case of Impressionist paintings, the window effect has the peculiar merit and attraction of being just about possible: the ladies *could* have been your acquaintances, the children *could* have been your own, and the gardens and landscapes, while they are better than the real view from your own windows, are not entirely out of reach of your pocket, your experience, your capabilities if you were really to try. Above all, they are not beyond the reach of your imagination. These pictures are views sometimes of gardens, sometimes of flowers alone, and sometimes of the orchards and domesticated (decorative) landscapes which, for the most part, any Parisian could have got the flavour of for themselves by gazing out of a train window only a few miles from the metropolis.

One caveat: a good deal of the foregoing is not true of Monet's late paintings, the great water lily pieces. Their scale alone is often monumentally undomestic. But these were deliberately intended by the old man as his gift to the nation – his own public monument, as it were. Their public destination is part of their character and poise. And, of course, they are further characterized by an intensification of the artist's commitment to the doctrine of visual truth, even though he was very nearly blind by then. They are, in short, a special, last, glorious case.

Vincent van Gogh (1853–1890) is different again, *very* different on the whole. So much so that I want to close this discussion of painterly gardens with some quite detailed observations on what is one of his very great paintings and one, *inter alia*, which draws us back to fundamental issues already considered. We'll be reminded again of Turner and the matter of the visual becoming a vehicle not just for vision but for the visionary, of the painting of a garden as – at least in some measure – an *objective* analogue for the garden but invested with *subjective* meaning. We'll encounter again the whole problem of seeing, where to *visualize* (to make an image, in Impressionist terms) has the compelling virtue of being so much more concrete than to *conceptualize*, but at the same time is so much less free than it would be if the injunction were simply to *imagine*.

In the summer of 1888 van Gogh was keenly awaiting the arrival of Paul Gauguin (1848–1903) at Arles in the South of France, to share conversation, a studio and his life. Theo van Gogh, the painter's brother, had struck some sort of deal with Gauguin whereby he (Theo, the art dealer) would take a proportion of Gauguin's work and pay him some sort of retainer – or at least his expenses.[6] To Gauguin, the idea of the garden had always been close to the centre of his vision, to such a degree that it had developed into the central component of the myth with which he had progressively fed more and more of his imagination, and by which he would eventually live (and die) once he had finally removed to the Marquesas Islands. There is a continuous line of development from the early Breton calvaries, with their bleached-out landscapes, gallows trees and all-too-dead Christs, to the rich paintings of Tahiti as if it were a garden, with their richly foliaged, richly fruiting trees, where the sting of the fruit of the tree of knowledge had at last been drawn. He placed in them scenes of almost explicit eroticism and generation, and his own self-portraits, his own painted presence – his homecoming, as it were – with his own face bearing a more-than-passing resemblance to that of his early Christs, but now with face and body vitally alive: the myth and the resurrection made flesh.

In a mood of intense excitement, van Gogh prepared the Yellow House for his guest – whitewashed throughout the interior, fresh yellow on the outside.[7] Gas was installed.[8] New paintings would have to be made to furnish the walls, and he set to work on those sunflowers we all know so well. He lived for four of those painting days mainly on '23 cafés . . . avec du pain'.[9] For Gauguin's room, he was working on a 'décoration, le *jardin d'un poète*', which comprised four paintings, including what we know now as *The Poet's Garden* (1888; illus. 31).[10]

The Poet's Garden was intended to welcome Gauguin to Arles, to make him feel spiritually as well as physically at home. As so often with van Gogh, his circumstances combined with his mental preoccupations to provide a sort of chromatic context for work in progress. His palette was his mood. In this case, the painting is almost entirely yellows and greens, but his mood (the joyful expectation of Gauguin apart) was grim. Earlier that year, in August, he had written to a characteristically worried Theo that those days, as far as material things went, were very long and hard ('ces jours ci sont matériellement d'une excessive dureté').[11] He was resentful of the poverty of his circumstances, his landlord fleecing him for the rent of his shanty ('sale baraque'). Thus, he painted his landlord's café as a form of 'revenge'. There, in *The Night Café* (1888), he expressed 'terribles passions humaines' by reds and greens: blood red and dull yellow for the room ('rouge sang and jaune sourd'), and the whole was a battle of glaringly different reds and greens ('un combat et une antithèse des verts et des rouges les plus differents'). The picture, he wrote (though in a jocular tone), was one of the ugliest ('un des plus laids') he had done.[12]

Opposite van Gogh's Yellow House in Arles was a public garden, the Place Lamartine (hence the name of the painting

– Alphonse de Lamartine being, but only incidentally, the 'poet'), and he began feverishly to sketch and to paint there, eventually working up to the finished picture. In effect, *The Poet's Garden* shows a tiny meadow, perhaps only a few metres across and deep, framed by a clipped, dome-shaped cedar (?) on the left and a weeping tree on the right. They are part of a receding concave grove: oleander bushes, dark evergreen shrubs charred by the intensity of the vision – withal, a dense group of six or seven intermingled trees, graded in height, and rising like a green-yellow fountain into the back of the picture. They mark the edge of the world. They stand, as it were, on a high cliff. Above and behind them is endlessly receding sky (or water, or the strange aqueous, aerial compound of both that van Gogh makes from time to time). Its surface is made up of blunt, brushed oblongs of green-yellow paint laid on like layered bricks, but almost invisibly so and, in any case, employing a bond unknown to ordinary builders of walls of light.

The great thing is the long-grassed meadow whose open space is like a stage. It takes up something like half the painting. Though a public park – and a French one, at that – it is un-mown, un-benched and conspicuously un-peopled here (in this respect alone like a late Monet, but unlike almost any Renoir, Sisley or even Pissarro). Its floor is spangled with flowers – yellow, greeny-white and, in the very front, some low-shouldered blossoms in a sort of bruised apricot. They aren't massed as in a conventional Impressionist painting. There are, however, a great many of them, and each bloom is individually rendered. Only a few stems are visible: the partially obscuring grass is long and uncut. The flowers, for all their corporeality, seem to float. Van Gogh doesn't want us to be troubled with their identification, and he was no botanist anyway. Some have the poise of columbines perhaps. Others might be narcissi. The squat ones in the foreground might be geums or rust-drenched poppies but for their lowly status. In even the most unspoiled meadow that hadn't been mown in living memory, you'd not find flowers like these. At any rate, they have an air of spring about them, while the oleander at the front of the fountain of trees speaks of high summer, and the bronze and coppery-yellow foliage of the trees towards the wall of light suggests early autumn. Like the tree in the ballad 'The Wife of Usher's Well', these are no ordinary plants submitting to a normal regime of the seasons. The birch in that poem

> neither grew in syke nor ditch,
> Nor yet in ony sheugh;
> But at the gates o' paradise,
> That birk grew fair eneugh.[13]

Likewise van Gogh's. This garden grows in the soil of the painter's visionary expectation of 'the poet' (Gauguin himself sometimes described his later paintings as 'poems') coming to take his place in an earthly paradise – the very thing Gauguin had been searching for.[14]

In the event, it didn't work out as van Gogh had hoped. He and Gauguin quarrelled. Two days before Christmas, while out walking at night, Gauguin was confronted by van Gogh brandishing a razor. He didn't strike or even threaten his friend. He turned and walked away. But that same night he cut off his own ear. Gauguin left. None of this makes any difference to the painting, however. The last thing in van Gogh's mind when he was painting it was failure, even if his close neighbour was madness.

The appearance in the painting of a unicorn would not be unlikely, though van Gogh eschews its literal presence. So does he every other animal or human presence, but the empty space in the foreground of the painting predicates some sort of imminent advent, something about to happen, someone about to arrive. The missing presence is that of Gauguin. Metaphorically – perhaps even literally – van Gogh expects Gauguin to paint himself into the picture.

14

Gardens and Music

Among Christopher Lloyd's gardening books there is at least one which has deservedly become a classic of the literature. It's called *The Well-Tempered Garden* (1970). The title sets up a resonant field of association: tuning and fine-tuning, harmony and counterpoint, Bach's *Das Wohltemperierte Klavier* – in a word, the art of music. The title apart, during the course of the book there is no further explicit reference to music, but the idea nevertheless underwrites it all: harmony, the melody of colour, something which, as he puts it quietly in his preface, 'is an art as well as a craft'.[1] He might have gone on to say that it is an art which involves difficulty and dissonance too (the *passus* of the Mass in B Minor, perhaps, or the removal of a venerable but dangerous tree), but which is necessarily viewed as part of the mystery involved in the processes of reconciling opposites: nature/human nature, consonance/dissonance, evolving into harmony, and then eventually into a perfect cadence. Human nature is not, it seems, necessarily consonant, not naturally consonant with nature itself.

I think there are indeed analogies, and correspondences too, between gardens and music, and that they are important and meaningful. But they're subtle. They're hard to objectify and – like music itself and also like what it is that makes a garden good – hard to grasp. At the same time, however, they do matter.

In the nature of such experience, not only are the links almost unyieldingly ineffable, but they are singular and private. Anyone who has been on a garden tour may remember painfully how much of their time was spent in trying to get away from the rest of the party. Anyone who has been gripped by music will recognize the guilty conscience they have felt sometimes when they discover an involuntary resentment of the trespass into their privacy by the person in the next seat with whom they are, in principle, sharing the concert. Andrew Marvell has it thus in 'The Garden' (1681): 'Two Paradises 'twere in one/ To live in Paradise alone.'[2]

It is a curious and perhaps revealing fact that it is going to be much, much easier to talk about 'music and gardens' than about 'gardens and music'. The literature of evocative garden music is very extensive indeed – Claude Debussy (1862–1918), Manuel de Falla (1876–1946), Ottorino Respighi (1879–1936), Arnold Bax (1883–1953), Michael Tippett (1905–1998), Ruth Gipps (1921–1999), Einojuhani Rautavaara (1928–2016), Toru Takemitsu (1930–1996) – the list could go on and on, but only one person, so far as I know, has actually modelled a garden on music: the composer Krzysztof Penderecki (1933–2020) in his garden at Lusławice in Poland. The two media – music and gardens – do not at first sight easily lend themselves to reciprocal translation, though there has been a good deal of traffic in one direction at least – to wit, all the music about gardens. What is evident, however, is that the effect upon us of both music and gardens is, in some respects, quite often similar, quite often mutually associative: private, restorative, integrative, harmonizing while remaining tantalizingly elusive.

In the cases of Olivier Messiaen (1908–1992) in the *Catalogue d'oiseaux* (1958) and Papageno's bird catching in *The Magic Flute* (1791), both music and musicians are self-consciously, deliberately, imitative of birdsong, and they are always performed indoors, but birdsong itself is the very spirit of virtually all music of whatever age or style, and that has always seemed to us to be a prefiguring. As if to make the point, allying human speech to birdsong – and vice versa – has been canonized in so many myths and legends, though, interestingly, rock music has seriously broken away from this, and that would seem to point to a watershed in music, its nature and our understanding of it. The beloved is still addressed as the singer's 'bird', but typically the sound is electrified, amplified, grunged, far beyond any plausible analogy with birdsong.

Aviaries, fairly common in English gardens a few years ago but rarer now, have come down in the world, the social world, at the same time as we have become more sensitive to a dissonance in the idea of incarcerating creatures to whom originally and essentially we were attracted by the perceived freedom of their spirits. Italian gardens of the late Renaissance knew no such scruples. What Mozart's Papageno was catching and selling birds for was the domestic market: birds to be kept in cages in ordinary people's houses, but the bigger money was in supplying birds for rich men's gardens. These places regularly featured a *ragnaia*, a thicket whose purpose was to trap songbirds. These evolved into elaborate and decorative zones of trellis and invisibly netted tunnels and arbours. Birds lured inside would delight visitors with their song, perhaps amplified by the confinement. And then the birds were slaughtered and served at dinner (the breasts of larks, finches and thrushes – minimalist meats if ever there were such) and deemed gastronomic delicacies. Or that great tour de force of the seventeenth-century kitchen: a succession of birds graduated in size and stuffed inside each other – and the more varieties, the greater the culinary feat – starting with the wren and climaxing with the swan.

There are ugly ironies, though, in our fascination with birds and gardens. Almost canonically it is eagles that we choose, frozen in stone, proudly to guard our gateposts. We no longer hear of the menus of banquets offering larks' tongues in aspic, and four and twenty blackbirds are throttled now only in the pies of nursery rhymes, though aviaries are still to be found in gardens from time to time. Milliners no longer make hats from the feathers of dead birds, and fashionable women no longer wear them . . . to weddings, to Ascot and so on. Like scalps hanging as trophies on the belts of Indian braves, they have been consigned to the history of 'barbarity'. Or simply of unthinkingness. The wren is still king for a day in parts of Ireland, Britain and Brittany (though the price is his life), but most of us now know about this only from *The Golden Bough* (1890).[3] We think we have moved on. We are more responsible, less unkind. Perhaps as a consequence, birdsong is prized probably as never before – but not, as of yore, for its musical qualities. Now it is seen (heard) as an index of ecological well-being in our gardens and the countryside. More and more, it is prized for its rarity. Its absence disturbs us and our consciences, even when we have forgotten the bitter poetry embodied in the title of the book that first stirred that conscience: Rachel Carson's *Silent Spring* of 1962 (and surely she must have been thinking of Keats's 'La Belle Dame sans Merci', where 'no birds sing').[4]

The presence of aviaries in gardens has its own musical logic, but it is also part of the tradition of using gardens to house exotic creatures – zoological gardens, in effect (illus. 36). John Tradescant's famous garden in seventeenth-century Lambeth was known as the Ark because it housed so many curious animals (albeit dead and stuffed), as well, of course, as plants. At Melbourne Hall in Derbyshire is a wrought-iron structure called – though perhaps only fancifully – the Birdcage. It was designed by Robert Bakewell and built between 1706 and 1711. Built during the reign (1603–25) of James I, the aviary in St James's Park occasioned the name Birdcage Walk for what is now the road on the park's south side.

Just as gardens are, in some respects, illusions of the 'natural', so we have often extended the trope in order that gardens, or parts of them, may appear to be the natural habitats of the birds, animals and reptiles that it has amused us to trap and keep. But

36 Gustave Doré's illustration of the Parrot Walk in London's Zoological Gardens, from Blanchard Jerrold, *London: A Pilgrimage* (1872). Fashionable society throngs – and largely ignores – the procession of captive birds strung up between the trees. All the flowers in evidence are artificial (on the women's hats), but the feathers (on the parrots) are real enough . . . and quite bizarrely inverted or hanging down like trophies in a poulterer's shop window.

conventionally (and conveniently) we overlook the bars and cages, just as our vision doesn't take in the pruning, weeding and mowing that actually distort the natural in a garden at the same time as we think of gardens as perfecting nature, consummating the natural. It is another of those tricks our minds willingly perform for us – a sleight of vision as well as, perhaps, of conscience. What we reckon on as perfecting (or conserving, or working with nature, or whatever creed we affiliate to) is so often the almost involuntary double-glazing that defends (and distorts) our perceptual experience from nature even as we endeavour to come to terms with the truly natural both within us and without.

At Schwetzingen, Nicolas de Pigage (1723–1796) designed between 1752 and 1795 a set of new garden buildings for the Elector Palatine. They include a 'Mosque', a Temple of Botany, a Temple of Mercury, a Bird Fountain and others. In their aggregate quality, their variety and their density, they represent one of the finest collections in Europe. In the case of the Bird Fountain – sometimes dubbed the Bird Theatre – a central, oval-shaped pool is enclosed by a suggestively 'Chinese' wooden balustrade, and, in the middle, an eagle-owl is on the point of taking flight.[5] In its talons it grasps a pheasant. From its beak it spouts water. Around the pool is a beautiful pavement of grey stone and small cobbles laid in geometric patterns. I imagine that seed to lure wild birds might once have been scattered here. Surrounding the whole space is a tall iron trellis which begins to curve inwards at a height of about 2 metres (7 ft) and, having done so, enables *Vitis* and *Parthenocissus* to make a canopy more or less over the pavement, but still to leave the pool open to the sky and the entire space visible to avian visitors. Along the edge of the overarching trellis, other birds – a hoopoe, a capercaillie, an exotic turkey, a goose and so on, made (in reproduction now) of durable copper plate but originally of painted steel – stand gazing rather menacingly down. When the fountain is functioning, these elevated birds spew water on to the eagle-owl – evidently in anger and disapproval, suggestively reminding the visitor perhaps of Aesop's Fables.

As far as human visitors are concerned, over whom the jets of water arch, the Bird Theatre is entered and quitted by means of long tunnels entirely enclosed by trellis and – in summer – by climbing plants. Thus, it is a suspended mystery that would lure the human visitors into the Bird Theatre, and an intriguing surprise that would greet them when they emerged out of the tunnels and into the open space. Once inside, you would find aviaries branching off from the walls of trellis, and captured songbirds would fill the air with sound all day long, resonating perhaps in the walls and on the pavement. In the autumn the foliage must look stunningly good too, the redness of the leaves hinting again at the Chinese. The longest axis leading out from this place supplies another vision of strangeness: the End of the World in a painted frieze designed to look both far off and paradisal.

John Evelyn mentioned the story of an elm near Toulouse which 'uttered a voice like . . . a mans [*sic*] as those of the Oracular *Dodona*'. The tree turned out to be hollow and its utterance no more than sounds echoing through its trunk.[6] This leads him on to notes about statues in gardens that 'spoke'. More literal, much more mechanical attempts to introduce music into gardens have been made since, most of them tripped up by the clumsiness of their own literalness, but there have been some imaginative ones too. Aeolus – god of the winds, who gave Odysseus a sack full of his bounty to speed him on his way (but his greedy sailors, thinking the sack contained more tangible treasure, opened it and let the winds escape) – is patron of the harp (the Aeolian harp) that still resonates with his voice occasionally in gardens. Wind chimes – metallic and wooden, with their flavour of the Japanese – are heard sometimes now. As children, we would play 'tunes' on the railings and palings we passed. In Arizona, Glenn Weyant banged mallets against the border fence apparently to produce 'sometimes ethereal' sounds.[7] The garden in Helsinki that surrounds the Finnish nation's memorial to its greatest son, Jean Sibelius (1865–1957), astonishes the visitor fortunate enough to be there very early in the morning (Sunday morning is best of all – the level of traffic noise in the distance is at its lowest). When a propitious wind blows off the nearby lake and over the tops of the hundreds of beautiful stainless steel pipes which comprise the great organ-like sculptural memorial, the strangest, ghostliest music imaginable steals through the spaces among the trees.

A claim for the most literal connection of all between music and horticulture might be made from the fact that Jethro Tull (1674–1741) was able to perfect his famous seed drill only because he was not just a farmer (and barrister) but an enthusiastic organist. The mechanism for the regulated introduction of seed into the drills was derived directly from the palettes: the opening and closing spring-loaded doors through which wind reaches the pipes standing on an organ's wind chest. The shape of the drills themselves was suggested by the tapered feet of organ pipes – a case of life feeding off art if ever there were one.

At the Villa d'Este in Tivoli, the spirit of Ovid (and so of imaginative metamorphosis) meets you at every turn. One thing leads to another; one thing becomes another. There's a fountain whose vertical jets and falling cascades suggest the most beautiful organ fascia you could ever imagine. But that's not all. As the falling water accumulates in the pools at the bottom, it brings pressure to bear upon a chamber of air – a bellows and wind chest, in effect. The air is allowed to escape into true musical pipes, and the sequence of their sounding is governed by a water wheel – cogged as in a musical box – which opens and closes valves to pipes according to the 'score' introduced into it. Franz Liszt (1811–1886) fixed both place and sound forever in music: *Les Jeux d'eaux à la Villa d'Este*, included in the third volume (1883) of his *Années de pèlerinage*.

There were several other Italian organ fountains dating from the sixteenth and seventeenth centuries: those in the Quirinal

Garden in Rome and at the Villa Aldobrandini in Frascati were probably the best known. Further examples are known in Austria and France. At the Villa Aldobrandini, an excess of zeal in the production of an aural garden seems to have taken hold of both the builders and the proprietors. The vast semicircular exedra built into the hillside and framing the fantastic cascade of water tumbling down into it from the steep, wooded slope above has large grottoes let into its walls, the central niche housing the god Atlas and, on either side, Polyphemus and a centaur carved with superb baroque theatricality. But the falling water originally activated acoustical machinery too: a horn played by the centaur and the panpipes played by the cyclops. You could also experience a variety of climates: mist, hail and thunder were available.[8] Within the Chamber of Apollo on one side of the exedra, the sound of an invisible organ, resonating perhaps with the wind (Aeolus) coming off the hill above the garden, could be heard. Charles de Brosses (1709–1777) left behind characteristically crotchety impressions of an Italian tour he made in 1739–40, and these include his considered opinion that the entire shebang at Aldobrandini was a dreadful row, 'déplorable', 'puérile' and 'sans agrément'.[9]

London's eighteenth-century pleasure gardens were full of music. Handel and Boyce, Avison, Arne and dozens of other contemporary musicians and composers must have found their biggest audiences in the crowds at Vauxhall, Marylebone and Ranelagh, but probably neither gardens nor music was central to why the crowds flocked there. These were fashionable venues both for those who had 'arrived' in society itself and for the still greater mass of people who believed themselves to be on their way. In our modern sense of arriving on the 'scene', these places were the theatres of social ostentation and aspiration, places in which to see and be seen, rendezvous for amorous assignations, pleasant but suitably expensive places in which to ingratiate yourself with prospective business associates, places for gormandizing and tippling. Music here was important, but only as the soft fabric of aural furnishing. It was the aural equivalent of the drapes and faux classical landscapes you posed in front of for society portraitists: an accessory you bought into temporarily to decorate the scenery of the stage of your life. The same was true of the gardens themselves, though one wonders how much of the horticulture was limited by London's sulphur-filled (coal-fired) air pollution. It must have made a difference, but, on the other hand, the relative lack of noise pollution would have made outdoor music possible to a degree that is hard to imagine now. Eighteenth-century London, in the pages of *The Spectator*, *The Tatler*, *The Idler* and elsewhere, revelled in a contagious and much-repeated description of itself as 'immersed in Sin and Sea-Coal'.[10] Tackling Vauxhall's reputation for sexual licence – 'This Spot seemed to be the Rendezvous of Cupid' – would have occasioned the magistrates to impose orders (in 1763 and again in 1764) requiring fences to be built and bright lights installed to prevent people from 'committing the indecencies so much complained of'.[11] Joseph Addison had his Roger de Coverley remark that he would be a more frequent customer of these places 'if there were more Nightingales, and fewer Strumpets'.[12]

The social cachet of those pleasure gardens is still true today of places which, superficially as it may be (or perhaps more substantially), resemble them, and an important association between gardens and music is maintained even now at Glyndebourne and Garsington. But the conjunctive association of gardens and music happens too frequently to be explained away merely as an occasional social event. Sometimes – stripped of its society glamour – you can get a glimpse of a connection with deeper roots and more compelling affinities. The nightly concerts in summer at the Tivoli Gardens in Copenhagen spread a kind of magic which derives almost as much from the garden context as from the music itself. You cannot reach the performance (in the concert hall) except by walking through the gardens. Nor are the paths direct. They wander through groves of trees, past water and through the haze of night-scented flowering plants. And so must you. Nor can you leave when the music has finished and straightaway exit into the bustle of the city's streets. You cannot but return by the slower, meandering route you took to reach it. The garden is unavoidably the context, the milieu. When I was there years ago, the programmes of music were shorter than you'd get at a regular concert hall (only an hour or so), so they didn't take up your whole evening, and you wanted to linger on in the gardens – for a walk, for a drink or dinner, for some amusement at one or more of the pretty kiosks and pavilions (have your portrait made in silhouette, shy for coconuts, visit the waxworks), or just to sit under the trees. Instead of having to leave at the close of the concert and join the scrum on a train, you emerged from one art and gently lingered on in another, for a while at least. Not having to plunge straight out into a noisy street with its busily moving lights, traffic, sounds and people allowed the music to seep more deeply into your reflective memory. And as the August twilight drew in, some beams of light, whose source was invisible, were played upon beautiful fireflies and dragonflies apparently in flight across the lake.

Something a little less high-minded perhaps but just as fine in its way, and just as soluble into the soul, occurs in the case of a band concert in a park. Lunchtime jazz in St Stephen's Green (one of the very finest of the world's public gardens) – shutting out traffic and commerce, Dublin and difficulty – is another among my happiest musical experiences. And such occasions must also rank as among our most successful attempts to integrate culture (the arts) with the rest of our lives, making connections with sense and the beautiful, with fun and the recreative, as credible as appointments at the office or the hairdresser. It is the context, the frame, which achieves the integration, and that too is not necessarily a common or simple feat.

Sometimes the nexus between music and gardens amounts to not much more than a contrived but happy holiday from the ordinary world. Sometimes, though, it intimates something more fundamental, while still obstinately resisting our best efforts to explain why it is so, why it *should* be so. That Jean-Baptiste Lully (1632–1687) should have written operas expressly for performance in the gardens at Versailles doesn't really seem any more significant than having the lawns mown in straight lines rather than (say) concentric circles, or having the gardeners dressed in green pullovers rather than (say) brown. Madame de Pompadour (1721–1764) commissioning ballets and operas for her gardens signifies just about as much, I think, as arrangements to keep the champagne cool. But other connections hint at more: Kundry's garden in *Parsifal* (1882) was said to have been modelled upon Wagner's memories of the gardens of Isola Bella. As I listen to the music I can believe it: the chromatic, ethereal otherworldliness is palpable. Wagner's music is one of the fixed points of reference George Sitwell (1860–1943) uses – in his classic *Essay on the Making of Gardens* (1909) – to develop his theme of what is really going on in the minds of people who make great gardens. Liszt's music from the gardens of the Villa d'Este digs deeper than merely a collection of holiday postcards in sound. The connection is not that of life lived just as a tourist passing through, but of this world becoming more than a merely transient house for us while we happen to be here, and beginning, moreover, to resonate more like our natural home.

Echoing William Wordsworth's poem 'Airey-Force Valley', Ivon Hitchens (1893–1979) spoke of his landscape paintings in terms of music, in terms of Wordsworthian 'eye-music'. 'I should like things to fall into place with so clear a *notation* that the spectator's eye and "aesthetic *ear*" shall receive a clear message, a clear *tune* . . . I seek to recreate the truth of nature by making my own *song* about it (in paint).'[13] Those italics are mine, but the recurrent metaphor places Hitchens's paintings in a powerful, long-standing continuum of perceiving music, poetry and painting as very closely allied indeed. Hitchens is an obvious incumbent in the line of

English succession from Gainsborough through Turner and Constable, Crome, Palmer, the Nashes and Sutherland. Indeed, shortly before he was selected to represent Britain at the Venice Biennale in 1956, he was plausibly identified as 'the most important English painter now living'.[14] Perhaps not coincidentally, he painted almost all his work only a mile or two from Turner's Petworth, in a 2.4 hectare (6 ac) wood he bought, lived in and watched grow for forty years.

Hitchens's paintings (again like Turner's Petworth landscapes) are typically oblong, often as much as three times longer than they are tall. The eye has to travel – conventionally from left to right – to take it all in, and there's no single avenue into the paintings (no golden section), but several consecutive ones in which verticals – trees as often as not, or shafts of light between trees – delineate periods, rather indeed as if one were listening to music (illus. 32). Thus, also, these suggestively parallel experiences are similarly intensely and literally chromatic. Hitchens's paintings lean towards the abstract; they resemble colours still on the palette, or in transitional movement towards form and representation, towards melody and harmony. The correspondences between music and his painting resist an explanation as merely accidental. It's hard too to ascribe to mere coincidence the fact that Hitchens's wife, Mollie, was a very accomplished pianist – an improviser as well as performer.

The rock musician Sting (b. 1951) developed over many years a fascination for the four-hundred-year-old music of John Dowland (*c.* 1563–1626). In 2006 this matured into an album of Dowland's music: *Songs from the Labyrinth*. Here, Sting plays this Elizabethan music with his Bosnian friend Edin Karamazov, a virtuoso on the lute. The results are intensely musical. There is, however, also a garden dimension to this, albeit an almost inscrutable one. Lutes enrich and amplify the sound of their strings being plucked in the characteristically swollen belly of their construction. When we speak about 'a body of sound', the expression becomes virtually literal in the case of a lute – much more so than in almost any other instrument. From this body, the enriched sound emerges through a sound hole. In the case of members of the violin family, these are italic *f*-shapes. In the case of the guitar, it's simply a round O, even though it's fringed with an inlay of linear purfling. In the case of a lute, the sound hole has a wooden fret across it, a sort of grille. This is its *rose*. From it, the sound blossoms. Its round shape apart, it does not resemble an easily recognizable (botanical) rose, but perhaps only because Islam resists the literal representation of living things, and the lute – the *oud* – was originally an Islamic instrument. Instead, the rose is stylized, geometricized. It will retain the original's symmetry and probably something of its concentricity, but

37 The rose of the author's cittern. Spruce, maple and ebony were used to construct the instrument as a whole, but the rose was carved from lime wood. Residual arms – residual anthropomorphic stumps – can be seen between the instrument's body and the neck.

the intensity of its workmanship, its beauty, as well as its abstraction, transcend mere imitation. The sound hole of a harpsichord is also called a rose and is often a similar tour de force of intricate woodcarving. So is that of the cittern, a close relative of the lute (illus. 37). This aperture is the mouth of the instrument, and the body and neck are still – despite a long, digressive evolution – discernibly anthropomorphic. It has indeed a neck, a body (an ear in the case of a violin, the so-called scroll) – and a mouth.

The roses of lutes developed – pre-Islamically – from that originating flower, but in the process they adopted the character, the schemata, of mazes. Roses and mazes both occur in gardens. Indeed, if you were to follow the pattern of the unfolding petals of a rose, it would take on the character of a journey, a maze. Of the rose belonging to his own lute, Sting says, 'I first came across this labyrinth design . . . in San Francisco, and found it very beautiful. It was based on the labyrinth in Chartres Cathedral, originally designed as a meditational tool.' In the garden of his Elizabethan house in Wiltshire, he set about echoing this labyrinth in the lawn. It took years to build, and he says he tries to 'walk it every day'. 'It's also become a metaphor for my journey in music. I'm constantly drawn towards the centre of things.'[15]

Almost last, but certainly not least, there's a deep – indeed, almost similarly compelling – affinity between the sort of mind which understands music and the mind which grasps a garden. I have argued in this book that memory plays a significant part both in what goes on in the minds of people making gardens and in the way we understand them. In the case of music – the appreciation of music – the demands made upon memory are well known and understood. You cannot make sense of the sonata form (in which all symphonic first movements, and many others besides, are cast) unless you remember the themes in the exposition, so that you recognize them as old friends in the recapitulation. Nor is it just a matter of themes or melodies: a symphonic exposition lays out its materials in a particular tonal context, a particular set of keys; then it generates tensions through tonal disturbances, finally resolving them through tonal and consonantal affirmations. It returns to its original key. To understand such music the listener must have registered and remembered the tonal context in which it began, but reflexively, almost intuitively, and certainly not because of a formal education in sonata form. Failing to have done so would mean the ultimate resolution (the return to that original home key) would afford no satisfaction, make no sense. The demands music makes on memory have no equal in the other arts of man.

In Xanadu did Kubla Khan
A stately pleasure-dome decree:
Where Alph, the sacred river, ran
Through caverns measureless to man
Down to a sunless sea.
So twice five miles of fertile ground
With walls and towers were girdled round:
And there were gardens bright with sinuous rills
Where blossom'd many an incense-bearing tree;
. . .
A damsel with a dulcimer
In a vision once I saw:
It was an Abyssinian maid
And on her dulcimer she play'd,
Singing of Mount Abora.
Could I revive within me
Her symphony and song,
To such a deep delight 'twould win me,
That with music loud and long,

I would build that dome in air,
That sunny dome!
SAMUEL TAYLOR COLERIDGE (1772–1834)[16]

Coleridge's vision of paradise takes the form, of course, of a garden, but it is a garden whose buildings are made of music. He anticipated what was to become one of the great projects of the Romantic imagination: the synthesis of all the arts of man. Walter Pater (1839–1894) famously marked out its central tenet: 'All art constantly aspires towards the condition of music.'[17] He meant that the degree to which an artwork had achieved an identity and integrity of matter and meaning determined its success, the matter of music (sound) being the same thing as its sense. So a painting – two-dimensional and made of canvas, flat forms and flat masses of colour – might achieve a seemingly three-dimensional representation of something, but it remained an illusion: what it actually is – its material substance – subsists physically distinct from what it means, and it will always remain so. Words on the page (onomatopoeia apart) remain more or less arbitrary verbal transliterations of nonverbal experiences, but their sounds don't correspond to the experiences themselves at all. Music, by contrast, is made of what it means. Matter and manner, matter and meaning, are one. In retrospect, we can see that this drive of the Romantic to fuse matter and meaning would tend towards ever more abstraction in the plastic arts, and so it has turned out, even in the work of those moderns who most stridently dissociate themselves from any Romantic antecedents. Or it has generated hybrids in other parts of the wood: son et lumière, cinema, lasers, strobes, projections and light shows at the disco, installation art in the late twentieth century and, of course, opera still ploughing the furrows of its own hybrid synthesis of music and drama: Wagner's *Parsifal* (1882), Rutland Boughton's *The Immortal Hour* (1914), Michael Tippett's *The Knot Garden* (1970) – all of them critically dependent upon their contexts: gardens.

Gardens naturally go a long way towards fulfilling Pater's principles. They are indeed made of what they mean. Gardens don't represent gardens; they simply are. As in music, there is an identity of subject and object, but also as with music, they locate and suspend us in the strange, largely unclaimed, unnamed territory which lies between life and art, between the natural world and the transcendent. We feel as if we belong in them, but we know ourselves to be finally only visitors.

Monet subscribed to the loose collective creed of Impressionism that all the arts have points in common, that there are harmonies and consonances in them that are self-sufficient, and that – in a painting – they affect us very much as a musical phrase or a chord can, striking us deeply. This returns us to somewhere close to where we began. We nod to an existential sympathy between gardens and music. We recognize a similarity between the effects upon us of both. Both allow a shortening of the distance between the materially real and the transcendently imagined, 'Annihilating all that's made/ To a green Thought in a green Shade'.[18] We see that, whatever the means and methods, whatever the connections, and however inscrutably they resist the analytical eye, they work. But identifying just what it is that they are made of is difficult. We set about to engineer associations and introduce pointers to analogy between the two: something as clumsy as a statue in a garden of a shepherd playing on a pipe on the one hand, or a complicated and abstract theory of harmonies in a manual of painterly aesthetics on the other: the rhyming and chiming of colours, texture, verticals, horizontals, foreground incidents and background space and so on. The well-tempered garden, whether in Bach's original or Lloyd's paraphrase, continues to elude our hermeneutics, just as it impresses our experience always with the fidelity and the reality of its earthy, down-to-earth physicality – the real facts of mould, mud and manure, hard bark, hard frost and hard graft – while suggesting always something metaphysical, stirred not just by the garden itself but (and very necessarily so too) by our *presence* in the garden.

According to legend, Amphion built the walls of Thebes with the music of his lyre, but the engineering remains elusive, more difficult perhaps than the psychology. After all, Joshua could topple walls with the sound of the trumpet, so why should not the reverse be within the scope of imagination? Coleridge's well-nigh definitive garden of music remains elusive too – elusive perhaps even to the poet himself as much as to us. To at least one of his contemporaries, he was the 'poeticopolitical, rhapsodicoprosaical, deisidaemoniac oparadoxographical, pseudolatreiological, transcendental meteorosophist, Moley Mystic'.[19] But there may still be a way through the mists of such metaphysics. If so, it runs like this: we apprehend almost everything first through our eyes, not through our ears, our noses or our sense of touch; and not least do we apprehend thus the wild and the natural, which we then translate in some measure into our gardens, and thus – if you allow a colossal leap of the imagination – into forms and meanings that mediate between the animal and the angel within ourselves. Sight is our most exercised sense, and so much so that the other four are, to a degree at least, sometimes occluded and, through lack of use, somewhat wasted away. And yet it is sound which conveys to us the most direct and immediate, the most compelling and visceral, information about the world around us: language and speech among ourselves, the soothing, menacing, rhythmic or inchoate sounds which reach us from speechless things (water, wind, animals, our own infants, our own heartbeats), and then music – sound in its most refined, most abstract form – which mediates between the worlds we know objectively and those other, better worlds we can otherwise only dimly perceive through the workaday clutter that confuses that other, perhaps better mode of perception, our imagination.

Our perception of the wild and the natural, and then of the gardens which mediate these to us, has become very narrowly visual. That may represent a distortion of what would be (and once was?) a more balanced, better distributed way in which we might take in and make sense of experience through the apertures of *all* our senses. Nevertheless, satisfaction, pleasure and gratification (with the way things are, and with the place we find ourselves in, or have made for ourselves, in the order of things), these are intuitions and circumstances we regularly express in musical, auditory terms. Pleasure and satisfaction again and again turn out to be paraphrases for what we really perceive of as harmonies.

The eye, however, identifies the object, the objective event, the concrete thing. It functions in empirical space and informs us of empirical matter and manners. The ear does that too, but much less. On the whole, the ear is involved with identifying things which take place in time, things whose essence is not event but process, and things (when there are more than one of them, as is usually the case) that move, moreover, simultaneously but not necessarily synchronously. This horizontal movement generates, through time, a motion in objects (or it generates melody by offering not just one note, but a sequence of them differentiated, if we're talking in terms of music). But it goes further too: it presents also the variety of their motions – the variety of their different rhythms and speeds, spans and patterns – simultaneously. By doing so, it allows us to see relationships both horizontally and vertically: thus, our apprehension of harmony and all the pleasure that that entails. Or, indeed, it may be of dissonance, and the jarring that results from that. But that – discordance, difficulty, discrepancy, contest – is the medicinal music of wisdom too.

The eye individuates, identifies, discriminates and eventually separates. The ear, however, moves, swims, goes with the flow of what must be, and then, in music, integrates and transcends. The harmony, the sense of oneness (and of properly belonging with oneself) that music induces in the interiorized regions of the soul, has one of its objective correlatives in the harmony we can sense – and be involved in – in a garden. Music is the reconciliation of the dissonant, just as gardens are the reconciling of ourselves with the world we no longer belong to: nature.

The music of Gerald Finzi (1901–1956) – one of the most characteristically English-sounding of all twentieth-century composers – is shot through again and again with a very beautiful, very crepuscular melancholy. His is the voice of a quietly understated sadness, a distilled sense of brevity and of its cousin beauty. Music apart, Finzi's passion was another version of Eden lost, but glimpsed again: he planted, tended, was often to be found in, his orchard of English apple trees.

15

Walls, Hedges and Fencing with Ourselves

Strolling along an English suburban street, you might be forgiven for thinking you're being mocked. Walls (and fences and the occasional hedge) define your progress from one end of the street to the other, but none of them could or would prevent you from entering the gardens behind them if you so wished. They're too flimsy, too low – alright for the gnomes some of them enclose, but no deterrent to the urban guerrillas who might kidnap the same and hold them to ransom.

The walls (and the fences too) don't stop the dumping of litter or the drift of falling leaves, the neighbours' cats or the neighbourhood's footballs. The paperboy used to jump over them (when he thought no one was looking). Even the snails, despite your best precautions, trudge up and over them. You have to wonder why they're there at all.

And then there are gates. The posts glare eagles or lions at you. Concrete cannonballs martially crown the pillars of the wall, and between them the wall itself bristles with little battlements. The curlicues in the wrought-iron gate don't now generally sport the family crest, but they do still faintly betray their origins in the medieval portcullis, yet it's all a fiction, really. At best, a game of property-respecting etiquette; at worst, a charade of baronial one-upmanship or pathetically transparent sabre rattling.

Robert Frost (1874–1963) pondered the matter of walls in quite a number of the poems in his second collection, *North of Boston* (1914). His 'Mending Wall' has the famous line: 'Good fences make good neighbors.' The speaker goes along with it. He repairs his side of the wall, though privately he wonders why. The neighbour, he feels, for all of his wiseacring wisdom, 'moves in darkness' and

> Not of woods only and the shade of trees.
> He will not go behind his father's saying,
> And he likes having the thought of it so well
> He says again, 'Good fences make good neighbors.'

But for his part, the speaker says:

> Before I built a wall I'd ask to know
> What I was walling in or walling out.

Yet his neighbour has no such practical (or philosophical) scruples. He'll have his wall, Frost implies, because, to him, there's something primitively necessary about it. How primitive? Palaeolithic, says Frost. The neighbour lifts a stone

> firmly by the top
> In each hand, like an old-stone savage armed.

Frost the modern, the progressive, is unconvinced. 'Something there is that doesn't love a wall,' he says in his own voice, and he's right.[1] Along the high road through the centre of our history, our wisdom, our very psyche, we have always been keen on walls, but at the extreme poles of our nature – the parts closest to our wild origins, and then the parts most remote – we resist them. And yet we put them up everywhere – or we put up the tokenist gnome-proportioned gestures of them insofar as planning laws permit – and, above all, we put them round our gardens. Garden walls, or hedges, don't really keep anything out. They aren't there to fend off wind and weather, and they don't support ceilings and a roof. They don't keep out burglars, cats or kids retrieving footballs. They'd never deter an invading army. John Evelyn's reputed rage at Peter the Great having himself pushed in a wheelbarrow through the hedges of his garden at Sayes Court in 1698 sounds as much like pique at the puncturing of the fiction of his hedges as impenetrable barriers as it does high dudgeon at the un-kingly, uncouth behaviour.[2]

Garden walls don't work in the opposite direction either: they're hardly efficient at containment, at keeping things in. Your colonizing plants, your cats, even your children, are barely corralled by your walls. But there must be something going on, or we wouldn't bother to build the walls in the first place, and we wouldn't bother to close the gate behind us either.

Richard Lovelace (1617–1657) famously had it in 'To Althea, from Prison' (1649) that 'Stone Walls doe not a Prison make.'[3] Because he is really comparing freedom of thought and conscience with freedom of movement, we take his point. Nevertheless, it is in the mind that walls – and most especially garden walls – work. And they work at their crudest as wishful thinking, at their best as metaphor.

Of course, walls identify property: they mark boundaries. In Britain, particularly, they flatter our little grip on the idea that our homes are our castles. They're manifestos of power and privilege, inclusion and exclusion – all the things that textbook Freudians would nod their heads sagely (and justifiably) about. But it is as metaphor, I think, that they're really interesting: as metaphors themselves and as parts of the larger metaphor that the gardens they enclose represent. We must return to Frost's advice to ask what it is that we are 'walling in or walling out'.

Hawthorn has been a favourite tree for hedging since the enclosures. The word itself comes from the Old English *haga*: 'hedge', 'enclosure'. The word *garden* – which means simply and essentially 'an enclosed outdoor place' – has a revealing range of cognates too: *yard*, *gird*, *girdle*. They all come from the same linguistic root, and most of them (like walls) work in two directions. It's in both of those senses that that most improbable of all hedges 'worked': those 4,000 kilometres (2,500 mi.) from Himalayan foothills to the Gulf of Bengal, planted by the British to protect their control of salt production. To employ a bit of current management babble, the words – like the concepts they represent – work both reactively and proactively.

Freud has it that 'the principal task of civilization, its actual *raison d'être*, is to defend us against nature,' which can't be a congenial idea for modern ecologists, nature lovers and even conscientious gardeners who, broadly speaking, are somewhat more likely now to think of civilization as the predator, not the prey, of nature.[4] On the whole, ancient wisdom would support this latter view rather than Freud's. And yet human history is the annals of building walls: around and above our bodies and against the elements (and in this respect the animal in us conforms to the pattern of animal behaviour in general: birds, bees, beavers and every sort of bobcat do exactly the same). We build walls around our cities and against our enemies, around our coasts and against the sea, along our frontiers and against our ethnic and ideological rivals.

Gardens are metaphors for culture coming to terms with wilderness, and for wilderness being tamed by culture. They represent and embody treaties we've made with the natural. We build walls around these treaty places to keep out rabbits, bark-eating deer, ground elder and human poachers – those who would steal our game or our privacy, our gnomes or our peace. But most of all, we want to keep out nature – that is, the real wilderness, the alien world outside human culture. (You might wonder what Freud would have made of the quite emphatically walled gardens we have so often made for those special neighbours of ours with whom we are rarely on easy terms: the dead.) The real thing, the real wilderness, is not in cultural terms our home at all, spiritual or otherwise. The reality of what we dub 'nature' and 'natural' (by which, all too glibly, we are likely to mean just 'pretty' or 'picturesque' or 'charming') actually lies elsewhere, in something we fear, something we envy: in short, wilderness. In part, that is because our nature is no longer exclusively natural. Whereas nature in the broader sense offers flowers as lures to sexual reproduction, we construe them largely in cultural and aesthetic – but not biological – terms. What we see in them is a construct of our own imaginations: beauty.

Where nature's imperatives are the survival of the collective, the species, humans perceive themselves as specific individuals. We know about death, and we guess at something beyond mechanical reproduction which we call 'love'. The two together make us see our own deaths as personal losses, and not really at all as setbacks for the species. Something in us – something apart from nature – makes us reluctant to conform to the way all other animals behave. We go down fighting not only against the fact, but against the principle, of personal extinction. In short, we're self-conscious, individuated and, to a degree, extra-naturally, supra-naturally driven creatures. We are, in the strictest sense of the word, unnatural.

Michelangelo didn't paint the Sistine Chapel ceiling to gain advantage for his genes. He did it to interpose between us and the real sky (the natural sky of scorching sun, fumbling darkness, drenching rain and, above all, appallingly empty endlessness) a new roof in which infinity and mystery were prefigured in the finite and the understandable: the fact of the fall of man's nature redeemed through the metaphor and fiction of his beauty. So it is with the mother who embroiders flowers on a pillowcase so that her children can sleep in a bed of them even when their eyes are closed; so it is with the man who hangs up his onions to dry, but plaits them first – all of those things extracurricular, gratuitous, extramural.

Gardens are the same. They're artifices, fictions, things for which we know no biological imperative. They're the places in which we reconcile the natural outside us with the human, the wilderness with the cultured, the biologically imperative (merely functional) facts of life with the aspirant fictions of our freebooting spirits. With walled gardens (*paradeisos*, the space walled round), we unconsciously hedge our bets, we seek to keep a foot in both worlds – that of nature and that of our own human nature. We strive both to have our cake (nature that is, respected and even marvelled at) and still to eat it, to exploit its materials to sustain our own less natural lives.

The trouble – the crisis we face now – is not that gardens are fictions (metaphors, artifices), but that wilderness has become a fiction too. There is nowhere left in which the degrading, destructive influence of man is not at work, for all that we designate this or that patch as an inviolable 'reserve', and for all that we have not yet literally set foot on absolutely every square inch of the planet. The forests, the seas, the ice caps, the mountains: all of them are now insidiously man-shaped if not exactly man-made. Tearing down the walls between us and nature, or at least changing the hinges on the gates so that they open both ways – reconnecting with nature as the eco-prophets would have us do, or like foxes relocating to cities – won't answer either, because the wilderness outside us isn't truly real any more, while the wasteland inside us really is. Exit, pursued, not by a bear (or even a teddy bear) but by guilt.

16

INTERLUDE
Two Gardens Enclosed

Ampthill in Bedfordshire merits three entries in Headley and Meulenkamp's *Follies, Grottoes and Garden Buildings* (1999), which suggests a local tendency to the idiosyncratic. The good burghers of the town prefer to present a more sober image, however. On tourist maps and on a board as you drive in, it is a 'Georgian Market Town', and in truth, if it does have an eccentric tendency, it hides it well. It's a small, tidy Georgian, pretty Regency, worthily decent Victorian sort of place. The Gothic church is handsome, but this is Bunyan country, so there's a gentle but discernible undertow of Nonconformity, a place not quite sure if it should have allowed itself to lapse into the genteel. It did but only quietly. Its antique shops would aspire (if they could) to a town with something of the air of Tunbridge Wells. But the real modesty of the place conspires against them, and all is satisfactorily unpretentious after all. It's the sort of place that puts you in mind of what a very pleasant thing indeed a row of terraced houses can be.

Behind the main London–Bedford street and those decent, sober houses is a field that slopes along the side of a shallow valley. A footpath – the King's Arms Path, away from the town and along the edge of the field – leads to what must once have been an outlying hamlet, now a fold in the skirt of the housing that rings the town. At the bottom of the path and the valley, but before it reaches its destination and still easily within strolling distance, there's a damp acre or so, once unregarded, but then it fell under the custodianship of a man called William Nourish (d. 1986), who made a garden here. Since 1987, King's Arms Garden has been tended by the Friends of the Garden on behalf of the town council – and it's a very remarkable place indeed.

There's a stout hedge between it and the public footpath. You can see through the hedge sometimes, over it sometimes. There's no road in or out of it, and no road along its perimeter. This is a place you can only walk to. Once inside, and after walking only a few paces, you're lost. You can't see the gate any more, and you're not sure which path led to it anyway, but there's the *Taxodium distichum*, the swamp cypress you saw (some of it, but never all, because of the visually obstructing hedge) as you walked the footpath into the town. But you never even guessed at those extraordinary, arthritic roots that radiate from its base. And then there's the sparkling cornus, the top of which so often caught your eye. Now at last you can confirm for yourself what you always suspected: those seemingly familiar trees – like people whose faces you've seen at a window but never met, and the inside of whose houses you have always had to imagine – appear now, seen at last in their entirety, quite different. They have bodies as well as faces, and they have rooms of their own. Beneath these trees, luxuries of woodlanders – ferns, anemones, shady winter aconites and summer geraniums – spread their easy naturalness everywhere. The paths are informal – no edges, no paving, no proscriptions, no obligations – and once again you're reminded of the freedoms of a private house where it's only the informal placing of the furniture that determines where you walk or how you cross a room.

There's no lawn here (though there is a rich variety of cultivated grasses). All the space is given over to the prosperity of plants. There are paths, though, and they're not mean or cramped, and there are seats to linger on if you will. Paths and seats, but none of the paraphernalia of a garden on its best behaviour: litter bins, directional signs, ostentations of botanical labels, educational activity questionnaires, tearooms, toilets and all the rest of it. It's as if there being no car park, all the rest of the clutter is pre-empted too – and, curiously, unlooked for.

Horticulturally the place is very rich indeed, yet the site isn't an easy one: damp, shaded, quite cold and with an unremittingly acid soil. You could certainly not grow anything and everything here. But by respecting these constraints and by not struggling against them – rather by working with them and imaginatively planting what really will thrive – the plants confirm the place, and that's a vital component of its sense. There are commoners as well as aristocrats here, natives as well as foreigners – a grand, mature *Liriodendron tulipifera*, a ginkgo, acers (lots and perhaps the best of them an *Acer tetramerum*). There's *Fagus sylvatica* 'Roseomarginata', wisteria climbing up two Scots pines, hollies – big, impressive specimen trees – and then cyclamen, hellebores, erythroniums, fritillaries, primulas, hemerocallis, kniphofias and astrantias. All of them belong here. All of them subscribe to the same commonwealth. That's remarkable too. How often does one find a rare plant coerced by a visually intrusive label to flaunt its address as it were, or, conversely, how often is one invited to applaud the planting of native species somewhere, and yet the place itself has absorbed nothing of a natural England at all? Not here.

With or without an apprehension of the invisible skill behind the planting of this garden, once inside you begin to see why paths go where they do. That they provide access to views for visitors (and indeed they do) is not what they're really for. In the first place, they're there to allow gardeners to reach plants. Leading the visitor on is really only an accident – but, when you stop to think about it, a perfectly natural one. The result is a garden where the paths go where you want to go, and this is to a degree extraordinary for a public garden. Something reciprocal about your being able to reach the plants begins to shape your sense of the place. The plants – their beauty and the happy naturalness of their flourishing – reach you without you having to strain, to reach for them. It is the paths and their work-shaped journeys that achieve this.

There isn't a straight axis anywhere (though you knew that the now invisible hedge along the footpath ran directly north to south), but this isn't artful *sharawadgi*, the cod-Chinese word for the seemingly random, seemingly artless style of gardening introduced by Sir William Temple in the late seventeenth century. It's the trees and the pond, and the boggy zones, that have naturally shaped the place, and you have to pull yourself up short to notice how remarkable a thing it is when in the case of nearly everywhere else, it would be a matter of a tree being fitted to a space rather than vice versa. Partly because of the density of the planting, partly because you cannot help but turn your head first one way and then another to enjoy a magnolia here, a rhododendron there, looking up to a flowering tree, looking down to a creeping moss – and all these endorsed by the wandering of the paths – you can't by any means accurately sense the size or the shape of the garden as a whole. It is indeed a place apart, an enclosed garden, with blessedly nothing at all of the usual 'references to the house', or borrowed landscape, or any imposed architectural form.

Before you came in, and on most of those occasions when you walked along the public path outside, you often heard birds – heard but not so often saw. Now you see them too, as if previously it was you who had been in a cage, walled out of sight as it were, but now, like them, you can pass freely.

The Friedsam *Annunciation* (*c.* 1445) in New York used to be attributed to Jan van Eyck (illus. 33). Now – but still a little cautiously – it's attributed to Petrus Christus. In it the Virgin is standing on the threshold of a part-Romanesque, part-Gothic doorway. She greets the angel with her raised right hand, and in her left she holds a book. She seems to have been reading when the visitor disturbed her.

We have been taught to 'read' paintings, and probably to have found that this is a particularly fruitful thing to do with Flemish paintings because so many of the compositional elements are obviously iconographic, and because so many more, though less obviously, may be. Scholars have had plenty to exercise their speculative eyes and wits upon. I mean, for example, that though the oranges on the windowsill and chest in Jan van Eyck's *Arnolfini Portrait* (1434) are so clearly emblematic, you're still intrigued by the tiny carved wooden animal which peeps out between the edge of the lady's dress and the pillar of the chair. So it is with the Friedsam *Annunciation*. It's a very beautiful painting in its own right, but it's also a catalogue of painterly conventions and culturally encoded emblems. Most of them are familiar: the white lilies in the pot which stands in the porch; the building itself, which might be a palace or a chapel. (Of course, actually it's both, and that's how the painter inflects the House of God to infer the Home of Humankind.) Then there's the sceptre in the angel's left hand, at the end of which are stylized and geometricized flowers that suggest, behind the petals, the seed vessels about to be fertilized. Above all, angel, lady and building are all conventionally set in a garden. Its turf is conventionally spangled with flowers, its safety conventionally secured by a surrounding wall.

But there's a problem with this wall. Very evidently, on the left-hand side as it leaves the picture, there's a breach. It's a large ragged gap, and it has been there for some time. At the bottom the turf has grown over where at least the foundations would have been visible. A little further back along the wall, the masonry has fallen out to half its depth, so we should infer that it's a case of a wall in decline rather than the work of intentional demolition. The gap – the big breach at the left – is quite wide. If you wanted to, you could easily use it to steal in or out. The problem for the person seeking to understand the painting is that the breach in the wall represents also a breach in conventions – painterly, social, even theological.

The conventional explanation of this unconventional feature is that the crumbling masonry points to a distinction between human history (bricks and mortar) and sacred time. The one decays while the other endures. The angel intervenes into the temporal, but the meaning and consequences of this event are eternal. Indeed, divine intervention acting through temporal means is, in any case, the whole sense of the Incarnation here being initiated. The things of humankind crumble (and possibly we're also meant specifically to infer allusion to fractures in the social order of fifteenth-century Bruges), but the purposes of God endure.

I have no quarrel with that reading, but insofar as the painting plays tunes on its own temporariness at the same time as it aspires to transcend its own time, and because I want to pay more than mere lip service to the old rhetoric that a work of great art, though made yesterday, is still news tomorrow, I wish to suggest another reading of it, one which would probably have been unlikely at the time the painting was made (but just about possible), and yet, if we imagined the panel as having been painted yesterday, would be almost impossible to avoid today.

The wall is a puzzle to us, but presumably not to the mid-fifteenth-century painter who intended and painted it. His problem was always going to be with the angel because, for all that angels generally get by on a ticket of metaphor (or something like that, so that we go along with the *idea* of angels), actually they don't happen. The painter here had to make the presence of his angel sufficiently cognate with ordinary visible reality to make it plausible, but still to retain enough of the supernatural to make him – and, in this specific instance, the angel Gabriel's visitation – almost (but not absolutely) extraordinary: to make the supernatural not so much an alternative to, or a critical replacement of, the natural, but somehow plausibly congruent with it at the same time as being numinous.

Gabriel has wings, exquisitely rendered here to suggest a bird of paradise if ever there were one. Like most of his kind in late medieval painting, he has forgotten to furl them, forgotten that he'll be blown or fall over if he doesn't – or else that he'll look like a fowl flourishing his plumage in courtship. In fact, that image, though unintended, is parallel to how we would read the painting if we were in any doubt whatsoever that its subject was religious and not secular. Here would be a handsome young prince paying court to his muse, and the expressive languages he's using are all easily legible as the usual conventions of courtly love. The attitudes (all except for his raised index finger requiring attention rather than an outspread hand supplicating reciprocation) are exactly those of just such a conventional scene: the girl, demurely removed from him, does not want to meet his eyes, nor to step across the threshold (of the building or of courtly convention) to touch or be touched by him. Her mind, if indeed it is inclined to love at all, is fixed on love as an abstraction, but we have evidence that in any case her thoughts are elsewhere. She was, after all, interrupted while reading a book. Not only these actions (and suspended interactions) but the *mise en scène* is consistent with the conventions of courtly love. This is the enclosed garden, the *hortus conclusus*, of hundreds of other conventional scenes of the declaration of chaste passion.

But I don't want in any way to suggest that this picture is a muddle. It's far too coherently beautiful, and far too confidently rendered, to be anything like that at all. In any case, the dove, showering beams of golden light down on to Mary's head, tilts the painting away from the ordinary, the natural, and towards the extraordinary through the intervention of the supernatural. Having said that, though, we're still left with the matter of the wall and the hole in the wall.

Outside the garden we'd conventionally expect to catch at least a glimpse of a contrastingly unsophisticated, ungroomed or uncultivated world: either peasants plodding like animals behind their ploughs and their oxen and completely untouched by, and indifferent to, the culturally refined world of palace and garden, or a rough dark forest, rough unhewn rocks to stumble over, and not a Christian soul in sight, so inhospitable would be the landscape. The painter here, however, gives us neither. It's true that flowers don't spring from the turf out there, but the turf itself is soft enough, its gradient gentle enough, and its surface not ravaged by rough winds. The trees – there are two of them – aren't flowering or fruiting, but they're shapely and beautiful things in their own right. And there are no thorns on their branches, no rocks to stumble over at their feet. What we see beyond the wall is no less pleasant than what we're presented with inside. That doesn't amount in itself to anything as violent as an explicit subversion of convention, but it does suggest at least an equilibrium between nature and culture, whereas we expected not balance but antithesis and tension.

Looking again at the world inside the garden, our normal expectations are, however, subverted nevertheless, for all that this is done quietly. There's a bare, rude cliff of rock (in the left foreground of the painting), and it's *inside* the garden. There are weeds, plants out of place, things growing independently of man's cultivation – they too are *inside* the garden. Growing on the chamfered tops of some of the buttresses there are adventitious weeds, and they're flowering as cheerfully as anything on the cultivated mead below. They might be wallflowers; they might be wild carnations. It's hard to read them as an accident of the painter's imagination, even though they're necessarily subject to our categorization as accidents of nature and not culture.

In view of these things, I don't think we can really carry on subscribing to a conventional reading of the *mise en scène* of the painting – nature versus culture – any longer. The garden metaphor here is less simple, more ambivalent, than that, and possibly more complex and interesting than in almost any other medieval religious painting we have.

We return now to that critical breach in the wall. We can't actually see through it (at least, through the bit of it that we're shown; the rest of it belongs out of the painting's left side, and we have already inferred that the gap – could we but see all of it – is quite wide enough for someone to pass in and out). What prevents us from being able to see through our bit of the gap is a bush. Quite clearly, it's growing from roots on the outside of the wall, but it's tall enough now to be growing over the top and to be beginning to tumble down the inside. It's also growing sideways into the breach and softening the broken edges of stone.

According to the conventions of the *hortus conclusus*, we should expect this plant to be, if not a noxious weed which, once inside, will strangle the plants of the cultivated garden, then at least a wilding, an interloper – something that quite literally doesn't belong here and may have the anarchic potential to be a threat. At its most extreme, the branches of this bush could be the ladder by means of which the serpent gains entrance to the garden and sets about its baleful work of undoing our bliss. But none of this is true here. The bush is clearly not a botanical Goth. There's nothing about it which suggests either literal or metaphorical invasion. Far from challenging the wall, it seems to be – in the manner of the best behaved of garden wall plants – only its happy partner. In fact, though growing outside the wall and only tentatively hanging over no more than the first few inches, it is far and away the most beautiful botanical element in the whole picture. It is bursting with flower, beautiful open trusses of flower.

So much for an easy reading of this garden as a conventional essay in culture versus nature, but what about the natural and the supernatural, and the painter's difficult task of making the angel immanent in nature and yet also somehow beyond it? The dove, for all its golden effulgence, flew in. That much is plain. It's still on the wing, hovering near the Virgin's head. Birds do that; it's in their nature, and so it doesn't signify, doesn't matter. We might also want to notice that in flying over the walls birds represent a breach of the principle that walls keep things in or out. What does matter, however, is how Gabriel got in.

Through the gate? That's what we'd suppose. It's out of the question that he too flew in. Angels don't fly in medieval paintings unless the scene is heaven itself. Their wings are a metaphor for their spirituality, not the engine of aviation. (It's easy to imagine why not when you think of what they become in later Renaissance and baroque painting: avian fantasies or fat kids with wings, sucking the toffee off their plump pink thumbs.) If we look for a gate in this painting, we'd expect to have found it lined up with the door of the chapel/palace a little to the left of where we stand in front of the painting. But it can't be there. That rocky cliff would block it. Nevertheless, and supposing the layout of the garden to have less formal geometry than a straight axis from gate to door would require, we'd look for a gate (or a path to a gate) a little further round to our right. Yet it isn't there, can't be there. The artist has been careful to paint in a fringe of turf (only very narrowly broken) along the bottom of the painting where the path we're looking for would otherwise have been. Moreover, Gabriel the visitor, who would have had to come in by the gate and have kept to the path too (howsoever transcendent he may be as an angel because, for the purposes of *this* mission, he must be grounded), is facing completely the wrong way to have entered the picture either from the front or from the right.

Gabriel, the painting leads us to infer, can only have entered the garden through the breach in the wall. What that says about nature and the *extra*, the *super*natural, I wouldn't presume fully to understand (though it's hard not gropingly to begin to guess), and our difficulty – our modern difficulty – with giving any sort of credence to the supernatural makes it even harder to make some sense of the picture in any terms other than purely as an aesthetic object. That Gabriel the Angel should enter our rational, material, cultured world through a gap in our defences (against the illogical, against the absurdly impossible, against – above all – the laws of nature) is a very neat trope on the painter's part and one that seems to have a kind of logic after all, even for the most hard-boiled of rationalists. But that he comes from (and belongs to?) nature, the wild and the wilderness has such a sharp stinging edge to it now (albeit probably quite unintentionally in terms of the painting as a cultural product of the late medieval mind) and has the consequence of speaking to our very contemporary preoccupation with the treaty we must strike, before it's too late, between nature and our own natures. That allows the painting to claim a most unusually significant place in the galleries of our own lives.

17

The Garden Party

Garden parties have a cachet that few other social events can rival. However glittering the company and well appointed the indoor venue, nothing can match the milieu of a garden. It is less formal, more relaxed and more spacious, but at the same time it has more about it of the sense of an occasion. There are only a few weeks in the year when it's possible, and then probably only a scattering of days during those weeks when the weather is truly sunny in the afternoon or balmy in the evening so that it really does complement the mood of a successful party. You can hold a party indoors at any time, but a garden party is special.

In the afternoon, there might be punch or sorbets, croquet, and then you drift away to watch the koi lazily swimming in and out of the shadows of lily pads. Something like the myth of the Edwardian golden afternoon intoxicates the air (that and the scent of the limes if you're at Buckingham Palace – everyone I know who's been to one of those parties seems to remember that smell above all, and the ubiquity of it). Something in the air that makes us careless, for just a few hours, careless of yesterdays or tomorrows. Something that makes lotus-eaters of us all.

In the evening, the air and the ambience, the mood and the moment can easily be charged with magic. Trees – soused in light during the day – now look mysteriously beautiful in ways we never normally see except (as now) when they're lit artificially. Now they're magical and otherworldly, as if the unwonted illumination reveals the secret life of their nocturnal groves which we've never noticed, never been vouchsafed, before. Shadows suggest mystery too, and lure you and your imagination to a degree that never happens in daylight. Unicorns are possible.

But most magical of all at night is being able to hear music, but not necessarily to perceive its source. It reaches you – like scent – with no visible agency. Like Prospero's enchanted island – an isle that's 'full of noises/ Sounds and sweet airs', says Caliban – everything (yourself included) is spellbound.[1]

As a theatre of love, the half-lit garden has no peer. The touch of a hand (when there's light to see only the ghost of a face) recovers an ancient sense of connection lost in the candour of daylight. That warmth, even in fingers – you'd never registered that calorific glow quite so closely as you do tonight. The tone of a voice when you can't see the lips absorbs your attention as if you were listening to music.

English literature, or literature in English, is full of great set-piece garden parties: Milton's *Comus* and the sheep-shearing festivities (a masque in all but name) in *The Winter's Tale* (and defying the play's title, not being set in winter at all) – and then Ariel's world, Shakespeare's masque in *The Tempest* (for all that Caliban chops wood for a winter's fire as well as the kitchen?), seems never to know the fall of the leaf. The Mad Hatter's tea party is hardly the most conventional of *plein-air* festivities, but it must be the most celebrated – and the origin of the best moments of many a Cambridge May Ball, I should think, not least because they actually take place in June. Weather permitting, these are essentially *garden* parties. But the most lavish and extraordinary of all imaginary, ideal parties must be those given by Jay Gatsby in his garden at West Egg on the shores of Long Island Sound:

> In his blue gardens men and girls came and went like moths among the whisperings and the champagne and the stars . . . enough colored lights to make a Christmas tree of Gatsby's enormous garden . . . The lights grow brighter as the earth lurches away from the sun, and now the orchestra is playing yellow cocktail music . . . Laughter is easier minute by minute, spilled with prodigality, tipped out at a cheerful word . . . The first supper – there would be another one after midnight – was now being served . . . champagne was served in glasses bigger than finger-bowls.[2]

So gardens, in summer, excite us to extraordinary fluencies of social intercourse, of appetite, of imagination. Clothes become looser, morals too perhaps, and it must be because gardens themselves are freer, airier, somehow more natural places than the houses we go back to in winter.

I don't think it's some regressive gene in us taking us back to life on the savannah, and – apparently in contradiction to so much of the foregoing – I don't really think gardens essentially have it in them to be social places. Rather the reverse, but perhaps it is this gift of a balmy evening and being invited to share someone else's rather private, rather special, space for a few hours that goes some way towards making the garden party the special occasion that it so often feels like. It's best at night, though, and perhaps that's the essence of the spell: the normally secret nocturnal life of the garden opens briefly and then closes again once the lights go out.

In 1875 a garden party was given by the Duke of Sutherland in the grounds of Stafford House in London. Social intercourse apart, it was also a promotional event to encourage the use of biodegradable wicker coffins, and the guests could tour the gardens and review the variously available models: 'the scene was anything but the dismal, but rather partook of the gay.'[3]

That must have strained the power of the garden to the limit, and no record survives of whether the event – as a party – was a success. I like to think of the withies behaving true to their nature (if indeed they were willows) and sprouting up again twelve months later, after the interment. As an essay in entertainment, the project seems to have little to offer, but as a garden party bizarre enough to outdo even Lewis Carroll's fantasy, it deserves consideration.

One of the most moving photographic images I know – and one of the most powerful evocations of gardens – is the portrait of Lady Augusta Gregory (1852–1932) sitting underneath the catalpa tree in the garden of her beloved Coole Park in County Galway (illus. 38). She is solitary, a small dumpy figure occupying only a very small part of the picture, seen in shadow and profile against the light at the end of the tunnel of leaves. The path goes on past her into the light and the rest of the garden, but our gaze stops, thinking about what she might be contemplating, thinking about what she might be seeing as she looks steadily away from us and out into the garden. You can see the features and the character of her face only dimly. It's clear that this is an elderly woman, stooped, shrunken, leaving. And though you know that even if the tree and the bench were to go on indefinitely – likewise Yeats's Seven Woods and his famous visions of the 'nine-and-fifty swans' – this is an image of things passing and reflecting on things past.[4] Something about her solitariness, and something graceful, paradoxically careless but still dignified, speaks of a woman whose presence, however old and derelict, need make no effort whatsoever to cut a figure.

Heaven knows, Augusta Gregory had cause enough for personal sorrow. Married at 27, she was widowed at 39. Then she had

38 Lady Gregory beneath the catalpa tree at Coole Park, 1927. The autograph tree – unlike the venerable catalpa in this image – still stands a little further on, to the right of the path.

lost her only son, Robert, in January 1918. 'Soldier, scholar, horseman' (as Yeats put it), he died while piloting a fighter plane in Italy.[5] He was a gifted painter too. Augusta's nephew Hugh Lane, whom she loved almost as much as her son, had been drowned when the *Lusitania* was torpedoed off the Old Head of Kinsale in 1915. But she had achieved much, nevertheless, and in the shape of an ancient copper beech, it is memorialized in the garden where her guests must so often have walked, sat, talked and worked. She herself wrote plays for the theatre and transcribed and collected Irish folktales. She was a co-founder of the Abbey (the National Theatre of Ireland). But, above all, in her house and garden, she entertained, encouraged, admonished, subsidized, edited, advised, fed and watered an astonishing number of the greatest writers of the twentieth century.

And there she is, in this photograph, in 1927. It's late summer. The catalpa's flowering is over, but Japanese anemones are blooming in the bottom left foreground. Her poise, the dignity, the same black clothes remind me very much of another gardener: Gertrude Jekyll (1843–1932), Edwin Lutyens's 'Aunt Bumps' in the 1920 portrait by William Nicholson (now in the National Portrait Gallery).

Lady Gregory kept a record, as it were, of her friends and their visits to her library, her house and her garden. The record is in the form of initials cut into the bark of that copper beech in the garden – ranging from Yeats himself to Sean O'Casey, from John Synge to George Bernard Shaw. Cumulatively, this tree bears witness to one of the greatest garden parties there can ever have been or ever will be.

From time to time, reference has been made in this book to London's eighteenth-century pleasure gardens – Vauxhall, Ranelagh, Marylebone and the rest – places, par excellence, of perpetual garden partying. It's also been noted that in our own twenty-first century the tradition lives on very successfully indeed in Copenhagen's Tivoli Gardens, in Garsington's and Glyndebourne's opera seasons. The nineteenth century seems dull in comparison, and the festive spirit to have retired indoors as if the umbrella had won after all. But Vauxhall didn't finally close its gates until 1859, by which time its seventeenth-century beginnings as Fox-hall had been blotted out entirely by the teeming urban growth of South London. Yet the cultural need for such places didn't die with it. Cremorne Gardens kept going until 1877, when it too closed. There was a theatre there, a banqueting house. There were dance rooms and, of course, gardens. It was, by all accounts, a cheerful, popular, raucous place (and probably an embarrassment to genteel Chelsea). On one famous occasion, a certain Madame Genevieve drew huge crowds by walking on a tightrope strung across the Thames from the gardens. As at Vauxhall, there were nightly fireworks and, on special occasions, the re-enactments of battles. Pyrotechnics were a great attraction, and it was these fireworks that were the subject of Whistler's *Nocturne in Black and Gold* (*c.* 1875) – the painting which provoked a splenetic Ruskin to accuse Whistler of having flung 'a pot of paint in the public's face' and Whistler to counter with a libel action (illus. 34).[6] (Technically he won, though the judge – living up to that time-honoured convention of British philistinism masquerading as lovable eccentricity – awarded him only a farthing in damages.)

The Battersea Pleasure Gardens for the Festival of Britain in 1951 carried essentially the same formula into the twentieth century. There seems to be something about the South Bank which even now erupts from time to time into junketing. And elsewhere too. Pop concerts, which are huge commercial parties really, are beginning to occupy a somewhat similar space in the public imagination. Many such events take place not exactly in gardens or even parks (and certainly not those at Reading or Glastonbury) but still outside, and still somehow outside the jurisdiction of accepted social conventions. As in the pleasure gardens of the eighteenth and nineteenth centuries, the ostensible attraction is the music, but in reality people go there for the atmosphere (and booze, and camping out, and drugs, and everything else). Not exactly apart from the music (but not entirely entailed in it either), pop festivals have become a very lucrative way of selling people freedoms of one kind or another.

However you see it, and whatever era or style you fix your attention on, what is special about *plein-air* parties is the suspensions they imply of the ordinary conventions of the world and even of the laws of nature. At least in the privileged precincts of your imagination, it never rains. People are friendlier. Tolerance becomes the norm, and not just the best behaviour of occasional political correctness. Class barriers are loosened – ditto, possibly, sexual mores, purse strings and conventions of dress. The absolute moment of this is struck in Édouard Manet's *Le Déjeuner sur l'herbe* (1863), but, like holidays, it's only temporary and, like the garden itself, an artifice.

At its very heart is a willing but temporary suspension of disbelief. For a few hours we behave as if nature – the weather above us, the earth below us on which we sit or lie, the trees and plants around us – is where we belong or, better still, where we really belong if we are to bring out the best in ourselves and other people, and be very happy indeed. This is where no one has to work, or grow old, or even succumb to sleep and go to bed. The illusion is that we behave most naturally (generously, openly, carefreely) when the context is nature – the garden, the fields at Reading, the picnic at Box Hill. When the sun shines on us – either figuratively or even actually – we emerge, like gilded butterflies, as ourselves at our very best. The garden party is an act of faith on our part. It is a sort of social naturism without necessarily the nudity. For a few hours we want to believe that there are no snakes in the grass after all, there are no biting insects in the air, no storm clouds on the horizon. And it's an illusion, but it still speaks of some deeply printed wish (almost invisible by now) to find ourselves *naturally* happy.

39 George Frampton, *Peter Pan*, 1912, Kensington Gardens. Charming by design but altogether improbable (a left-handed pipe?), the bronze sculpture has become a national icon.

18

Peter and Pan

One of the strangest facts about the history of gardens is the identity, in the ancient world, of the deity who presides over these places. It is not a bit what we would expect now. In the first place, it wasn't female but male. We would have expected perhaps Chloris or Demeter – spirits of spring and agriculture and regeneration – or Hegemone or Persephone. Or, if not them, someone less rustic perhaps, someone more domesticated, more suggestive of the comfortable good life those patrons only hint at. Flora or Pomona perhaps. But actually not so. None of those is tutelary spirit of gardens in the ancient world.

The true identity of the god of ancient gardens delivers one of those shocks of the old which tug at the rug under the feet of our smug modernity. To the ancients and, through their legacy, to the succeeding phases of European history right up to the Renaissance, the god of gardens was not demure Flora, abundant Pomona or shape-changing Vertumnus, the giver of fruits. It wasn't even one of the nymphs or one of the dryads, those spirits of trees. No, the god of ancient gardens was Priapus – randy, flagrantly pornographic, exhibitionist Priapus.

Son of Aphrodite and wild Dionysus, Priapus had a mixed portfolio. He was patron of shepherds, fishermen and farmers, but essentially a god of fertility and generation, and only thus, by extension, of gardens. And Priapus' patronage of gardens still strikes us – like his brandished penis – as somewhat earthy, to say the least. That he should have held on to this position (as well as his 'post') well into the seventeenth century is perhaps more surprising still, but he did, at least in Italy, if not in Protestant northern Europe.

On the one hand, we have a vision of decorous, refined, intellectually articulated Renaissance gardens, and on the other this ridiculous, phallic exhibitionism – all those things they didn't tell you in classics lessons at school, but which you found out anyway: the candour in some of Catullus, the phallic altar at Delos, the priapic wall paintings at Pompeii. It's indeed true that Horace, Tibullus and Martial all wrote humorously and disparagingly about him, just as they did about the whole riotous tribe of satyrs and sileni. In their version of history, Priapus was really a bit of a joke, a sort of scarecrow – face painted red and perky phallus only signalling a warning at the garden gate to ward off carrot thieves – a sort of Mr McGregor with his trousers down. The *coup de grâce* to his dignity was reckoned (in sophisticated circles at least) to be the fact that his preferred sacrifice was that of a donkey: notoriously lustful but ultimately ridiculous.

The Greeks owned no angels. It's a curious omission, and one whose explanation would probably have to take account of two things. The first is that characteristically Greek tendency towards realism. Too hard-headed to allow of anything as fey as angels, Greek intellectuals would have perceived them as objects of ridicule much as we do now in the case of fairies, and at least partly so because angels were insubstantial, incorporeal, asexual – in a word, unreal. And the second explanatory factor is that the distance between the human and the divine, as it was perceived by the Greeks, was not so great as to allow of much room for some intermediate creatures anyway. It wasn't so much that humans were almost gods – though in Greek sculpture there's really no differentiation at all – as that the gods were, as often as not, all too human.

But the Greeks did give time and thought to transitional creatures who tended in the opposite direction – away from the human and towards the animal – most famously, the man-bull hybrid, the Minotaur, but also the fauns, those creatures, gentle on the whole, who give us our modern word *fauna*, and whose spirit Claude Debussy caught so languorously in the *Prélude à l'après-midi d'un faune* (1894). Then there were the centaurs, lustful, rapacious, clumsy, dipsomaniac creatures paradoxically so much at odds with their original, Chiron, who numbered among his student protégés Achilles (instructed by Chiron in the arts of war and music) and Asclepius (father of medicine, schooled in all the arts of healing). But then there were the satyrs – shaggy-legged, donkey-penised lords of misrule – credible enough as projections of men at their worst, their most exhibitionist, their most coarse.

Finally, there's the most mysterious, the most interesting of them all, and the one who came eventually to haunt the wilder fringes of gardens, or the margins of the true wilderness where it abuts on to the human: Pan. If Priapus was nominally the deity of gardens, in practice it seems that the role was actually far more

40 Thomas Robins's drawing of Pan's Lodge, Painswick, 1757, pen and ink on paper. Behind the fence in the foreground: PAN DEUS ARCADIÆ.

frequently filled by Pan from at least late antiquity onwards. Gradually Priapus was replaced by Pan. Or perhaps he changed himself into Pan, or Pan absorbed him, just as, in a sense, he drew *all* the gods into himself. You can see the blurred demarcations between Pan and Priapus in Nicolas Poussin's *A Bacchanalian Revel Before a Term* (1632–3). The 'term' (or herm, the upright pillar which becomes the torso of a man) has the head of Pan, but below the waist he's not hairy and goatish – and not demonstrably priapic either – but simply anatomically male.

Exactly when Pan completed his supplanting of Priapus is impossible to establish. Two small sightings of the process – something going on beneath the polished surfaces of culture, dealing perhaps with something essentially subversive – in England and Italy will serve to show the difficulty. Timothy Mowl uncovered some years ago evidence of what seems to have been a cult of Pan in the Gloucestershire town of Painswick. One of the finest houses there (Beacon House, built in 1757–9) has superb rococo plasterwork containing arcane references to, as well as explicit images of, Pan and his pastoral world. A mile and a half away, at a now lost pavilion dubbed Pan's Lodge, there seems also to have been a popular festival of Pan in the mid-eighteenth century. These annual processions were revived in the 1880s while a certain W. H. Seddon was vicar there, only to be discontinued under another vicar in the mid-twentieth century. Thomas Robins's 1757 drawings of Pan's Lodge and its surroundings make the connection very plain (illus. 40). Some of them even spell Painswick as 'Panswyck'.[1]

Some thirty years later, Richard Payne Knight (1751–1824) – member of Parliament and of the Society of Dilettanti – published *An Account of the Remains of the Worship of Priapus* (1786). He was also the author of a poem widely read and influentially attacking 'Capability' Brown: *The Landscape: A Didactic Poem* (1794). In its turn, this provoked a parody – John Matthews's *A Sketch, from The*

Landscape, a Didactic Poem (1794) – which closed with Knight envisioned as Priapus himself. Knight's *Account* is in the field of what we would now call cultural anthropology, and like many a work of anthropology since (especially if illustrated, and this one most emphatically is), in certain lights it could be read (albeit prudishly) as pornography. The first part of the book describes what the author understood to be the survival of an ancient cult of Priapus in the Italian town of Isernia. The second part is a survey of ancient archaeological remains (coins, gems, bronzes and sculptures – many of them from Knight's own collection) pertaining, as he saw it, to the widespread original practices of the cult in the ancient world.

Pan in England (albeit clad in the garb of folkloric and antiquarian scholarship) and Priapus in Italy (but recorded by an Englishman), and both of them within a few years of each other: it's impossible to see exactly where the one begins and the other ends.

Why should Pan have supplanted Priapus? Perhaps it was because, randy though he often is, Pan is still a good deal more modest than Priapus. He's never rampantly and explicitly priapic. His genitals are often quite modestly covered by the copious hair on his legs. As a result, he is much less seriously or embarrassingly ridiculous, but at the same time he is much more seriously interesting. Goat (and mindlessly generative, coarse and basely animal) below the waist, above it he is human – often beautifully human – and even spiritual as he conjures the mystery of music from his pipes. Pan evolved – perhaps even began – as a metaphor for the translation of animal lust into (remorseful) human love, for inspiration (literally, the act of breathing into) and for music. Listen to the closing movement of Francis Poulenc's *Sonate pour flûte et piano* (1957): towards the end of all the hectic, terpsichorean bustle of that finale, there's a brief but unmissably poignant, head-hurting wail. For 'flute' read 'pan-pipes'; for 'moment of musical dolour' read 'primeval *cri de cœur*': all the comfortable certainties of life we take for granted are dissolved, and even the music itself – the sureties of tonality, the elemental security of a steady pulse – is arrested for an age-long moment of *panic*.

For all his amorous chasing of the nymphs, Pan is, like them, a shy creature, a haunter of secret groves and mysterious caves where, if he can be glimpsed at all, he remains nonetheless elusive. His dwelling place is Arcadia, a region shaped partly by our own experience but also partly created by our imaginations, where intoxications of exhaustion or passion may grant visions of sublimity, and where the human may prefigure perhaps the divine. It's that compromise zone that was imagined then by the Greeks as Arcadia and that we recognize now, appropriately enough, as one of the most formative models of our gardens.

From time to time, over the centuries, it has always been possible to watch people taking up positions regarding Pan or his less modest alter ego, Priapus. John Evelyn implausibly (and rather comically) wrestles with his own prudishness. There is, he insists, nothing 'immodest' about Priapus in gardens, whom he reckons to have been a sun god; what the god holds in his right hand is 'a Scepter' ('to denote his regiment over Land & Sea') and, in his left, the genital 'because he sowes the Earth with Seedes'.[2] It is the context, however, that makes this shape-shifting – and our moralistic shadowboxing – both interesting and complicated.

To the cursory eye, taking in the literal superficies of appearances, most gardens are pagan – statues of classical deities perhaps, or it may be a vague but general apotheosis of Mother Nature, or something like that. Gardens have not often been, even in the heyday of Christendom, Christian places (where Pan might have morphed into the Good Shepherd, for example). But nor, beneath the surfaces, are gardens confessionally pagan places either. Instead, they're essentially Arcadian, pre-confessional. The same – but with a different confessional complexion – can be said of those gardens which, in the Middle Ages, were made explicitly to identify with and conform to the cult of the Virgin Mary. Only the literal surfaces (and lapidary, sculptural accessories) of these places conformed. The rest – the subtexts – resisted.

Thus it is that Pan – the idea of him, the ideas that he embodies – has outlived all his classical peers, just as he also antedates them in ways that we've been noticing. His name is cognate with the Sanskrit Pushan – a god of nomadic herdsmen – and far more ancient than the gods of Olympus or even the Titans. So ancient, so primitively primal is he that he represents in himself – and in the constellation of ideas that he incarnates – something like the very essence of what gardens have always meant, and not just in the past but even perhaps particularly now.

Of course, he is a fiction. And gardens are not. But fictions are the inventions – artful constructions of compression, selection and deletion – we employ to express the otherwise inexpressible. They're the lies we tell to find, and then to find words for, truths. This is the essence of our respect for and understanding of the nature and dynamics of myth. We've learnt respect for imagination (fiction, untruth, lies, if you like – and gardens *in the mind* are certainly exempla of those fictions) not only as a creative and recreative faculty, but as a cognitive one.

Like children, Pan is pre-religious, pre-confessional, but he's also – the top half of him at any rate – spiritual. In specifically English culture, and in the popular as well as the cultivated imagination, he seems to have shape-shifted sometimes into Puck, Hobgoblin, Robin Goodfellow – in Shakespeare, of course, but then in an ongoing succession from Drayton's *Nymphidia* (1627) to Kipling's *Puck of Pook's Hill* (1906) – and he's still with us: the child, the outlaw of gravity, the fairy (but an earthy one). His tutelage of gardens seen in this light seems suddenly and unarguably appropriate. And insofar as Pan is only impressionistically but somehow really emblematic of the spirit of gardens – that primal energy and wildness syndicated with the practice of highly sophisticated designing and shaping and cultivation – gardens themselves become slightly more identifiable as the spiritual places we all sense them to be anyway, even though we can't find the words to articulate what we feel. And if we use Pan, and what he stands for, as something like a magnetic metaphor which draws into itself the various and disparate components that go to make up our vision of what gardens are, what they are for and how they work their meanings into the tissues of our minds, then the matter becomes clearer still, though without, of course, allowing us to reach any necessarily hard and fast conclusions. We are, after all, postmodern castaways ourselves.

There's a subclause to this. Just as Pan probably represents one of the gods of the infancy of our race, one of our first intimations of ourselves as creatures of spirit as well as of matter, so do we need to identify and recover some of the child in ourselves in order to understand our relations with and need for gardens. And yet at the same time, we don't want to lose sight of our adult selves either. We need, therefore, both to be pre-confessional, pre-educated innocents, open to the numinous, the atavistic and the wonderful – to be, in short, capable of enchantment – and to be post-educated, disillusioned, realistic, honestly enlightened, post-Weberian, disenchanted adults.

The Greeks had a word for how we do it: *poiesis*, 'making' – originally the making of anything from a loaf of bread to the making of sense, but eventually the word settled down in favour of the last, and gave us our word *poet*, sense-maker. And the tools and materials these makers – be they poets, painters, musicians, architects or gardeners – used to make their sense were metaphors: abstractions in principle but verities in realization, such as tragedy and comedy, personifications such as gods – impulses, metaphors all of them – to give form to the longings and fears inherent in the human condition (love, death, impermanence, value and so on). In that way we're invited to trust the metaphor and the metaphorical vision and put our heads in the clouds, while still keeping our feet on the ground and our hands in the soil: *homo topiarius*, man the gardener.

On an individual as well as on a collective level, gardens enable us to keep in touch with and even to recover some of our own remembered happiness as children. On a cultural level, as we've seen over and over again, gardens represent to us the recovery of our mythic Edens. This – as in the case of the national parks of the USA, and there not on a personal level but collectively – can be worked out on a huge and impersonalized scale. And that's an index of something deeply important.

At any rate, and be that as it may, gardens for adults are still the playgrounds of their imaginations. They're the places where the originally childlike connections between freedom and happiness, security and happiness, freedom and carefreeness, the natural and being happy, are remade, places where work is redeemed from labour (and mind-numbing, muscle-gruelling grind), where that curse on Adam, who must eat his bread 'in the sweat' of his brow (and Eve too, who shall indeed 'bring forth children' but 'in sorrow', for fertility and fecundity are stunted, begrudged even),[3] may be mitigated, and so there's no necessary dichotomy between *living* and *having to make a living* – a sort of recovered wholeness uncannily reminiscent of allotment keeping, actually. Cockaigne, the pan-European medieval conceit of a land of licence, plenty and easy living, became one of this utopian spirit's peculiarly English manifestations, a pseudonym for London itself, particularly the city's East End, where the Cockneys lived – a throwback to Eden itself, where work is not labour, where food grows effortlessly and is there for the eating.

To children, gardens are simply places to play. No one ever told a child to go out into the garden and work. Or go out into the garden and contemplate beauty. Or go out into the garden and grow up. To a child, the place and its purpose are self-evident. And this taking things for granted – all the things they see – betokens something prelapsarian, something Edenic. That, I suppose, is in essence why so many pieces of garden sculpture – so many of the actors we place in the theatre of our garden imaginations – are representations of children. And if they're not of children, they still suggest innocence, even (or is it especially?) the nudes. We could even say that gardens, or at least the way we use them as sculpture parks, evince tendencies to infantile regression in us. But in the vast majority of gardens and gardeners, it's not that simple, or crude, or embarrassing, at all. For adults, it's surely much more a case of the child in us, having been father to the man, seeking an expression of the impulse to keep alive the embers of primal imagination, primal play, the impulse to make the world all over again, and thus to make sense of it.

There's a vast sump of sentimentality in all this, though. Children aren't really like that at all. Or rather, if they are like that, they're also other things as well. But we persevere with our preferred versions: at one extreme, coy little shepherdesses and doe-eyed boys hugging the necks of Bambis and, at the other, the sexless, intellectualized nakednesses of a Venus born out of Botticelli or a David emasculated out of Michelangelo. Realistically – if we really did subscribe to a belief in an equation between innocence and the wild, if we really weren't shy of the thrush in our gardens smashing hell out of the snail, or the cat terrorizing the bird, or the bird ripping apart the worm – we should be having casts made not from Botticelli or Michelangelo (and still less from Disneyland or Marie Antoinette's fantasy world of milkmaids and jolly young swains), but of the *Laocoön* or that ancient bronze lion bringing down an agonized gazelle.

But we don't. We much prefer the prettified, the romanticized and the sanitized. Sir John Clerk of Penicuik's remarks in 1727 about Lord Cadogan's Caversham Park ring true for many another garden right up to the present day. The gardens, he said, had been recently laid out at 'vast expense' but 'without either taste or judgement'. Of the sculpture he observed: 'very bad . . . His Lordship . . . brought several large marble statues from Holland. There are several Godesses but of such a clumsy make as one may See they were made in a Country where women are welcomed by the pound of A–se' – from which one infers that he didn't like Rubens either.[4] There is indeed a clumsy, pretty tasteless, clothes-shedding, kitschy, sentimentalizing tendency in an awful lot of garden sculpture.

Even Pan – though he never was simply a thoroughgoing villain, a mere rapist – has often been subjected to the same sanitizing, romanticizing treatment. There he is in Kensington Gardens (though, of course, we know him there now as Peter Pan). Instead of his original's rough hairiness below the waist, he sports a modest, androgynous skirt. Instead of Pan's pipes, formed out of Syrinx's fear of rape, we have the little boy tootling away on his one-handed flute (actually an aulos), and beneath him the whole squirrelly, butterflied world of nature dances artlessly to his tune. Charmed they all are, and charming, but not real. Thus George Frampton's sculpture of 1912 (illus. 39).

Nevertheless, the real Pan won't go away. He too has a kind of innocence. When Syrinx metamorphoses into reeds before his very eyes, he is as genuinely sorry and uncomprehendingly distressed as Lennie in John Steinbeck's *Of Mice and Men* (1937), who cannot stop himself from crushing the mice, rabbits and puppies he sought really only to caress. Pan is not the opposite pole to Peter. Pan is not civilized and educated, trained and culturally conditioned (like children, eventually), but nor is he truly wild either. He belongs instead to the place occasionally glimpsed but much more often imagined: the half-understood, half-lived-in world of Arcadia, the place the ancients identified as our real spiritual home, though we might call it the land of heart's desire.

All the more strange it is then – because we had always taken it to be a fiction – to learn that Arcadia is a real place too. It is the remote interior of the Peloponnese, but so remotely perceived as the back of beyond by the original Attic sophisticates that it morphed into the mythical even while it really existed. It thus became – for them and indeed for us – a case of something like an inversion of the old Voltairean adage about God: if Arcadia really did exist, it would be necessary to dematerialize it, make a myth of it.

The early Christian Church noticed Pan's cloven hooves, and that was quite enough to disqualify him from reinvention as a refurbished Christian saint in the way that quite a few other deities, Greek and Celtic, were. The Church didn't bother to look for redeeming, compensating features: his beautiful, musicianly hands, for example. Before them, the Greeks, albeit obliquely, had sensed something of their own nature in the plight of the sacrificial goat, goat below the waist but with something like a theophany above it. Their explanation of the human condition – that we do what we will, but we cannot necessarily will what we do – evolved into the great metaphor we know as tragedy. According to this model, in the end we're doomed, but we can be magnificent in our struggle against that doom: *tragedy*, the word, comes from *tragos*, which means 'goat'. Only listen to the plaintive bleat of a goat being led to the slaughter, and it's easy to see (to hear) the connection. It's easier still, however, to miss the irony that this imagery must have had its origins in the public slaughter of goats – the ritual sacrifice, the bloodletting of the scapegoat – which everyone would have witnessed and willed because it appeased the gods, and it softened the rod of Fate upon the backs of humankind. Why it should have been a goat that was deemed both appropriate and sufficient is a fascinating problem, and one very close to the heart of the psychological territory we are discussing with respect to gardens.

So Pan is not quite all he appears to be. He actually replicates and embodies psychological truths about human nature which – almost uncluttered in his case by sentimentality – turn out to be emblematic of our relations with nature at large. Pan, being half-goat, is the very pattern of humankind's 'goatish disposition' – the *real* thing, the 'poor, bare, forked animal', the unregenerate beast, 'forked', bifurcated.[5] But in the case of Pan (and his ilk, the fauns), not all base animal either.[6] Pan makes music, intuits harmony. The angel in him seeks to balance, and mysteriously to complement, the beast.

Peter – the other half of Peter Pan – is not quite all he seems either. He's certainly not necessarily the castrated *puer aeternus* of our fantasized daydreaming. But nor is he the Beast, the Lord of the Flies, the lieutenant of Fallen Satan that William Golding (1911–1993) uncovers for us when the veneers of civilization and education are gradually stripped away from his boys on their paradise island, their untouched original Eden. Peter is the best of childhood, as well as the sentimentalized, the impossibly idealized. He is all the things we've mislaid in the course of becoming adult. He is, for example, the refusal to grow up because, in some senses, it's a trap – to put on a uniform to shoot his fellows in war, to leave a beggar's hand empty on the street, or first to sympathize with the cry of the stricken goat but then to eat it. He has no knowledge of death. Like all children, he behaves as if he were immortal. And therein lies, I suppose, the heart of our affection for children, our fascination and distrust of childhood. And of our careful envy and protectiveness.

We are to visit, finally, two gardens. They belong, as I believe gardens should, to both Peter and Pan. And then, to close, I want briefly to return once more to Kensington Gardens.

We go first to Pangbourne in Berkshire, on the banks of the lazy Thames, still young and nowhere near grand enough yet to make its entry into London. Toad – he of the egregious driving offences – has been apprehended at last. All those promises of reform he gave came to nothing. Even Badger's last-ditch attempt to force him to mend his ways by confining him to his bedroom until he categorically promised to behave himself had been undone by Toad's guile. Badger, Mole and Rat planned to have kept him there until 'the poison [had] worked itself out of his system' and he really had been 'converted' to 'a proper point of view'.[7] But he escaped and reoffended.

Toad is tried, convicted, and duly and dreadfully conveyed away to incarceration. Shocked but ruefully grateful for the peace which has descended upon the River Bank now that Toad is locked up, the animals are settling again into the naturally lazy rhythms of summer. Ratty, free now from the exertions of trying to reform Toad, has resolved to keep the promise of his long-deferred visit to Otter. On this errand he has been gone for some hours, and a balmy twilight is closing in on the high summer's evening. Mole is asleep, out of doors because of the heat, in the cool shade of some dock leaves, but he rouses himself when he hears Ratty's returning footsteps. Mole expects speech. But Ratty sits down, 'gazing thoughtfully into the river, silent and pre-occupied'.[8] There's something on his mind.

Eventually, Mole learns what it is. Little Portly, Otter's son and apple of his father's eye, has gone missing. That's often been the case before, but never for so very long. Otter and all his kin have searched high and low, but they've found no sign anywhere of him. Otter, despairing, his mind full of the spectres of dangerous weirs, of traps, and of a child who can barely swim, has been reduced to a solitary nocturnal vigil by the shallow pool where he first introduced his son to water and where Portly had caught his first fish.

Ratty and Mole can't think of going to bed with such disturbing news in their heads. Instead, they take to the river in their boat. Ratty does the skulling. Mole steers. And upstream they go, on and on, till the moon eventually rises. And something unnatural, some sort of spellbound mood, takes over. The world about them – 'meadows wide-spread, and quiet gardens, and the river itself from bank to bank' – was familiar enough, 'but with a difference that was tremendous'.[9] The difference is not exactly identified, but it impresses itself upon the two night-searchers with an intensity which suggests – rightly, as it turns out – a kind of awe. They change places and Mole rows.

They search the banks systematically but find nothing. The moon slides down the sky and is gone. The night is almost finished. The edge of the sky begins to glimmer again, but this time in the east with the duller light of day and the failure of their quest. A bird suddenly sings and then, equally suddenly, falls silent. A light breeze moves the reeds to rustle. Mole casts a glance at Ratty. He's transfixed with the effort to listen, but to listen to what?

Piping, he says. 'Such music I never dreamed of, and the call in it is stronger even than the music is sweet! Row on, Mole, row! For the music and the call must be for us.'[10]

Mole obeys but can hear nothing. On creeps the light, on and in. Ratty, 'rapt, transported, trembling', drops the rudder strings. They reach a place where the river divides, and they follow a backwater whither the sound is luring them. Magical sights begin to complement magical sounds. Crepuscular flowers of purple make their presence felt as no ordinary flowers. They are 'gemm[ing] the water's edge'.[11]

Then Mole catches the music too. Awestruck, he notices tears on his listening companion's face, and he too 'bow[s] his head and underst[ands]'. In response to this awe-inspiring, summoning, ethereal music, they move across the water. Once more, sight reinforces sound, and scent joins in too. The meadow grass, emerald in that early morning light, is of a 'greenness unsurpassable'. 'Never ha[ve] they noticed the roses so vivid, the willow-herb so riotous, the meadow-sweet so odorous and pervading.' They're the first discoverers of a riverine Eden on the morning of the first day of a new world. Miraculously, they pass without harm through a weir and draw the boat up on the banks of the island that lies beyond it, 'behind a veil' of solemn, silent expectancy. Speechless, they know they have been called by the music, 'called and chosen'. They climb out of the boat and up the bank until they reach level ground, a 'little lawn of a marvellous green set round with Nature's own orchard-trees – crab-apple, wild cherry, and sloe'.[12]

Like an explorer stumbling upon an aboriginal, unspoilt, hitherto undiscovered world – powerfully, if serendipitously,

41 Front board of the first edition of Kenneth Grahame's *The Wind in the Willows* (1908), showing the Great God Pan. Ratty and Mole crouch in awe in the foreground. The bulrushes quietly suggest the safety of the woven cradle made for Moses in the Bible.

anticipating Bruce Chatwin's *The Songlines* (1987) indeed – Rat whispers: 'This is the place of my song-dream, the place the music played to me . . . Here, in this holy place, here if anywhere, surely we shall find Him!' (illus. 41).[13]

The capital 'H' is not mine. It's there in the text of this extraordinary central chapter of *The Wind in the Willows* (1908), where, for a few pages, all the high jinks of Toad, the great adventures of the Wild Wood, the grand comedy of the Billingsgate barge-woman and the gangsterism of the venial stoats are suddenly suspended. Mole and Ratty are vouchsafed, but only for a moment, a vision of a god.

Kenneth Grahame (1859–1932) artfully slips into his text – at the moment that they step into this perfection of all gardens (but before their gaze strikes upon the god) – the remark that Rat and Mole feel 'no panic terror', and yet it is indeed Pan that they behold. He smiles at them, his pipes relaxed in the moment after leaving his lips. And 'nestling between his very hooves', fast asleep, lies Little Portly. Grahame doesn't actually name this epiphany. Rat and Mole were, he says, looking into the eyes of 'the Friend and Helper'.[14]

And then the vision is closed. The rising sun wipes their eyes with another sort of light. Suddenly, the birds sing again. A 'capricious little breeze' blows over them, bringing with it 'instant oblivion'. 'I beg your pardon; what did you say, Rat?' asks Mole, rubbing his eyes. 'I think I was only remarking,' says Rat, puzzled, 'that this was the right sort of place, and that here, if anywhere, we should find him.'[15] That earlier 'H' shrinks into the everyday, a dull, quotidian lower case 'h'.

Portly wakes up. Only two telltales remain to support the truth of their experience. Portly searches, and searches more and more frantically, for something unnamed but lost. Then he bursts into tears to signal the 'black moment' when he knows that, whatever it is he has been seeking, it'll never again be found. Rat pauses 'long and doubtfully at certain hoof-marks' imprinted deeply in the sward. 'Some – great – animal – has been here,' he murmurs slowly.[16]

On the way back, both Rat and Mole think they hear the music again – or is it only the wind in the reeds, the wind in the willows? – and they think there may even have been words to the music, but only in the sense that the beautiful sound 'passes into words' – the open window of language – and then out again. Almost all they can glean of these mysterious lyrics is the repeated charm, the spellbinding mantra '*forget, forget*'.[17]

This chapter ('The Piper at the Gates of Dawn') at the very midway point (and perhaps at the heart) of the book adds only a little to the plot and nothing to the ostensible themes of the book as a whole. Indeed, it suspends both narrative and theme in its clouds of mystery. Some later editions of this much-reprinted book simply leave the chapter out altogether. 'Sensitive abridgement', the blurb may call it. But I think something else is going on too. Something of protective censorship?

What did the eight-year-old boy, Grahame's son, Alastair ('Mouse'), the original recipient of the story, make of it? We don't know and never shall. He died, apparently by suicide, crushed by a train, while still an undergraduate at Oxford. It's tempting, though, to think that he too would have been puzzled as well as charmed by this Great God Pan episode. Tempting, but actually it's unlikely. He would not have been old enough to have read two of his father's books which had already been published – *The Golden Age* (1895) and *Dream Days* (1898), both of them reminiscences of childhood (and the former a great favourite with Kaiser Wilhelm II of all people) – but Mouse must have sensed his father's extraordinary care for the memory of his own childhood and for the setting of it in the geographical milieu of the middle reaches of the River Thames, a lazy river running through rich, fertile meadows. This region of the mind as much as of the literal geography must surely have been familiar to him too from his father's so frequent and so affectionate remembering of his own childhood in Cookham Dean, a few miles further downriver from Pangbourne. Grahame – the author of these books – had been brought up there by his grandmother, his mother having died when he was five and his father having abandoned his children, gone off to France, never being seen again. In any case, at least in terms of topography, it's the same willowy, watery idyll of childhood as Alastair's Pangbourne. And as for the strange chapter we've been looking at, Mouse may not have known that his father's first published book was called *Pagan Papers* (1894), but the ideas and attitudes that inform that book must surely have coloured the gentle way in which he too had been brought up.

We might take these books – *The Wind in the Willows* included, and indeed its kin 'The Pied Piper of Hamelin' in the Grimm brothers' fairytales and Browning's poem – as subversive, anti-Christian polemic. But we would be wrong. Explicitly, the book for Alastair is not religious – or anti-religious – at all. It's really just an affectionate, animal fantasy story for children, but Grahame does place special value in it upon the *vision* of children: those ingenuous, untutored perspectives that exasperate parents who want their children to grow up, and those unfamiliar ways of seeing familiar things which charm and fascinate those parents who don't. In Grahame's terms – and there was a sort of vogue for 'pagan' posturing in the air at that time anyway (the first decade of the twentieth century) – that peculiar vision of children is itself 'pagan'. It is pre-religious, innocent and illuminating to the jaded eyes of adults.

We shall probably never know everything about the genesis of *The Wind in the Willows*. Was it perhaps prompted by something as simple and elemental as the boy not getting his tongue around the *g* in Pangbourne, and inquiring thus whether Pan lived in 'Panbourne'? But that the book represents a golden vision of life, and of a place to live in, seen through the eyes of a child (or of small animals, and Mouse was one of those), and that the mysterious heart of this place-of-the-mind is a fabulous, numinous garden, both natural and supernatural – the end of their quest, the goal of their longings – none of that can be denied or fail to cast its spell. For evidence of the last, we have only to look at its classic afterlives (books, films, ballets, stage plays) and the generations of children who have obliged their parents to 'read that to me again, please'.

Perhaps the essence of this epicentral episode is that children are apt to take gods – their reality – for granted. And then that they feel neither especially alarmed nor privileged by encountering them. And lastly that they are most likely to do so in a garden. But what is going on in the mind of an adult is possibly something more curious still. Adults have not a memory for the thing itself, but register nonetheless the *forgetting* of it. We don't so much forget to remember as remember to forget. Or perhaps it is that though we can't remember its presence yet, even years later we're not entirely unaware of its absence. In any case a psychological distance has been imposed whose telltale is that sense of loss which a good deal of this book you are reading now has been concerned with. At the same time, however, there remains also enough of a residue – of delight, of the sense of a charmed life in a charmed world, of those 'clouds of glory' that Wordsworth says we were 'trailing' behind us when we came into this world – so that we're still quietly but compulsively driven to try to recover it.[18] 'The Child' – as Wordsworth again has it – is indeed in some sense 'Father of the Man'.[19]

We're still at Pangbourne, but this time in the company of the painter John Singer Sargent (1856–1925), and the occasion is not Kenneth Grahame's long, golden Edwardian afternoon, but a late summer evening in 1885. *Huckleberry Finn* – another outdoor idyll of childhood and rivers – has just been published; Johannes

Brahms is completing his fourth and last symphony, Louis Pasteur is making the first successful inoculations against rabies, and Queen Victoria's Golden Jubilee is only two years away. Monet's new garden at Giverny is just two years old. Whiling away pleasant hours in a boat on the Thames is about to become the late Victorian vogue (Jerome K. Jerome's *Three Men in a Boat* was published in 1889) whose eventual swansong we might see as *The Wind in the Willows*.

Sargent himself was out in a boat on the river. The night was just beginning to draw in, and he saw on the bank 'a charming thing . . . Two little girls in a garden at twilight lighting paper lanterns among the flowers from rose-tree to rose-tree'.[20] The impression of it (there's a good deal of Impressionism about his English vision) – fleeting but so vivid – gripped him. Working through the late summer and autumn, he made a start, at first with the idea of painting only a single figure, and then with two figures, Polly and Dolly, the eleven- and seven-year-old daughters of Frederick Barnard, the illustrator. Special white dresses were made for the girls. Masses of sketches and studies in pencil, and then oil sketches of the effects of candlelight on faces and flowers, went hand in hand with the making of the finished picture, but it wasn't easy. There were reports of Sargent wiping out the previous day's work time after time. The shape and size changed too, from oblong to almost square, a rather 'modern' thing to do, in fact. Sargent's painting is now reckoned a landmark in English painting in general and 'perhaps the greatest of all garden paintings' (illus. 35).[21]

This isn't a portrait, but nor is it quite a landscape. Neither of the girls' faces is clearly represented. Instead, they're both looking down, and their faces glow softly as if they too were emanations of the lamps they're lighting, and that glow, both reflected by and seemingly emanating from the faces, hints at the same 'glory', the nimbus of light that envelops the child in Wordsworth's 'Immortality' Ode. This painting – eighty years on – is at some level a gloss on Wordsworth's great poem.

It follows that the real subject of the painting is light: the natural, muted, half-light of the evening and the artificial glow of creamy-pink and orange light from the paper lanterns the girls have lit and hung in the trees. These lights play on the girls' white dresses, their white faces, on the tall white lilies above their heads and the very dusky-red roses and carnations which cluster around their waists and shoulders. Given that the lily is the time-honoured wand of Mary, the Virgin, there's a faint echo of innocence, holiness.

The title *Carnation, Lily, Lily, Rose* duplicates a line from a music hall song, 'The Wreath' by Joseph Mazzinghi, but I'd like to think it may have been first suggested by the mild confusion of instructions that must have arisen often enough as the two girls posed for the painting: *Dolly stand here*; *Polly turn your head a little*; *Polly look down*; *Dolly give Polly your Lolly . . . no, I mean your Lily* . . . Dolly, Polly, Lolly, Lily.

The painting combines three great themes: gardens (and the magic of certain lights in gardens), flowers (and the traditional symbolism of flowers) and the children's beautiful, original innocence. Not very far away are Sargent's oblique allusions to paintings of the Annunciation – all those old masters, of course, but Dante Gabriel Rossetti's *Ecce Ancilla Domini* of 1850 too – and to the *hortus conclusus* of the Virgin's bower, with all those iconographical associations of roses and lilies in the vocabulary of medieval and Renaissance paintings. But this painting is essentially secular. Some precedent exists in John Everett Millais's *Ophelia* (1851–2). Sargent must have known the picture. A similarly dense impression of an enclosed world apart is achieved in it by the reeds, branches and flowers so close up to the figure. The *Ophelia* is itself a sort of valedictory gloss upon the stock attitude and gestures of centuries of Annunciations. If you turn the picture upright through ninety degrees, you'll see better what I mean. Seen thus, the figure will be standing, her face transfigured, one hand making the conventional Marian gesture of modesty, and the other holding a wand of flowers.

In Sargent's picture, the translation from the sacred to the secular is complete, and it is convincing, and yet even after it's done, there's a further translation back into something magical, mysterious, luminous and numinous: a garden at twilight. Both the children – perfectly secularized as pieces of white-dressed chinoiserie – and the lanterns suggest the Chinese, or the westernized vogue for things Chinese which was all the rage in the 1880s. But the girls here are the originators, and sole inhabitants, of a new world, a place set apart, a place of their own making through the power of their poetic imaginations. In this painting, new planets hang in the firmament all around them, and each girl – suggestively moon-faced, as in the conventional western perception of an Asian face – is about to set one more planet into place as the globes in their hands (which they have just lit) are hung up in the trees. Above them the almost literally star-shaped blooms of the lilies spangle the mysterious green spaces of this new cosmos, and beneath their feet the lesser lights of small roses and carnations glimmer in a stellar vastness of dark grey-green. There's nearly something Blakean about this, as in the older painter's last illustration to the Book of Job, where, all travail over, 'the morning stars sang together', as they did in the first days of Creation.[22]

It could be argued that all this is about paintings – or literary evocations – of gardens rather than about the gardens themselves, but that's my very point: more often than we probably realize, real gardens are – metaphorically and imaginatively – constructed as pictures in the mind's eye. Gardens are pictures of paintings, and those paintings are made up of all the elements of the cultural, pre-cultural and personal resonances, reverberations and baggage accumulated in our lives so far, both as individuals and as a species. To be talking about paintings rather than 'real' gardens is not an evasion or a displacement. It's almost the very heart of the matter.

The child in us fathers the adult, and the adult – the one who makes the places we call gardens – returns to these places something precious from their childhood recovered, restored and re-placed. All the rest of the things gardens *can* mean – territorial possession, the hobby of a retired person, the obsession of a plantsman, the passion of a real enthusiast, the vision of an artist, the laboratory of scientific horticulture, the showcase of snobbery, of macho-machine operations and of fussy orderliness – all these are types of gardens and gardening we would recognize, but so are those other gardens in which mechanical time is re-cogged into more temperate, natural rhythms, a locus of peacefulness, artfulness. They're true too, at least for some people, some of the time.

But if Kensington Gardens were to be allowed to stand, for a moment, as a map of these worlds compressed into the single space of only a few acres, something revealing occurs. Peter Pan stands in one corner surely enough. It's the part where J. M. Barrie (1860–1937) used to walk his Newfoundland dog, Luath, the model for Nana in the story of *The Boy Who Wouldn't Grow Up*. But elsewhere in these same gardens, and not far away, Harriet Westbrook (1795–1816), first wife of the poet Percy Bysshe Shelley (1792–1822), drowned herself in the Long Water. It was winter of the year 1816, frosty and – as it seemed to her – friendless and meaningless. Shelley had dumped her and their two children in favour of Mary Wollstonecraft Godwin, who would become his second wife and, in due course, author of *Frankenstein* (1818). The lines quoted below, first published after Shelley's own death under his widow's supervision, were (deliberately or to put people off the scent of something shameful?) dated to 1815, but latterly have been widely thought to be Percy's dirge for Harriet, the woman he had so wronged, and – if this is the case – could not have been written before December 1816. Probably not accidentally, they borrow the image of 'the visiting moon' from Shakespeare's *Antony and Cleopatra*, the story of another abandoned woman.[23]

The moon made thy lips pale, beloved –
The wind made thy bosom chill –
The night did shed on thy dear head
Its frozen dew, and thou didst lie
Where the bitter breath of the naked sky
Might visit thee at will.[24]

That this lonely, terrible thing should have happened in what we think of as the companionable, familiar Kensington Gardens is grim and shocking. In an analogous way, *The Wind in the Willows* – the book par excellence of the garden of England – must have become for Kenneth Grahame not only the idyll of a golden, pagan world of childhood but the awful reminder of his son's death.

In myth, a garden is where, as children in the earth's history, we came from. In fact, it is also where we – most of us in one form or another – end. But it is what we do, however, between those beginnings and endings that matters, just as what we do in between the sometimes contradictory, sometimes complementary poles of our natures – the Peter and the Pan, as it were – is often what matters so much more than we can generally see clearly in the patterns of our lives and in the shapes of some of the things we do, the making of gardens in particular. It is Pan who begets Peter; Peter who begets Pan. Elizabeth Barrett Browning (1806–1861) has it thus in one of her poems: Pan as both beast and creative energy.

Yet half a beast is the great god Pan
To laugh, as he sits by the river,
Making a poet out of a man.[25]

Because gardens are metaphors, I want to close with one, and I'm taking it from Shelley's 'Hymn of Pan' (1820). The old god plays his instrument, and even the seas cease their movement and listen, dumbstruck like everything else in nature – birds, the 'wind in the reeds', 'bees on the bells of thyme' – by this wondrous sound:

> The Sileni, and Sylvans, and Fauns,
>   And the Nymphs of the woods and waves,
> To the edge of the moist river-lawns,
>   And the brink of the dewy caves,
> . . . all that did then attend and follow
> Were silent . . .

Silenced, in their cases, by the spell of Pan's 'sweet pipings'. But Apollo too – no slight musician himself – is stopped in his tracks and stands silent. In his case, however, it is not only 'love' that he feels but 'envy'.[26]

The idea that there are moments in our lives – our otherwise clumsy, ramshackle, inconsequential, uneventful lives – that even the gods (and they, surely, are metaphors themselves) could envy seems quite a good one. It offers itself as some means to measure our achievement after all, just as metaphors (and gods) are our best means sometimes to try to identify and understand things which are evident but not otherwise easily grasped in our lives. So we *can* imagine moments in life when even the gods (whether they be real indeed or simply our creations, our necessary fictions) might envy us: the first time we hear and understand Beethoven's late string quartet, opus 131; those moments when we stand like Keats's Cortez, 'Silent, upon a peak in Darien'; the first steps of the visitor into Sissinghurst's first court on a late May morning when, just for a moment, everything makes sense and the occasion fills us with awe.[27]

But it's harder, much harder, to imagine the gods ever envying us our material world. Could they ever pause and think, 'I like the look of that so much, I could live there'? Unlikely, I think, of cities; impossible now of churches and temples somehow; and ridiculous of palaces and holiday resorts, government chambers and corporate or multinational premises. They could perhaps, like us, linger, pause sometimes, in books, sometimes in the theatre, the concert hall and the cinema, and sometimes inside our heads. Indeed, to a degree, that's precisely what does happen, but never for very long, and never long enough for us entirely to satisfy our (or their) longing just to live . . . in places and in ways that simply make sense per se, instead of always having to be making it – having to manufacture sense, that is – for ourselves.

But there's one place – our gardens, the best of them – where I can imagine those gods being brought up short. They'd pause, look around perhaps, and then think: *Yes, even I could live here*. But it wouldn't just be a rapture, or a falling in love, or a *petit mort* of their confining immortality. There would have to be envy too. Sooner or later, they – the gods, past, present, future – would have to understand that it is we, not they, who made these places, these gardens, and, having had to do it – having been compelled to make them by something in us that we barely understand – it is we, not they, who got there first. It is we, not they, who deserve to belong.

REFERENCES

Introduction

1 Voltaire, *Candide, ou l'Optimisme* (Geneva, 1759), p. 294.
2 Horace Walpole, *Anecdotes of Painting in England* (Strawberry Hill, 1762–71), vol. IV, p. 138.
3 Dylan Thomas, 'The force that through the green fuse', in *18 Poems* (London, 1934), p. 17.

1 Mazes and Labyrinths

1 James Barclay, *A Complete and Universal Dictionary of the English Language* (Bungay, 1812), p. 589.
2 G. N. Maynard, 'The Ancient Labyrinth or Maze at Saffron Walden', *Essex Naturalist*, III (1889), pp. 244–7.
3 T. S. Eliot, *Four Quartets* (New York, 1943), p. 11.
4 Jacob E. Nyenhuis, *Myth and the Creative Process: Michael Ayrton and the Myth of Daedalus, the Maze Maker* (Detroit, MI, 2003), p. 140.
5 Francesco Colonna, *Hypnerotomachia Poliphili: The Strife of Love in a Dream*, trans. Joscelyn Godwin (London, 1999), p. 15.
6 Ibid., p. 19.

2 Gardens and Time

1 Walt Whitman, 'When lilacs last in the door-yard bloom'd', in *Sequel to Drum-Taps* (Washington, DC, 1865–6), p. 3.
2 William Shakespeare, *Antony and Cleopatra*, ed. John Wilders (London, 1995), p. 124.
3 Evelyn Carrington, 'Singing Games', *Folk-Lore Record*, III/2 (1881), pp. 169–73.
4 A. E. Housman, 'Loveliest of trees, the cherry now', in *A Shropshire Lad*, illustrated by William Hyde (London, 1908), p. 15.
5 Hugh Keyte and Andrew Parrott, eds, *The New Oxford Book of Carols* (Oxford, 1992), pp. 436–7.
6 Emily Dickinson, 'The vastest earthly Day', in *The Poems of Emily Dickinson*, ed. R. W. Franklin (Cambridge, MA, 1998), p. 1147.
7 ''Twas later when the summer went', ibid., p. 1133.
8 Thomas Browne, *Religio Medici, Hydriotaphia and the Garden of Cyrus*, ed. R.H.A. Robbins (Oxford, 1997), p. 189.
9 Ibid., p. 76.
10 Ibid., p. 128.

11 Edward Thomas, 'Fifty Faggots', in *The Annotated Collected Poems*, ed. Edna Longley (Tarset, 2008), p. 90.
12 Gerard Manley Hopkins, *Poems*, ed. Robert Bridges (London, 1918), p. 51.

3 The Garden as Theatre

1 Todd Longstaffe-Gowan, *English Garden Eccentrics* (London, 2022), p. 66.
2 W. B. Yeats, 'The Stolen Child', in *The Poems*, ed. Daniel Albright (London, 1992), pp. 44–5.
3 Nikolaus Pevsner, *The Englishness of English Art* (London, 1964), pp. 173–8.
4 John Keats, 'On a Grecian Urn', *Annals of the Fine Arts*, IV (1820), pp. 638–9.
5 Horace Walpole, *Anecdotes of Painting in England* (Strawberry Hill, 1762–71), vol. IV, p. 138.

4 INTERLUDE: Ilnacullin, County Cork, Ireland

1 Nigel Everett, *Wild Gardens: The Lost Demesnes of Bantry Bay* (Bantry, 2001), p. 167.

5 The Green Chapel

1 For the Middle English text, W.R.J. Barron, ed., *Sir Gawain and the Green Knight* (Manchester, 1974), p. 50.
2 Ibid., p. 114.
3 J. G. Frazer's *The Golden Bough* (London, 1890–1915) remains the classic source of information. Jessie Weston's *From Ritual to Romance* (Cambridge, 1920), particularly the chapter entitled 'The Symbols', is rich in ideas, and Joseph Campbell's *The Masks of God: Creative Mythology* (New York, 1968) proposes persuasive syntheses.
4 Churchill quoted in Jane Brown, *The Pursuit of Paradise: A Social History of Gardens and Gardening* (London, 1999), p. 82. Robert W. Rogers, *Outlines of the History of Early Babylonia* (Leipzig, 1895), p. 4.
5 Song of Solomon 4:12–15.
6 John Evelyn, *Elysium Britannicum, or The Royal Gardens*, ed. John E. Ingram (Philadelphia, PA, 2001), p. 31.
7 E. K. Chambers and F. Sidgwick, eds, *Early English Lyrics: Amorous, Divine, Moral and Trivial* (London, 1966), p. 148.
8 Wendell Clausen, *A Commentary on Virgil: Eclogues* (Oxford, 1994), p. 11.
9 Percy Bysshe Shelley, *Hellas: A Lyrical Drama* (London, 1822), p. 51.
10 Emily Dickinson, 'A narrow fellow in the grass', in *The Poems of Emily Dickinson*, ed. R. W. Franklin (Cambridge, MA, 1998), p. 952.
11 Nikolaus Pevsner, *The Leaves of Southwell* (London, 1945), p. 19.

6 INTERLUDE: St Mary's Churchyard, Mundon, Essex

1 Nikolaus Pevsner, *The Buildings of England: Essex*, 2nd edn, rev. Enid Radcliffe (London, 1965), p. 303.
2 Thomas Browne, *Religio Medici, Hydriotaphia and the Garden of Cyrus*, ed. R.H.A. Robbins (Oxford, 1997), p. 79.

3 Robert Frost, 'The Strong are Saying Nothing', in *A Further Range* (New York, 1936), p. 53.

7 The Green Study

1 Horace, 'Epistles II.II', in *Satires, Epistles, and Ars Poetica*, trans. H. Rushton Fairclough (Cambridge, MA, and London, 1929), p. 426.
2 Pliny, 'To Julius Naso', in *Letters and Panegyricus*, trans. Betty Radice (Cambridge, MA, and London, 1989), vol. I, p. 253.
3 'To Clusinius (?) Gallus', ibid., p. 139.
4 Ibid., p. 141.
5 Ibid., pp. 133–43.
6 Pliny, 'To Voconius Romanus', in *Letters, Books VIII–X, Panegyricus*, trans. Betty Radice (Cambridge, MA, and London, 1997), pp. 89–91.
7 Pliny, 'To Domitius Apollinaris', in *Letters and Panegyricus*, vol. I, p. 343.
8 Ibid., p. 351.
9 Ibid., p. 355.
10 'To Calpurnius Macer', ibid., p. 385.
11 'To Domitius Apollinaris', ibid., p. 355.
12 Alexander Pope, *An Epistle from Mr Pope to Dr Arbuthnot* (London, 1735), p. 1.
13 Alexander Pope, *The Works of Alexander Pope*, ed. Whitwell Elwin and William John Courthope (London, 1871–89), vol. VIII, p. 337.
14 John Serle, *A Plan of Mr Pope's Garden* (London, 1745).
15 Alexander Pope, *The Works of Alexander Pope*, ed. William Warburton (London, 1751), vol. IX, p. 203.
16 *Supplemental Volume to the Works of Alexander Pope* (London, 1825), p. 63.
17 Alexander Pope, trans., *The Odyssey of Homer* (London, 1725–6), vol. V, p. 279.
18 William Shenstone, *The Works in Verse and Prose, of William Shenstone* (London, 1764), vol. II, p. 125.
19 Joseph Spence, *Anecdotes, Observations, and Characters, of Books and Men* (London, 1820), p. 144.
20 Horace, *Satires, Epistles, and Ars Poetica*, p. 480.
21 Gilbert West, *Stowe, the Gardens of the Right Honourable Richard Lord Viscount Cobham* (London, 1732), pp. 14, 3.
22 Thomas More, *Utopia*, trans. Ralph Robinson, ed. J. H. Lupton (Oxford, 1895), p. 29.
23 Pope, *Epistle*, p. 6.
24 Pope, *Works* (1751), vol. I, p. 58.
25 Andrew Marvell, 'The Garden', in *Miscellaneous Poems* (London, 1681), p. 50.
26 Emily Charlotte Boyle, ed., *The Orrery Papers* (London, 1903), vol. II, p. 3.

8 INTERLUDE: Green Thoughts

1 Henry James, *English Hours* (London, 1905), p. 249.
2 Ibid.
3 F.W.H. Myers, *Essays Classical and Modern* (London, 1921), p. 495.

9 Garden Follies

1 Gwyn Headley and Wim Meulenkamp, *Follies, Grottoes and Garden Buildings* (London, 1999), pp. 501–5.
2 James Barclay, *A Complete and Universal Dictionary of the English Language* (Bungay, 1812), p. 359.
3 William Blake, *Blake's Poetry and Designs*, ed. Mary Lynn Johnson and John E. Grant, 2nd edn (New York and London, 2008), p. 72.
4 Oswald Zenker, *Schwetzingen Castle Gardens*, trans. Ernest Herbster, 5th edn (Schwetzingen, 1991), pp. 44–5.
5 For some of the facts here, Mark Amory, *Lord Berners: The Last Eccentric* (London, 1998).
6 Edward Lear, 'The Owl and the Pussy-Cat', *Our Young Folks*, VI/2 (1870), pp. 111–12.

10 INTERLUDE: Some Favourite Follies

1 Thomas Pakenham, *Meetings with Remarkable Trees* (London, 1997), p. 123.
2 James Bettley and Nikolaus Pevsner, *The Buildings of England: Essex* (New Haven, CT, and London, 2007), p. 135.

11 The Garden of England

1 William Blake, 'Jerusalem', in *Blake's Poetry and Designs*, ed. Mary Lynn Johnson and John E. Grant, 2nd edn (New York and London, 2008), p. 147.
2 Charles Dickens, *Great Expectations* (London, 1861), vol. II, pp. 95–6.
3 Ibid., p. 96.
4 Ibid., pp. 93, 96.
5 Ibid., p. 98.
6 Ibid., p. 98.
7 Ibid., pp. 214–16.
8 Oscar Wilde, *The Importance of Being Earnest* (London, 1899), p. 103.
9 W. Alexander Harvey, *The Model Village and its Cottages: Bournville* (London, 1906), p. 24.
10 Quoted in Standish Meacham, *Regaining Paradise: Englishness and the Early Garden City Movement* (New Haven, CT, and London, 1999), p. 29.
11 A 1939 song by Ross Parker and Hugh Charles.
12 *Cobbett's Weekly Register*, XLI (1822), column 1609.
13 Henry Grabar, *Paved Paradise: How Parking Explains the World* (New York, 2023), p. 71.
14 Royal Horticultural Society, 'Why We All Need Greening Grey Britain', www.rhs.org.uk, accessed 30 October 2023.
15 Jonathan Swift, *Travels into Several Remote Nations of the World* (London, 1726), vol. II, pp. 22–3.
16 Ibid., p. 16.
17 Ibid., p. 63.
18 Edward Thomas, *In Pursuit of Spring* (London, 1914), pp. 36–44.
19 Blake, *Poetry and Designs*, p. 148.

12 Gardens and Painting

1 Quoted in Joseph Spence, *Anecdotes, Observations, and Characters, of Books and Men* (London, 1820), p. 144.
2 Quoted in Donald F. Bond, ed., *The Spectator* (Oxford, 1987), vol. III, p. 552.
3 See, for example, Book 2 of John Milton, *Paradise Lost* (London, 1667): 'the dark'nd lantskip' (line 491).
4 Jourdan Le Cointe, *La Santé de Mars* (Paris, 1790), pp. 325–8.
5 Dorothy Stroud, *Capability Brown* (London, 1984), pp. 68–9.
6 George Jones, *Sir Francis Chantrey, RA: Recollections of his Life, Practice, and Opinions* (London, 1849), p. 122.
7 Thomas Creevey, *Thomas Creevey's Papers*, ed. John Gore (Harmondsworth, 1985), p. 293.
8 *The Examiner*, 18 February 1816, p. 109.
9 George Santayana, *Soliloquies in England and Later Soliloquies* (New York, 1922), p. 30.
10 John Fisher Murray, *A Picturesque Tour of the River Thames in Its Western Course* (London, 1845), p. 118.
11 John Ruskin, *Modern Painters* (London, 1843–60), vol. II, pp. 11–17.
12 Andrew Wilton and Rosalind Mallord Turner, *Painting and Poetry: Turner's 'Verse Book' and his Work of 1804–1812* (London, 1990), p. 50.
13 John Keats, *Selected Letters*, ed. Robert Gittings and Jon Mee (Oxford, 2002), p. 62.
14 Ibid., p. 63.

13 INTERLUDE: Essex and Suffolk, Giverny and Arles

1 Beth Chatto, 'Sir Cedric Morris, Artist-Gardener', in *Hortus Revisited*, ed. David Wheeler (London, 2008), pp. 14–21.
2 See Tony Venison's entry in Gwynneth Reynolds and Diana Grace, eds, *Benton End Remembered* (London, 2002), pp. 109–12.
3 Tony Venison quoted in Janet Waymark, *Cedric Morris: A Life in Art and Plants* (London, 2019), p. 130.
4 Andy Friend, *John Nash: The Landscape of Love and Solace* (London, 2020), p. 53.
5 'Le motif est quelque chose de secondaire, ce que je veux reproduire, c'est ce qu'il y a entre le motif et moi'; see 'Citations', www.claudemonetgiverny.fr, accessed 5 October 2023.
6 Mark Roskill, ed., *The Letters of Vincent van Gogh* (London, 1963), p. 72.
7 Vincent van Gogh to Emile Bernard, 22 May 1888, in *Vincent van Gogh: The Letters*, ed. Leo Jansen, Hans Luijten and Nienke Bakker, https://vangoghletters.org, accessed 6 October 2023.
8 Vincent to Paul Gauguin, 17 October 1888, ibid.
9 Vincent to Theo van Gogh, 8 October 1888, ibid.
10 Vincent to Paul Gauguin, 3 October 1888, ibid.
11 Vincent to Theo van Gogh, 18 August 1888, ibid.
12 Vincent to Theo van Gogh, 8 September 1888, ibid.
13 *Minstrelsy of the Scottish Border* (Kelso, 1802), vol. II, p. 112.
14 See, for example, Gauguin's description of *D'où venons-nous? Que sommes-nous? Où allons-nous?* (1897–8). Ronald Alley, *Gauguin* (Feltham, 1968), p. 19.

14 Gardens and Music

1 Christopher Lloyd, *The Well-Tempered Garden* (New York, 1971), p. 9.
2 Andrew Marvell, 'The Garden', in *Miscellaneous Poems* (London, 1681), p. 50.
3 J. G. Frazer, *The Golden Bough: A Study in Comparative Religion* (London, 1890), vol. II, pp. 140–47.
4 John Keats, 'La Belle Dame sans Merci', *The Indicator*, I (1820), p. 248.
5 Michel Saudan and Sylvia Saudan-Skira, *From Folly to Follies* (Cologne, 1997), pp. 110–11.
6 John Evelyn, *Elysium Britannicum, or The Royal Gardens*, ed. John E. Ingram (Philadelphia, PA, 2001), p. 230.
7 Cindy Carcamo, 'Musician Turns Border Fence into Wall of Sounds', *Los Angeles Times*, www.latimes.com, 30 January 2014.
8 Vivian Russell, *Edith Wharton's Italian Gardens* (London, 1997), p. 185.
9 Charles de Brosses, *Le Président de Brosses en Italie*, ed. M. R. Colomb, 2nd edn (Paris, 1858), vol. II, p. 313.
10 Donald F. Bond, ed., *The Spectator* (Oxford, 1987), vol. IV, p. 390.
11 [John Lockman], *A Sketch of the Spring-Gardens, Vaux-Hall; In a Letter to a Noble Lord* (London, [1751]), p. 20. David Coke, *The Muse's Bower: Vauxhall Gardens 1728–1786*, exh. cat., Gainsborough's House (Sudbury, 1978), not paginated.
12 Bond, *The Spectator*, vol. III, p. 439.
13 Quoted in Andrew Lambirth, *Ivon Hitchens: The Painter in the Woods* (London, 2019), p. 31.
14 Ibid., p. 12.
15 John Allison, 'A Step Back in Time', *Seven*, 15 October 2006, pp. 12–14.
16 Samuel Taylor Coleridge, *Christabel: Kubla Khan, a Vision; The Pains of Sleep* (London, 1816), pp. 55–8.
17 Walter Pater, *The Renaissance: Studies in Art and Poetry*, 3rd edn (London and New York, 1888), p. 140.
18 Marvell, 'The Garden', p. 50.
19 Thomas Love Peacock, *Melincourt* (London, 1817), vol. III, p. 25.

15 Walls, Hedges and Fencing with Ourselves

1 Robert Frost, *North of Boston* (London, 1914), pp. 11–13.
2 William Bray, ed., *Memoirs, Illustrative of the Life and Writings of John Evelyn*, 2nd edn (London, 1819), vol. I, p. xv.
3 Richard Lovelace, *The Poems of Richard Lovelace*, ed. C. H. Wilkinson (Oxford, 1953), p. 79.
4 Sigmund Freud, *The Future of an Illusion*, trans. James Strachey (New York, 1961), p. 15.

17 The Garden Party

1 William Shakespeare, *The Tempest*, ed. Alden T. Vaughan and Virginia Mason Vaughan (London, 2011), p. 254.
2 F. Scott Fitzgerald, *The Great Gatsby* (New York, 1925), pp. 47–57.
3 'The Coffin Question', *Chamber's Journal of Popular Literature, Science, and Art*, XII/604 (1875), pp. 465–7.

4 W. B. Yeats, 'The Wild Swans at Coole', in *The Poems*, ed. Daniel Albright (London, 1992), p. 180.
5 'In Memory of Major Robert Gregory', ibid., p. 183.
6 John Ruskin, *Fors Clavigera* (Orpington, 1871–87), vol. VII, p. 201.

18 Peter and Pan

1 Timothy Mowl, 'In the Realm of the Great God Pan', *Country Life*, CXC/42 (1996), pp. 54–9.
2 John Evelyn, *Elysium Britannicum, or The Royal Gardens* (Philadelphia, PA, 2001), pp. 207–8.
3 Genesis 3:16–19.
4 Quoted in Richard Wilson and Alan Mackley, *Creating Paradise: The Building of the English Country House, 1660–1880* (London and New York, 2000), p. 84.
5 William Shakespeare, *King Lear*, ed. R. A. Foakes (London, 1997), pp. 187, 279.
6 See, for example, Faune Dansant, a sculpture by Eugène-Louis Lequesne (1815–1887), in the Luxembourg Garden, Paris. It has no trace of the bestial or the base.
7 Kenneth Grahame, *The Wind in the Willows* (New York, 1908), pp. 128–9.
8 Ibid., p. 145.
9 Ibid., p. 149.
10 Ibid., p. 151.
11 Ibid., p. 152.
12 Ibid., pp. 152–4.
13 Ibid., p. 154.
14 Ibid., pp. 154–5.
15 Ibid., pp. 156–7.
16 Ibid., p. 158.
17 Ibid., pp. 161–2.
18 William Wordsworth, 'Ode: Intimations of Immortality', in *Poems, in Two Volumes* (London, 1807), vol. II, p. 151.
19 'My heart leaps up when I behold', ibid., p. 44.
20 Quoted in Elaine Kilmurray and Richard Ormond, eds, *John Singer Sargent* (Princeton, NJ, 1998), p. 114.
21 Christopher Woodward, 'Introduction', in Andrew Lambirth, *Ivon Hitchens: The Painter in the Woods* (London, 2019), pp. 7–9.
22 Job 38:7.
23 William Shakespeare, *Antony and Cleopatra*, ed. John Wilders (London, 1995), p. 269.
24 Percy Bysshe Shelley, 'Lines', in *The Works of Percy Bysshe Shelley in Verse and Prose*, ed. Harry Buxton Forman (London, 1880), vol. III, pp. 146–7.
25 Elizabeth Barrett Browning, 'A Musical Instrument', *Cornhill Magazine*, II (1860), pp. 84–5.
26 See Shelley, 'Hymn of Pan', in *Works*, vol. IV, pp. 36–7.
27 John Keats, 'On First Looking into Chapman's Homer', *The Examiner*, 1 December 1816, pp. 761–2.

ACKNOWLEDGEMENTS

Martin Ventris-Field diligently and skilfully took many of the photographs in this book, without which some of the pages would be blind.

The ghost and even the voice of Jackie Webb visits these pages sometimes, especially those concerned with the Nourish Garden in Ampthill.

Kate Rhodes – the paragon of the ideal reader – brought her wisdom, inimitable experience and a profound generosity to this book.

Richard Cappuccio and Ann Marshall always ask the right questions, and they are patient, even with the wrong answers.

Peter Chadwick followed the evolution of the book with never-failing encouragement.

To Jeremy Elloy, scourge of pretentiousness, ally of looking thoughtfully, I'm always grateful.

Thanks also to Judyta Frodyma and Hal Robinson for lending me their eyesight and insight.

All the hospitable gardeners who have allowed me into their plots and sometimes shared their intuitions, I salute you.

And then to Jane Barry, who always listens for the voice in what I write. And to Ray and Ruth Hedley – such good friends, such loyal readers.

PHOTO ACKNOWLEDGEMENTS

The author and publishers wish to express their thanks to the sources listed below for illustrative material and/or permission to reproduce it. Some locations of artworks are also given below, in the interest of brevity:

American Academy in Rome, Photographic Archive: 21; Art Institute of Chicago: 31; from W. H. Bartlett, *The Scenery and Antiquities of Ireland* (London, 1842), vol. I, photo Martin Ventris-Field: 4; Beinecke Rare Book and Manuscript Library, Yale University, New Haven, CT: 18; from *Birket Foster's Pictures of English Landscape* (London and New York, 1863), photo Getty Research Institute, Los Angeles: 24; Boston Public Library, MA: 13; British Library, London (Cotton MS Nero A X, fol. 129v): 15; © Chloë Cheese, photo Martin Ventris-Field: 29; from Francesco Colonna, *Hypnerotomachia Poliphili* (Venice, 1499), photo McGill University Library, Montreal, QC: 5; Detroit Institute of Arts, MI: 34; from *L'Enfer de Dante Alighieri* (Paris, 1861), photo Bibliothèque nationale de France, Paris/Wikimedia Commons: 1; © Estate of Cedric Morris, all rights reserved 2025/Bridgeman Images, photo © Colchester and Ipswich Museums Service: 30; © The Estate of Ivon Hitchens, all rights reserved, DACS 2025, photo © Manchester Art Gallery/Bridgeman Images: 32; from John Evelyn, *Silva; or, A Discourse of Forest-Trees* (York, 1786), photo Martin Ventris-Field: 2; from Kenneth Grahame, *The Wind in the Willows* (London, 1908): 41; from Brothers Grimm, *Little Brother & Little Sister and Other Tales* (London, 1917), photo Archivist/AdobeStock: 10; from Johannes Hofer, *Dissertatio medica de nostalgia, oder Heimwehe* (Basel, 1688), photo Universitätsbibliothek Basel: 25; from David MacRitchie, *Fians, Fairies and Picts* (London, 1893): 3; The Metropolitan Museum of Art, New York: 14, 19, 33; Nationalgalerie, Staatliche Museen zu Berlin, photo Andres Kilger: 12; from A. Welby Pugin, *An Apology for the Revival of Christian Architecture in England* (London, 1843), photo Getty Research Institute, Los Angeles: 6; courtesy Colin Smythe: 38; Tate, London: 9, 27, 35; Tufts University, Digital Collections and Archives, Medford, MA: 36; photos Martin Ventris-Field: 7, 8, 16, 22, 23, 26, 37, 39; Victoria and Albert Museum, London: 28, 40; from Giuseppe Rocco Volpi, *Vetus Latium profanum*, vol. X, part I (Rome, 1745), photo Archäologisches Institut, Universität zu Köln: 17; Yale Center for British Art, New Haven, CT: 20; Yale University Art Gallery, New Haven, CT: 11.

INDEX

Illustration numbers are indicated by *italics*